Essaying Shakespeare

ESSAYING
SHAKESPEARE

KAREN NEWMAN

University of Minnesota Press
Minneapolis
London

The University of Minnesota Press gratefully acknowledges the financial
assistance provided for the publication of this book from the Department
of English, New York University.

For publication history of previously published material in
this book, see page 189.

Published by the University of Minnesota Press
111 Third Avenue South, Suite 290
Minneapolis, MN 55401-2520
http://www.upress.umn.edu

Library of Congress Cataloging-in-Publication Data
Newman, Karen
Essaying Shakespeare / Karen Newman.
p.   cm.
Includes bibliographical references and index.
ISBN 978-0-8166-5589-2 (acid-free paper)
ISBN 978-0-8166-5590-8 (pbk.: acid-free paper)
1. Shakespeare, William, 1564–1616—Criticism and interpretation.
I. Title.
PR2976.N49 2009
822.3'3—dc22
2008035346

Printed in the United States of America on acid-free paper

The University of Minnesota is an equal-opportunity
educator and employer.

15   14   13   12   11   10   09   10   9   8   7   6   5   4   3   2   1

To my students

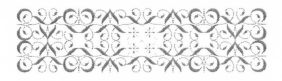

CONTENTS

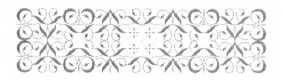

ACKNOWLEDGMENTS

THE ESSAYS COLLECTED HERE OFTEN BEGAN AS LECTURES OR conference papers presented in colleges and universities both in the United States and abroad; subsequently they appeared in print in various scholarly journals and collections. My thanks to the many colleagues and friends who extended such invitations over the years and to the journals and publishers who allowed me to republish them here. I wish in particular to acknowledge the anonymous readers of this collection, along with Richard Morrison at the University of Minnesota Press, for their generous judgment of my work and their confidence that these essays continue to have a shelf life beyond their initial publication. Thanks as well to Jonathan Goldberg for encouraging me to undertake this project, and to Margaret Ferguson for her generous and incisive reading of both the initial prospectus and the present Introduction. I am grateful to Ross Knecht and Kathryn Vomero for their conscientious help with the many mundane tasks involved in putting this book together, from scanning to permissions.

I learned much about Shakespeare from early teachers—Jonas Barish and Louise George Clubb—whom I wish to acknowledge and to thank, but much of what I know about Shakespeare I have learned from my students, both graduates and undergraduates, over many years of teaching at Brown University and recently at New York University. I dedicate this book to them with thanks.

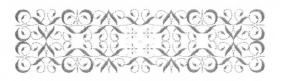

INTRODUCTION

ESSAYING SHAKESPEARE BRINGS TOGETHER WORK WRIT-
ten and published over the past twenty-five years during what
has been an intensely productive period for Shakespeare and
early modern studies. It also offers several new essays that have not yet
appeared in print and ends with a prolegomenon for new work under
way. The so-called linguistic or poststructuralist turn, psychoanalysis,
new historicism and cultural materialism, feminist literary criticism
and gender studies, cultural studies, critical race theory, the history of
sexuality, English nationalism and colonial expansion, visual culture,
print culture, and the appropriation of and globalization of Shakespeare, among other topics of critical and interdisciplinary inquiry,
echo through the various essays collected here. Not only do these
essays illustrate recent topics and critical approaches; they are also in
conversation with the work of many scholars writing on Shakespeare
and early modern English letters and culture, including Harry Berger
Jr., Walter Cohen, Margaret Ferguson, Jonathan Goldberg, Stephen
Greenblatt, John Guillory, Ann Rosalind Jones, Stephen Orgel, and
Peter Stallybrass, among others. Many engage theoretical work of
twentieth-century thinkers in other fields, such as Theodor Adorno,
Louis Althusser, Jacques Derrida, Michel Foucault, Freud, Jean Joseph
Goux, Luce Irigaray, Jacques Lacan, Claude Lévi-Strauss, Marx, Gayle
Rubin, Michel Serres, and others. The collection traces a trajectory of
recent Shakespeare criticism and maps out changes in approaches to
reading and teaching his work over the past twenty-five years. Thus it

offers not only readings of individual plays but also what I hope will be a useful overview of recent Shakespeare studies.

No effort has been made to "update" the already published essays collected here beyond incidental changes to conform to the house style of the University of Minnesota Press. Because part of the reader's interest in the collection will be the critical history it traces, I have arranged the essays chronologically. Though some essays are well known and have appeared in easily accessible journals or in my *Fashioning Femininity and English Renaissance Drama,* others have appeared in less accessible places such as conference proceedings, festschrifts, or specialty journals not often read by Shakespeareans. Only three of the essays in the collection are presently available through online data banks.

The earliest piece, "Myrrha's Revenge: Ovid and Shakespeare's Reluctant Adonis," began as a paper for a conference on Ovid and Ovidian influence held at Brown in 1979 during my first year teaching. It subsequently appeared in a special collection on Ovid and Renaissance literature published by *Illinois Classical Studies* in 1985. The essay considers the relation of Shakespeare's *Venus and Adonis* to Ovid in the context of psychoanalysis and feminist criticism, then dominant approaches to the study of gender. Psychoanalysis was at that time the only field to theorize sexual difference, to recognize and value the effects of material embodiment and its attendant passions, and to offer a language with which to analyze desire and affect. "Myrrha's Revenge" addresses a traditional problem in Shakespeare studies—his sources and borrowings—but from what was then a new perspective that continues to have purchase today.[1] It also reflects my training as a comparatist with a secondary field in Latin literature since my argument about Shakespeare's epyllion depends on a reading of book 10 of Ovid's *Metamorphoses* and its Renaissance commentaries. It is followed by "Hayman's Missing *Hamlet,*" a note, really, that originally appeared in *Shakespeare Quarterly* in 1983 and that foreshadowed the recent burgeoning interest in visual culture. It considers how visual representations of Shakespeare in the eighteenth century, as his reputation grew and new editions multiplied, present readings of the plays, and it traces choices made by some of Shakespeare's earliest editors and illustrators, including Thomas Hanmer and Francis Hayman.

"Renaissance Family Politics and Shakespeare's *The Taming of the Shrew*" and "'And wash the Ethiop white': Femininity and the

Monstrous in *Othello*" are in many ways the anchors of this volume. "Renaissance Family Politics" originally appeared in *English Literary Renaissance* in 1985 and subsequently became a chapter in *Fashioning Femininity and English Renaissance Drama* (1991). The early eighties were the heyday both of feminist criticism of Shakespeare and of what we loosely term poststructuralism. Like many young scholars of that heady time, I was reading not only the scholarship on Shakespeare and Renaissance literature but also French theory: Althusser, Barthes, Derrida, Foucault, Irigaray, Kristeva, and Macherey, among others. Their work called into question mimetic models of literary production that dominated much feminist work in the 1970s and 1980s. In a 1982 review that appeared in *Signs* of a number of books on Shakespeare, Carolyn Heilbrun described what she viewed as two stages of feminist criticism. The first generation, she argued, saw Shakespeare's heroines as positive representations of women's power and Shakespeare as managing, presumably because of his genius, to overcome male-governed hierarchy and patriarchal culture. In the second stage, feminist critics had begun to take a considerably more pessimistic view: Shakespeare was the "orchestrator of men in power" (184) who failed "to recognize the possibilities of female autonomy and growth" (186). Heilbrun ended her review elegiacally by writing that "we are overcome by a sense of loss in surveying Shakespeare's essential conservatism and phallocentrism" (185). I did not then, nor do I now, feel a part of that presumed "we" that betrays nostalgia for a universal Shakespeare, the great writer who once provided identitarian models for emulation but whom "we" must now acknowledge as limited and imperfect.[2] Both of Heilbrun's stages also seemed to me trapped in a too simple and unmediated mimetic mode in which literature is believed to *reflect* reality. Theories of representation were only beginning to have an impact on Shakespeare studies, and though as a feminist engaged in ideological critique I presume in my work a relation between cultural productions and socioeconomic power, my interest then, and now, remains the way in which features of form and style mediate that relation. The first issue of the journal *Representations* had yet to appear, and as unimaginable as it may now seem, in 1982 it was hard to conceive of historicist work that took into account questions of rhetoric and representation and in which gender was a category of analysis. "Renaissance Family Politics and Shakespeare's *The Taming of the Shrew*" was a response to what seemed then a critical impasse. It brought to bear on the reading and interpretation of Shakespeare the growing interest in history that was coming to be called "new historicism"; it worked with gender as an analytic category; and it attempted to take seriously poststructuralist theories of language and representation.

The essay begins with a classic new historicist anecdote that I owe to Susan Amussen, who was then finishing her doctoral work at Brown; it is a transcription of an early-seventeenth-century court record from the Public Records Office of a skimmington or charivari aimed at a shrewish wife and her hapless husband. It helped me pose a question that remains salient today: given ideologies of femininity in early modern Europe often summed up in the trinity "chaste, silent, and obedient," how do we account for Kate's speaking the most important speech in the play in which, paradoxically, she articulates women's silence and subjection? Using Luce Irigaray's notion of mimeticism and Joan Riviere's of female masquerade, it argues for a critical practice that exposes the "conflicts Shakespeare's plays display between the explicitly repressive patriarchal ideology governing Kate's speech and the subtext or implicit message communicated by representing a powerful female protagonist speaking the play's longest speech at a moment of emphatic suspense."[3] However real the constraints, exclusions, and repressions of women's lives, they are not effective everywhere, all of the time, but rent by sites of resistance, failures, moments of excess or lack that can also be productive and circumvent or disable subjection and domination.

"'And wash the Ethiop white': Femininity and the Monstrous in *Othello*" first circulated in a seminar at the World Shakespeare Congress held in Berlin, GDR, in April 1986; the essay subsequently appeared in *Shakespeare Reproduced,* a collection that issued from that seminar, and then in *Fashioning Femininity.* The essay anticipated the recent preoccupation with race in Shakespeare studies and literary studies more generally and was followed by a series of books concerned with questions of race and racialist thinking in early modern drama, including *Gender, Race, Renaissance Drama* (1989); *Women, "Race," and Writing in the Early Modern Period* (1994); *Things of Darkness: Economies of Race and Gender in Early Modern England* (1995); *Turks, Moors, and Englishmen in the Age of Discovery* (2000); and *English Ethnicity and Race in Early Modern Drama* (2003), among many others.[4] "'And wash the Ethiop white'" considers how racialist thinking marks Shakespeare's rhetoric and produces what I term "rhetorical miscegenation." It addresses relations between gender and race, for which it has sometimes been criticized, reputedly for eliding black masculinity with white femininity. The essay is said to conflate "the particular histories of white women's sexual oppression with the enslavement of black men" in what is termed a "neat elision."[5] But *elision* means not only a reduction or abridgement, as implied here, but also splitting, rending, severance, even mutilation. Instead of conflating black masculinity and white femininity, "'And wash the Ethiop white'" participates in the theoretical expansion that took place throughout the eighties and nineties whereby difference came to be split apart, to be plotted on multiple axes, not only gender and race but nation, religion, sexuality, social status and degree, among other differences.[6]

"Portia's Ring: Gender, Sexuality, and Theories of Exchange in *The Merchant of Venice*" first appeared in 1987 as "Portia's Ring: Unruly Women and Structures of Exchange in *The Merchant of Venice*" in a special issue of *Shakespeare Quarterly* dedicated to work on gender from a predominantly new historicist or cultural materialist perspective. As its title suggests, it takes anthropology as its theoretical model, particularly the work of Claude Lévi-Strauss on women and exchange and of Marcel Mauss on the gift. Using Natalie Zemon Davis's appropriation of anthropological theories of inversion and the woman on top, and the French feminist thinker Luce Irigaray's demystification and critique of social theories of exchange, it traces the exchange of rings from Portia and Nerissa to Bassanio and Gratiano, back to Portia and Nerissa disguised as Balthasar and his man, and finally again to Bassanio and Gratiano in the play's final scene that turns on bawdy sexual jokes and cuckoldry. Missing from the earlier version of this essay was consideration of its "heterosexual fix" and Antonio's relation to, and loss of, Bassanio.[7] In 1996, when I was asked to revisit the play for a collection of critical essays on *The Merchant of Venice,* queer theory and work in the history of sexuality had changed the critical landscape of gender studies.[8] It was no longer possible to read gender relations in the play without considering Antonio's desire and loss. Furthermore, critiques of the unified subject had begun to undermine what had fast become a repetitive paradigm about the exchange of women.[9] The essay reprinted here reframed "Portia's Ring" to consider anew the exchange paradigm and to indicate the impact of work in the history of sexuality on the study of gender.

"Ghostwriting: *Hamlet* and Claude Chabrol's *Ophélia*" appeared in a festschrift for a colleague at Brown in 1991.[10] Part of the growing interest in appropriations of Shakespeare, particularly Shakespeare on film, it demonstrates how Chabrol's thriller, *Ophélia*, is also a reading of Shakespeare's play. It also anticipates my current interest in cultural translation and Shakespeare in France.

"Englishing the Other: 'Le tiers exclu' and Shakespeare's *Henry V*" (1991) was written expressly for *Fashioning Femininity and English Renaissance Drama*. It participates in the burgeoning interest in nationhood perhaps most influentially articulated in Richard Helgerson's *Forms of Nationhood: The Elizabethan Writing of England* that appeared the following year. It is concerned with what Stephen Greenblatt has termed "linguistic colonialism," with the development of English nationhood in the context of early exploration of the so-called new world, and with the production of Englishness in relation to its indigenous peoples and to gender. Were I writing the essay today, I would want to explore more fully Frobisher's encounter with the Inuit as well as the significance for *Henry V* of the French phrase books and dialogues published in the 1590s such as *The French Garden* studied so interestingly by Juliet Fleming in an essay that appeared after *Fashioning Femininity* had gone to press.[11]

"Cultural Capital's Gold Standard: Shakespeare and the Critical Apostrophe in Renaissance Studies" began as a conference paper, "Rereading Shakespeare's *Timon of Athens* at the Fin de Siècle," first presented at the International Shakespeare Association meeting in Los Angeles in 1996 and included in its published proceedings that appeared in 1998. In dialogue with John Guillory's influential *Cultural Capital: The Problem of Literary Canon Formation,* it considers the problematic status of *Timon* in the Shakespeare canon. It also addresses homosocial relations in the play and, like "Myrrha's Revenge: Ovid and Shakespeare's Reluctant Adonis," considers Shakespeare's sources in unexpected ways that "queer" our understanding of the playwright's debt to Plutarch. The essay published here is an expanded version of the chapter that subsequently appeared in a collection titled *Discontinuities: New Essays on Renaissance Literature and Criticism.*[12] During the ten years since that essay's publication, I have worked on Shakespeare in a number of contexts for a recently published book on early modern cities, *Cultural Capitals: Early Modern London and Paris,* but I have only occasionally written an essay devoted primarily to Shakespeare. One such piece is "Charactery," an unpublished review essay of Harold Bloom's *Shakespeare and the Invention of the Human.* It was prompted by my experience teaching the large Shakespeare lecture course at Brown University for many years. Heavily promoted by the press, inexplicably praised for its "irreverent common sense," and touted as directed particularly to "performers and everyone who studies Shakespeare outside the academy," Bloom's book was being read by students despite its 750-some odd pages, and the results were noisome. Bloom encouraged students to believe in an idea of genius more appropriate to romanticism, his scholarly field, than to the collaborative practices of early modern playwriting. By claiming that "Shakespeare's uncanny power in the rendering of personality is perhaps beyond explanation," Bloom's book prompted students to believe, and even to claim, that his plays could not be analyzed. Worse, it encouraged prose like this example of Bloom's own: "He is a system of northern lights, an aurora borealis visible where most of us will never go. Libraries and playhouses (and cinemas) cannot contain him; he has become a spirit or 'spell of light,' almost too vast to apprehend."[13] "Charactery" offers a critique of Bloom's book and addresses the question of Shakespearean character in the context of the early modern genre of the *character* and by way of recent approaches to character and the new textual studies, particularly the work of Jonathan Goldberg and Randall McLeod.

"Sartorial Economies and Suitable Style: The Anonymous *Woodstock* and Shakespeare's *Richard II*" began as a working paper for a Shakespeare Association of America seminar and appears here in print for the first time. I returned to it only recently in response to the interest in Elizabethan and Jacobean dress that has focused almost exclusively on sartorial extravagance and elite costume.[14] This essay considers instead the clothing of the poor and reflects on the meaning and "unconscious" of the recent critical preoccupation with elite dress, on commodity fetishism, and on our compulsion to serve the market by enjoying what Jean Baudrillard dubs the "fun system" of consumption.

The final essay, "French Shakespeare: Dryden, Vigny's *Othello,* and British Cultural Expansion," offers a prospectus for a new project on Shakespeare and cultural translation. Cultural globalization is usually assumed to be a late-twentieth-century imperialist phenomenon, the result of an expansion and acceleration in the movement and exchange of ideas, commodities, and capital over vast distances and porous boundaries.[15] My new project aims to rethink current claims about the globalization of culture and western cultural hegemony by considering a longer historical frame in which cultural competition needs to be understood. It considers the long cultural rivalry between England and France by examining two chapters in that history, Dryden's *Of Dramatic Poesy* and the French romantic poet Alfred de Vigny's translation of *Othello*. Vigny's translation was prompted by the spectacular success of a group of English actors who came to Paris seeking new markets in 1827 and who performed Shakespeare in English on the French stage for some ten months. The essay sketches the outlines of what will be a longer study of the reception and translation of Shakespeare in France and francophone cultures, but with the broader, theoretical purpose of showing that the globalization of culture has a much longer history than has generally been allowed.

Bringing these essays together in one volume has inevitably also made me consider absences or omissions. In considering the past two decades of Shakespeare studies, in which the history of the book has recently played such an important role, missing from this collection is a more sustained study of Shakespeare and print culture. Though the concerns of the new textual studies make their appearance in several essays, a fuller consideration awaits the development of the new project outlined above. Already in the essay that ends this volume I consider the earliest advertisement for the First Folio that appeared in the appendix of English works at the end of the *Catalogus uniuersalis pro nundinis Francofurtensibis* (1622), an English edition of the half-yearly advertisement known as the *Mess-Katalog* that listed books available at the important book fair held every spring and autumn at Frankfurt-on-the-Main. But there is more work to be done. Also largely missing from my work is any serious attention to religion and religious controversy, an important force field in early modern England and a significant area of recent research in Shakespeare and early modern English studies. Perhaps the present political environment with regard to religion, in both the United States and the world, has made me chary, even unwilling, to undertake such study at such a temporal and geographical distance as the sixteenth and seventeenth centuries in England. It would seem that the Wars of Religion have never ended but instead are endlessly morphing on the expanding world scene.

My ambition is for this volume to be of interest not only to Shakespeareans but to both graduate and undergraduate students and to the general reader interested in Shakespeare and Shakespeare studies. That, dear reader, is for you to decide.

Essaying Shakespeare

MYRRHA'S REVENGE
Ovid and Shakespeare's Reluctant Adonis

I N ALL THE CONTROVERSY OVER SHAKESPEARE'S *VENUS AND
Adonis, commentators agree on one issue: "Shakespeare's Adonis,
contrary to the whole tradition, scorns love."[1] This fundamental change in the myth has never been satisfactorily explained, for
though Adonis complies with Venus's desires in the earliest versions,
in the Ovidian account that is generally regarded as Shakespeare's primary source, we are told almost nothing of Adonis's response to her
advances except that he does not reject them outright.[2]

Critics have advanced various biographical, historical, and literary arguments to explain Shakespeare's unwilling Adonis. At the time
Shakespeare wrote and published *Venus and Adonis,* the Earl of Southampton, to whom the poem was dedicated, was fighting an arranged
marriage with Elizabeth Vere. Shakespeare must have known of the
young earl's unwillingness to marry.[3] Those interested in psycho-biographical causes explain Shakespeare's preoccupation with the motif
of older women and young, inexperienced men by citing his own marriage at eighteen to Anne Hathaway, who was eight years his senior.[4]
Panofsky proposes that Shakespeare's lover was influenced by the
visual arts, specifically Titian's *Venus and Adonis* in which Adonis
actively evades Venus's embrace. William Keach refutes his argument
by pointing out first that Titian's virile young hunter is strikingly at
odds with Shakespeare's effeminate Adonis, and then that "nothing in
the painting proves that Titian thought of Adonis as having resisted
Venus throughout the encounter."[5] Adonis, after all, traditionally

ignores Venus's warnings and evades her protectiveness. Neither biographical nor historical arguments provide a completely satisfactory explanation for Shakespeare's unwilling Adonis.

Recent literary studies of Venus and Adonis have more often explored the psychology of Shakespeare's reluctant lover than the sources for his reluctance. Wayne Rebhorn claims that Adonis is part of a long line of Renaissance epic heroes who fear being "reabsorbed symbolically into the womb of this seemingly benevolent but really quite deadly mother."[6] Adonis's rejection of Venus's advances, then, is positive and places him in the good, if surprising, company of Spenser's Guyon and Tasso's Rinaldo. For Coppélia Kahn, Shakespeare dramatizes the narcissism characteristic of adolescent boys who fear the devouring mother and project that fear outside themselves.[7] She looks elsewhere in Ovid to explain Shakespeare's restive young man, to the myths of Hermaphroditus and Narcissus.[8] T. W. Baldwin long ago pointed out that the common denominator of the Ovidian myths of Adonis, Hermaphroditus, and Narcissus is "the irresistibly beautiful youth wooed by the over-ardent female."[9] Though Ovid's presentation of these diffident young men certainly influenced Shakespeare's portrayal of his reluctant lover, we should not jettison too hastily Ovid's tale of Venus and Adonis. Preoccupation with Adonis's predicament obscures rather than clarifies the mystery of the unwilling Adonis, for as classicists have long recognized, the main psychological interest in all three Ovidian tales is the frustrated female lover.[10]

The active reluctance of Shakespeare's Adonis can best be understood not by looking at other unwilling boys in Ovidian myth but by looking at the structure of the *Metamorphoses,* at its later commentaries, and at Shakespeare's Venus, from whose point of view after all, most of the poem's action is recounted. This shift in perspective from Adonis's unwillingness to Venus's desire demands a reevaluation of the poem in psychological as well as literary terms. What follows is first a reading of Ovid that suggests how Shakespeare's contemporaries understood the tale of Venus and Adonis; next I consider the implications of both recent and not so recent readings of the poem itself; and finally I reevaluate traditional psychological interpretations of the myth in terms of a feminist analysis that offers a new perspective on Venus's central position in the poem.

Shakespeare and Ovid

The myth of Venus and Adonis ends book 10 of the Metamorphoses, but the central story recounts the incestuous passion of Myrrha for her father, Cinyras. Adonis is the son of their unnatural union that Venus has caused by enflaming Myrrha with desire for her father. Implicit in Shakespeare's poem is the submerged irony that Venus's love for Adonis is incestuous, like Myrrha's for her father in Ovid. Myrrha's revenge on Venus for inspiring her unnatural passion is worked out through Adonis's rejection of the goddess of love.

Frustrated love motivates much of Ovid's narrative, and in books 9 and 10, unnatural love, particularly that generated by the female libido, causes situations that can only be resolved through death and metamorphosis. As Brooks Otis points out in his study *Ovid as an Epic Poet,* the series of tales beginning with the story of Byblis and climaxing in the story of Myrrha recounts the vagaries of perverse love and sexual desire.[11] The story of Caunus and Byblis, which begins with a warning "that girls should never love what is forbidden" ("ut ament concessa puellae," *Metamorphoses* 9.454), initiates the themes of incest and frustrated love that link the two books. Byblis loves her brother, but her love, as Ovid emphasizes throughout the tale, is unnatural, not fitting between brother and sister. Inspired by an erotic dream of sexual pleasure with her sibling, Byblis writes him confessing her love. Caunus rejects her proposal and flees. She is driven mad and eventually her tears of grief are metamorphosed into a fountain bearing her name. The Byblis story, in which unnatural love remains unconsummated, occupies the central position in book 9; it is paralleled by the tale of Myrrha in book 10 whose incestuous love is actually satisfied.

Book 10 begins with the story of Orpheus and Eurydice, but its avowed subject, as Orpheus tells us, is boys beloved of gods and girls frantic with forbidden fires so as to merit punishment ("dilectos superis, inconcessisque puellas / ignibus attonitas meruisse libidine poenam," *Metamorphoses* 10.154–55). The climactic episode and the center of the book is the story of Myrrha's unlawful passion to which Ovid devotes 222 out of 735 lines. After her father discovers he has been tricked into incest with his daughter, Myrrha flees to escape his wrath. Praying to an unnamed goddess, she is changed into the myrrh tree from which the incestuously conceived Adonis is born. The tale ends with a brief parody of the epic genealogy: Adonis is born from his sister and his grandfather: "ille sorore / natus avoque suo" (*Metamorphoses* 10.520–21).

Ovid's emphasis on the strange circumstances of Adonis's birth should also remind us that Myrrha's own father was the result of an unnatural union, for he is the grandson of Pygmalion and the statue that Venus had brought to life. Following the account of Adonis's birth, Ovid describes his unnatural beauty by comparing him to the Amores (*Metamorphoses* 10.516), Cupid-like cherubs who appear frequently in Roman art with wings and quivers.[12] The link between Adonis and Cupid is made explicit, however, in the medieval and Renaissance commentaries and translations: in the *Ovide moralisé*, for example, Adonis "le dieu d'amour ressemblast"; Golding translates Amores simply as "Cupids."[13] Ovid begins Adonis's own tale with yet another description of his beauty that pleases Venus but, more significantly, avenges the desires of his mother ("matrisque ulciscitur ignes" *Metamorphoses* 10.524). Ovid says outright that Venus's love for Adonis avenges his mother's unnatural passion, a passion that most versions of the myth attribute to Venus's inspiration.[14] The poet goes on in the next line to describe Venus as a mother herself: while giving his mother ("matri") a kiss, Cupid wounds her accidentally with one of his arrows; the result of this wound is her love for Adonis. In two lines, the word *mater* refers first to Myrrha, then to Venus, and thereby implicitly joins their guilty passions. For if we remember that Adonis has been explicitly identified with the Cupid-like Amores, and in the medieval and Renaissance traditions with Cupid himself, we can recognize the irony implicit in Ovid: Venus's love for Adonis, like Myrrha's for her father, is incestuous.[15] Though Shakespeare does not refer specifically to Myrrha myth, Baldwin points out that "in Shakespeare's day, that knowledge could be assumed."[16] Both the *Ovide moralisé* and its humanist successor, the Regius commentary (1492), make Adonis's origins explicit:

> Venus, la mere au dieu d'amours,
> Le fil Mirre ama par amours.
> (3703–4)

Venus, the mother of the god of love, was in love with Myrrha's son.

> Adonis ex incesto patris ac filie coitu natus.[17]

Regius goes even further in his gloss at the beginning of the tale by setting up a careful equivalence between Venus and Myrrha: Venus delighted in Adonis no less than Myrrha in her father ("Adonem cognominatus quem non minus Venus dilexit quam illa patrem Cinyram dilexerat beneficio Cupidinis").

In his seminar on Poe's "Purloined Letter," Jacques Lacan demonstrates the importance of what is absent to psychoanalytic interpretation.[18] Literary critics and theoreticians have transferred Lacan's insights to literary analysis by showing how the not-said or silences of a text are analogous to the overdetermined details of dream or the analytic session. Such details make manifest what is absent or latent—a past trauma or event not overtly present in the patient's discourse.[19] Silences can signify, sometimes more eloquently than what is spoken aloud. In the case of Shakespeare's *Venus and Adonis,* what is absent shaped the Renaissance reader's understanding of the poem in significant ways, for the poet undoubtedly recognized this submerged theme of incest and exploited its ironic potential.

When Venus presents her argument on behalf of procreation, her allusions to Adonis's own begetting would inevitably have recalled to Shakespeare's audience, so familiar with Ovid, the unnatural circumstances of Adonis's conception and birth. "Sappy plants" she reminds him, are made "to bear" (165), certainly an odd end to the series which begins "Torches are made to light" (163), but a reminder to a knowing audience of Ovid's etiological tale that explains Adonis's birth in terms of the bole that exudes the myrrh tree's sap. Venus ends the stanza with the exhortation "Thou wast begot; to get it is thy duty" (168). She also chides Adonis for his reluctance by reminding him of his own mother's willingness and obliquely links her frustration with Myrrha's:

> "Art thou a woman's son, and canst not feel
> What 'tis to love? how want of love tormenteth?
> O, had thy mother borne so hard a mind,
> She had not brought forth thee, but died unkind."
>
> (201–4)

Shakespeare also wittily recalls Adonis's unnatural descent from Pygmalion and his statue when he has Venus characterize Adonis as

> cold and senseless stone
> Well-painted idol, image dull and dead.
> Statue contenting but the eye alone,

Thing like a man, but of no woman bred!
                    (211–14)

Venus is not only an aggressive masculine wooer, she is also from the poem's outset a loving mother.[20] The notorious image of the goddess plucking Adonis from his horse and tucking him under her arm suggests not so much Venus as the "bold-faced suitor" of the first stanza but Venus as a mother, lifting and carrying her small child. Shakespeare describes Adonis here as "the tender boy" thereby establishing our sense of him as a child. Later he is "like the froward infant stilled with dandling" (562). Venus's solicitous care for Adonis and her fear of his hunting wild animals, certainly inspired in part by Ovid's portrayal of Venus, suggest the motherly concern that critics often remark on without noting its incestuous implications. Don Cameron Allen, for example, points out:

> Adonis is a child with her. When she swoons, he fusses over her as a boy might over his mother. He will readily kiss her goodnight when it is time for bed. The goddess takes advantage of the filial-maternal relationship which is really all Adonis wants.[21]

Venus, however, wants much more. Later in the poem she is described as a "milch doe" seeking to feed her fawn and, of course, a park which beckons Adonis to "Feed where thou wilt" (229–40). But the maternal-filial imagery is nowhere more obvious than in the poem's penultimate stanzas:

> "Poor flow'r," quoth she, "This was thy father's guise—
> Sweet issue of a more sweet-smelling sire—
> For every little grief to wet his eyes;
> To grow unto himself was his desire,
>   And so 'tis thine; but know, it is as good
>   To wither in my breast as in his blood.
>
> "Here was thy father's bed, here in my breast;
> Thou art the next of blood, and 'tis thy right.
> Lo in this hollow cradle take thy rest;
> My throbbing heart shall rock thee day and night:
>   There shall not be one minute in an hour
>   Wherein I will not kiss my sweet love's flow'r."
>   (1177–88)

Venus crops the Adonis flower and her invocation of "thy father" reminds us of its direct, familial tie to Adonis. Having lost the father, she will have the son. Shakespeare alludes to Adonis's descent from Myrrha when he has Venus call Adonis "a more sweet-smelling sire." She places the flower in her breast, which she calls "thy father's bed"; in "this hollow cradle" she will rock it "day and night."[22]

We can now see the significance of this imagery and its relationship to Shakespeare's Ovidian source: Adonis's rejection of Venus's advances is Shakespeare's self-conscious elaboration of Myrrha's revenge for her own disappointed love. He portrays Venus loving a mere boy in an incestuous relationship, which wittily reverses the myth of Myrrha and Cinyras in which daughter loves father. For Shakespeare and the reader, mother Venus loves her unwilling "son" Adonis and his death is analogous to Myrrha's loss of her beloved father. The audience for which Shakespeare wrote his poem, the Earl of Southampton and his sophisticated coterie of friends, were sure to be amused by the deliberate working out of Myrrha's revenge, which medieval and Renaissance glosses of Ovid make explicit:

> Adonis a vengeance prise
> De la grant honte et du mesfait
> Que Venus à sa mere a fait
> Quant el li fist amer son pere
> Or revenche Adonis sa mere.

Adonis took vengeance for the great shame and wrong Venus did to his mother when she made Myrrha love her own father. Now Adonis avenges his mother. William Barksted's *Mirrha* (1607), a poem generally agreed to be prompted by Shakespeare's *Venus and Adonis,* provides further testimony of this revenge motif:

> Wel, wel (quoth she) thou hast reveng'd the spight
> Which from my accurst sons bow did fowly light
> On thy faire Mother, O immortall boy
> Though thou be faire, tis I that should be coy.[23]

Ovid's incestuous story of Myrrha informs the poem, acting as a witty and ironic subtext to the text itself.

Reading *Venus and Adonis*

By focusing on the incest theme and frustrated female desire, the Myrrha story, Ovid's tale and its later commentaries serve, in addition to psycho-biographical and historical arguments, to explain Shakespeare's reluctant Adonis. They also point to a central problem in the poem that has always disturbed commentators. The Shakespearean narrator's distance from Venus's desire, manifest in his often-noted comic exaggeration of her size and ridicule of her overbearing lust, conflicts with a shift in our sympathies in the last section of the poem. After Adonis's departure to hunt the boar, the narrator, and consequently the reader, becomes increasingly sympathetic toward Venus's feelings. This shift makes the poem more emotionally powerful than is often admitted. Modern archetypal and psychological interpretations identify Venus and the boar with opposing aspects of the Great Mother and Adonis with the figure of her son-lover who in adolescence begins to differentiate himself from the unconscious and affirm his masculine otherness.[24] As E. Neumann describes it in *The Origins and History of Consciousness:*

> He is her lover as well as her son. But he is not yet strong enough to cope with her, he succumbs to her in death and is devoured. The mother-beloved turns into the terrible Death Goddess. . . . The masculine principle is not yet a paternal tendency balancing the maternal-female principle; it is still youthful and vernal, the merest beginning of an independent movement away from the place of origin and the infantile relation.[25]

The boar is a complicated symbol in myth, its phallic character, according to Neumann, a trace from that period when masculine and feminine are united in the uroborus or Great Mother. It is associated in Ovid with the wood and the cave, the womblike realms of the *turrita Mater,* and by implication, with Venus, who causes the lovers Atalanta and Hippomenes in their interpolated tale within Ovid's Venus and Adonis story to copulate in Cybele's cave. Such an interpretation of the myth certainly fits Ovid's larger narrative structure, for this tale, which ends book 10, is followed by the death of Orpheus at the hands of the Maenads, the maddened, destroying matrons of Thrace.

Traditional psychological interpretations such as Neumann's adopt a peculiarly masculine perspective toward Venus's desire; they project male fears of female sexuality onto Venus by attributing the boar and its destructiveness to her. An alternative and less limited view is to see the boar as a symbol of male virility, both in physical appearance and in myth. A. T. Hatto in fact argues that Venus is jealous of the boar with whom she competes for Adonis' affections.[26] He documents the medieval and Renaissance identification of the boar with male sexuality and points out that in Shakespeare's poem mention of the boar inevitably leads Venus to discourse on jealousy.[27] Her explicit sexual description of the slaying of Adonis supports his argument: the boar "thought to kiss him, and hath killed him so" (1110) and "by a kiss thought to persuade him there; / And nuzzling in his flank, the loving swine / Sheathed unaware the tusk in his soft groin" (1114–16). Adonis, who seeks to avoid sexual love with Venus, encounters it with the boar. The late classical and Continental sources of this conceit reinforce such a reading, for in pseudo-Theocritus and the Italian versions, the boar himself describes his act as a kiss and thereby makes the rivalry between Venus and the boar explicit.[28]

If Venus is cast as mother in this poem, and Adonis as son, the boar suggests not so much the Great Mother, as conventional psychological interpretations claim, but her rival, a kind of sexual father whose violence reinstates the sexual difference that Adonis's beauty and Venus's incestuous love endanger. Venus can avenge her wrong only by prophesying an endless chain of reciprocal male violence in love that will punish men: "It shall be cause of war and dire events / And set dissension 'twixt the son and sire" (1159–60).

Shakespeare's poem, Ovid's tale, and indeed the myth itself reenact that primitive act of violence that René Girard describes in his *Violence et le sacré,* but with a difference.[29] Girard liberates desire from its specifically Freudian familial model by arguing that all desire is mimetic. The Oedipal desire of son for mother is generated not from some inherent sexual urge toward a particular object at an early stage of development but simply by the desire to imitate those with power. Men contend for a sexual object, or indeed any object, in endlessly reciprocal "mimetic desire," which leads to what Girard terms a crisis of difference. By desiring the same object, father and son lose their individual identities and become doubles whose rivalry leads to reciprocal violence. Girard contends that such violence can only be arrested by collective aggression against a surrogate victim, an outsider, whether slave, child, foreigner, or *pharmakos,* whose death restores difference and, therefore, order. The implied threat of incest in Venus's love for Adonis, present for author and audience, is deflected through his death and metamorphosis, thereby maintaining the incest taboo with its widely recognized, almost universal civilizing function.

But neither Ovid's tale nor Shakespeare's poem wholly conforms to Girard's model, for the conventional syntax of the Oedipal complex is inverted: mother, not father, is desiring subject, and Adonis, that epicene representative of sexual desire itself, the object of her desire. For Venus, the boar represents the father and phallic power that destroys her love object; by doing so he reestablishes the familial bonds upon which patriarchal culture depends. Both the boar and the narrator of the poem, like Orpheus in *Metamorphoses* 10, are the bearers of patriarchal order.

By ending book 10 not only with the death of Adonis, who rejects women, but also with the death of Orpheus at women's hands, Ovid subverts that patriarchal order. At the end of book 9, we find the tale of Iphis and Ianthe in which both women are desiring subjects whose desire works within and across gender lines. In that tale, Iphis's mother, ordered to expose her female child, violates patriarchal command and instead obeys the Great Mother's behest to raise Iphis as a boy. She is eventually transformed into a man and thereby enabled to marry Ianthe. Throughout books 9 and 10, Ovid counterpoints the overvaluation of love that crosses gender lines in the incest tales with the tales of Pygmalion and Orpheus who undervalue love by refusing women or loving boys; the tale of Iphis and Ianthe is subversive because it upholds *and* obliterates sexual difference.

Shakespeare's poem, unlike the *Metamorphoses,* contains and controls these subversive suggestions, for in *Venus and Adonis,* Venus is left with only the delicate purple flower that was Adonis, a flower which Shakespeare reminds us will "wither," a mere ornament instead of the flesh and blood object of her unnatural desire. In *Venus and Adonis* the witty conceit of Myrrha's revenge focuses our attention on Venus's frustrated love, a focus in keeping with Shakespeare's Ovidian source. This shift in perspective generates for the reader a reinterpretation of the myth itself to represent woman as desiring subject in a changed position in conventionally represented sexual and familial configurations, but that changed position is finally undermined by the Shakespearean narrator's distance from, even punishment of, Venus's desire.

Myth and Feminine Desire

In closing we should consider the nature of myth itself and what differentiates it from other narratives. Myth, unlike other stories, seeks to contain or overcome oppositions and improbabilities.[30] A general theory of myth is perhaps as hard to formulate as a definitive reading of *Venus and Adonis,* but S. Clark Hulse makes a useful suggestion in his essay on Shakespeare's poem and the mythographic tradition. Despite their differences, he remarks, all the various theories of myth are preoccupied with mediation. For Frazer and the ritualists, myth mediates between the sacred and profane; for Freud and Jung, between the unconscious and the conscious, the collective and the individual; for Lévi-Strauss and the structuralists, between the opposing terms and contradictions of a given social system.[31] In classical versions of the ancient tale as well as in Shakespeare's poem, Adonis mediates between opposites. In his fascinating book on the system of dietary, vegetable, and astronomical codes attached to the ritual of the Adonia in ancient Greece, Marcel Detienne recognizes in Adonis erotic powers of attraction capable of bringing together opposing terms.[32] As a mortal who attracts the goddess of love, he brings together heaven and earth; as the progeny of the union of Myrrha and Cinyras, he links those who should be poles apart, daughter and father. Adonis is not a husband, nor even a man, but a lover whose effeminacy, his mediating status between masculine and feminine, is always emphasized by the Greeks' description of his appearance and his association with the perfume myrrh. In its ambivalence, in its multiple contrarieties, and in Adonis's role as mediator, Shakespeare's *Venus and Adonis* resembles these earlier versions, for Shakespeare's transformation of Adonis into unwilling lover, Venus into loving mother, and boar into jealous father rings another change on the mediated oppositions characteristic of myth.

Shakespeare's use of antithesis in this poem has been often remarked: red and white are united in Adonis' complexion and in the purple (*purpureus,* red, dark, violet) and white flower that is Adonis metamorphosed. Venus manifests the same antithesis because of the conflicting feelings of fear and desire he generates in her. Adonis's beauty is androgynous: he is "rose cheeked," "the field's chief flower," "more lovely than a man," with a "maiden burning in his cheeks." This sexual ambiguity is suggested even in the Ovidian tale, for in the story of Atalanta, Venus emphasizes the young runner's beauty by saying she was as beautiful as Venus herself, or Adonis "if he were a woman." Adonis also plays a mediating role in joining the two hunts of the poem, for he is first the quarry of Venus's sexual chase that begins the narrative; then a hunter in the literal hunt; and in a final reversal of roles, the victim of the boar.[33] Adonis also mediates between the sun and moon, for his beauty shames "the sun by day and her [Cynthia] by night." The sun, as classicists have pointed out, frequently suggests danger and destruction in the *Metamorphoses*. It is a masculine symbol of sexual power and energy "frequently represented as the unwelcome obtruder shunned by hunters and virgins."[34] And Adonis's own words link Venus with the sun: "Fie, no more of love! / The sun doth burn my face—I must remove" (185–86). Both animals and gods act contrary to their natures because of Adonis: wild beasts are tamed by seeing his beauty and Venus is transformed from an ardently sought object of love to an aggressor who "like a bold faced suitor gins to woo him." But she is more frequently described not as a mortal but as a beast of prey—a parodic elaboration of Ovid's description of Venus as huntress. The effect of Adonis's beauty, which from the first is described as unnatural, upsets the cosmological order; he threatens that order by endangering or abolishing the sexual, natural, familial, and cultural distinctions upon which peace, order, and fertility depend.

The riddle of Shakespeare's reluctant Adonis can be solved not through the discovery of some new source but by a more careful attention to the larger narrative structure of books 9 and 10 of the *Metamorphoses*. Ovid provides not only a source for the plot of this poem and its psychological configurations but also a beginning for its most frequently cited stylistic feature, antithesis. And Shakespeare's use of antithesis and paradox in his portrayal of Adonis, though characteristic of the intellectual and rhetorical climate of his age, can also be better understood by considering the nature of myth itself, which seeks to represent in language the multiple contrarieties and oppositions of human desire.

2

HAYMAN'S MISSING *HAMLET*

PAINTERS AND ILLUSTRATORS OF *HAMLET* CHOOSE TO render the play scene (3.2) more frequently than any other scene from the play, and these visual renderings are remarkably similar in their organization of figures and action, from the eighteenth century through to the present day.

Francis Hayman's drawing for Hanmer's illustrated Shakespeare of 1744 (Figure 1) establishes the central conventions that are repeated so consistently into the twentieth century: the "murder of Gonzago" is placed back center stage, with two groups ranged on either side, Claudius, Gertrude, and Polonius on the one, Hamlet, Horatio, and Ophelia on the other. The position of the dumbshow, in the background with the two audiences in the foreground on either side, makes the scene doubly theatrical by calling attention to the play-within-the-play and to the role of the other characters as spectators—an interpretation certainly consonant with modern readings that seek to emphasize the metadramatic dimensions of Shakespeare's plays.[1] Another important detail that is repeated in later versions is the position of Hamlet with body extended, at Ophelia's feet, which serves to link the two separate audience groups. The position of the viewer of this illustration is that of the dramatic audience itself, and it is commonly believed that Hayman's design renders with verisimilitude the actual staging of the play at Drury Lane in this period.[2] Such attention to contemporary staging is typical of eighteenth-century illustration and of Hayman's work in particular, since he was for many years a scene painter at Drury Lane.

Figure 1. Hayman's watercolor design for the *Hamlet* frontispiece to Hanmer's edition of Shakespeare, 1744. Reprinted by permission of the Folger Shakespeare Library.

To demonstrate the continuity of Hayman's organization of this scene, both onstage and in the visual arts, let us consider several representative examples from later periods: from the early nineteenth century, an engraving of Forrest playing Hamlet in the 1830s in which the influence of the proscenium stage is evident (Figure 2); Maclise's

Figure 2. Forrest in the play scene. Courtesy of The Harvard Theatre Collection, Houghton Library. Reprinted by permission.

Figure 3. Maclise's painting of Macready in the play scene. Courtesy of The Harvard Theatre Collection, Houghton Library. Reprinted by permission.

painting from about the same period of Macready, Forrest's rival, in an even more elaborate staging of the dumbshow (Figure 3); Booth's Hamlet in action (1864, Figure 4); Sothern as the Prince (1904, Figure 5); and finally Barrymore in Robert Edmond Jones's design (1923, Figure 6). Though there are marked differences in the actors'

Figure 4. Booth in the play scene, ca. 1864.

Figure 5. Sothern in the play scene, 1904. Courtesy of the Billy Rose Theatre Division, The New York Public Library for the Performing Arts, Astor, Lenox, and Tilden Foundations. Reprinted by permission.

interpretations of both Hamlet and other figures in the scene, in lighting, in periodization, and the like, the continuity of these visual representations is remarkable, from Hayman's early illustration in 1744 to Jones's scene design for Barrymore almost two hundred years later.

Such continuity makes Francis Hayman's painting for the Prince's Pavilion at Vauxhall Gardens all the more extraordinary, for unlike any other visual rendering of the scene, it does not include Hamlet (Figure 7).

Figure 6. Barrymore in *Hamlet* on Robert Edmond Jones's set, 1923. Courtesy of
Getty Images. Reprinted by permission.

Figure 7. The play scene in Francis Hayman's *Hamlet*, Vauxhall Gardens Pavilion.

This absence is all the more amazing if we remember, as W. Moelwyn Merchant points out in his *Shakespeare and the Artist,* that this was the Age of Garrick, and that "Hamlet was one of Garrick's greatest parts, . . . played at Drury Lane almost every year during his career"; that a scene painter from the theater would do a large painting of the play scene without the main character, Hamlet, inevitably raises questions.[3]

If Hanmer's instructions to Hayman for illustrating each play are indicative of contemporary attitudes toward the enterprise, as the illustrated editions seem to indicate, such an omission is indeed striking, for Hanmer recommends the most straightforward visual renderings. In most cases he asks for major scenes in which the main characters are present, such as the unhooding of the Duke in Act 5 of *Measure for Measure,* or the wrestling scene in *As You Like It.*[4] Unfortunately Hanmer's instructions do not include *Hamlet,* but the drawing itself conforms to the general directions and principles of illustration he gives for other plays: all the major characters are included, and the organization of figures evidently accords both with contemporary staging and with indications given in the text. We must conclude, therefore, that Hayman was not conforming to pictorial or dramatic convention but chose intentionally to exclude Hamlet from his painting.

How might we account for the Prince's absence from this large canvas, which decorated the Prince of Wales's Pavilion at Vauxhall Gardens? We should begin by comparing the painting with the illustration, also by Hayman, for the Hanmer edition (Figures 7 and 1). What we notice immediately, aside from Hamlet's absence, is the changed organization of the scene: the play scene is played forward, in the right-hand corner of the canvas and at the base of the throne rather than back. The central interest of the scene is, as Merchant notes, "where it psychologically lies, on the character and reaction of the King."[5] In order to emphasize the importance of Claudius' reaction, Hayman paints Polonius and Gertrude, those characters most likely to attend to and worry over Claudius's response, watching the King. He has started from his throne and grasps the hilt of his sword.

Merchant suggests that this painting was probably based on an actual theatrical production in which "the Presence" is placed, as it was on the Elizabethan stage, in the dominating position upstage center:

> It is possible, indeed even probable, that the play-scene would be
> played forward, towards the apron, both because its dumb show would
> in that way be more intimately shown and the King's reactions be the

more apparent. If that is so, Hayman will have produced in a closely knit composition the essential features of the theatre presentation; . . . he has isolated the essential dramatic moment in the text, and cutting out all inessentials, has rendered it with economy both of emotion and characterization.[6]

His comments explain the changed organization of the painting and the center staging of the King, appropriate certainly for a painting commissioned to decorate the Prince's Pavilion, but they fail to account for Hamlet's absence. I think that a closer look at the painting and at the text of the play may suggest an explanation for the missing Hamlet and point to an interesting artistic experiment on the part of Hayman.

We should begin by recalling Hamlet's own emphasis at the beginning of this scene on watching. In his comments to Horatio, he says:

> I prithee, when thou seest that act afoot,
> Even with the very comment of thy soul
> Observe my uncle. If his occulted guilt
> Do not itself unkennel in one speech,
> It is a damned ghost that we have seen,
> And my imaginations are as foul
> As Vulcan's stithy. Give him heedful note,
> For I mine eyes will rivet to his face,
> And after we will both our judgments join
> In censure of his seeming.
> (3.2.78–87)[7]

Remark the emphasis Hamlet places on the act of watching: "with the very comment of thy soul / Observe my uncle." The caesura contributes to this emphasis, as do the other verbs of seeing and Hamlet's striking verb "rivet." Hayman's organization of the painting and his placing of Claudius in the center of the canvas with Polonius and Gertrude watching him, not with fear or anxiety but "innocent concern," make us watch him as well.[8] The Ophelia figure, who in conventional renderings of the play scene often watches Hamlet, here seems to gaze toward someone or something outside the represented scene.[9] "Who watches whom" is the subject of Hayman's painting, but the principal watchers, Hamlet and Horatio, are both missing from the scene.

Both the painting and the text of the play that frames Hayman's representation locate the spectator in the role of Hamlet himself. Instead of watching Hamlet watch the others, as we do in other renderings of the play scene, we share Hamlet's point of view. To have ordered and composed the scene from the Prince's perspective was particularly appropriate when we recall that this canvas adorned the Prince of Wales's Pavilion at Vauxhall.[10] Hayman has superimposed the painter's gaze as he composed the painting, and the spectator's gaze as he views the representation, onto Hamlet's gaze. Though ordinarily the perspective of the painter and viewer are not represented because they come together at a point exterior to the picture, here any spectator familiar with the *Hamlet* text is necessarily reminded of the missing Hamlet, whose point of view organizes the scene.[11] The organization of the canvas, the text of *Hamlet,* and Ophelia's gaze all function to restore the absent Hamlet to the perception of the audience. By removing Hamlet from the painting and placing him in what is ordinarily our relation to the representation, Hayman usurps our conventional passive position as spectators and makes us participate in Hamlet's perception and interpretation of the play scene.[12]

We need to look finally at another painting of the play scene by Hayman, this one from the Folger Shakespeare Library, a very small canvas, 13 × 10½ inches (Figure 8), and compare it with the Vauxhall Gardens canvas. In it we see the representation of this very lack of the group of watchers for whom the action of the first painting takes place, Horatio and Hamlet (in his characteristic pose at the feet of Ophelia). As spectators, our relation to the scene and the painting is entirely changed by the addition of the group. Instead of the superimposed perspectives of the other painting, which locate us in Hamlet's point of view, we are watching the play *Hamlet.* The various lines of vision in the painting represent a closed world—the King watches the dumbshow; Gertrude, Polonius, Horatio, and Hamlet watch the King; and Ophelia watches Hamlet. In this design, as in the illustration, the theatrical illusion is preserved: as audience we stand outside the painting and the action it represents. Here Merchant's description of the larger painting, which I quoted earlier, that "the center of interest is where it psychologically lies, on . . . the king," is true; it is emphasized by Hamlet's watching within the painting from the feet of the King. Merchant suggests that this is "a study uniting elements from both the previous versions."[13] I think it more likely that this painting was a study for the larger painting which it very much resembles: the figures are the same, the throne and background are repeated, but without

Figure 8. The play scene from Hayman's *Hamlet*. Reprinted by permission of the Folger Shakespeare Library.

the same detail. In painting his larger canvas, Hayman experimented with point of view in a way that has puzzled commentators ever since, but in a way that can be understood if we consider the striking effect of the painting on its spectators.[14] Every commentator on this painting, from the early article on *Shakespeare's Pictorial Art* in *The Studio*, to Boase's major piece on Shakespearean illustration in the seventeenth and eighteenth centuries, to Merchant's work, which I have mentioned, puzzles over Hamlet's absence.[15] In doing so, each commentator demonstrates the incredible impact of that absence on the spectator who is superimposed on Hamlet and thereby takes his position in relation to what is represented, and in relation to the action of the play. That this kind of identification is at least one effect of *Hamlet* testifies to Hayman's achievement in rendering the play scene as he does, in calling attention to an absence that makes us the more aware not only of our intended relation to the action at this point in the play but also of the artist's representation itself and his experiment with point of view.

3

RENAISSANCE FAMILY POLITICS
AND SHAKESPEARE'S
THE TAMING OF THE SHREW

ETHERDEN, SUFFOLK. PLOUGH MONDAY, 1604. A drunken tanner, Nicholas Rosyer, staggers home from the alehouse. On arriving at his door, he is greeted by his wife with "dronken dogg, pisspott and other unseemly names." When Rosyer tried to come to bed with her, she "still raged against him and badd him out dronken dogg dronken pisspott." She struck him several times, clawed his face and arms, spit at him and beat him out of bed. Rosyer retreated, returned to the alehouse, and drank until he could hardly stand up. Shortly thereafter, Thomas Quarry and others met and "agreed amongest themselfs that the said Thomas Quarry who dwelt at the next howse . . . should . . . ryde abowt the towne upon a cowlestaff whereby not onley the woman which had offended might be shunned for her misdemeanors towards her husband but other women also by her shame might be admonished to offence in like sort."[1] Domestic violence, far from being contained in the family, spills out into the neighborhood, and the response of the community is an "old country ceremony used in merriment upon such accidents."

Quarry, wearing a kirtle or gown and apron, "was carried to diverse places and as he rode did admonishe all wiefs to take heede how they did beate their husbands." The Rosyers' neighbors reenacted their troubled gender relations: the beating was repeated with Quarry in woman's clothes playing Rosyer's wife, the neighbors standing in for the "abused" husband, and a rough music procession to the house of the transgressors. The result of this "merriment" suggests

Figure 9. "A skimmington," *English Customs,* plate 9. Reprinted by permission of
the Folger Shakespeare Library.

its darker purpose and the anxiety about gender relations it displays:
the offending couple left the village in shame. The skimmington, as
it was sometimes called, served its purpose by its ritual scapegoating
of the tanner, and more particularly, his wife. Rosyer vented his anger
by bringing charges against his neighbors in which he complained not
only of scandal and disgrace to himself, "his wief and kyndred," but
also of seditious "tumult and discention in the said towne."[2]

The entire incident figures the social anxiety about gender and
power that characterizes Elizabethan culture. Like Simon Forman's
dream of wish-fulfillment with Queen Elizabeth, this incident, in
Louis Montrose's words, "epitomizes the indissolubly political and
sexual character of the cultural forms in which [such] tensions might
be represented and addressed."[3] The community's ritual action against
the couple who transgress prevailing codes of gender behavior seeks
to reestablish those conventional modes of behavior—it seeks to sanc-
tion patriarchal order. But at the same time, this "old country ceremony" subverts, by its representation, its masquerade of the very

Figure 10. Thomas Cecil, "A New Yeares guift for shrews," broadside, ca. 1620.
Copyright the Trustees of The British Museum. Reprinted by permission.

events it criticizes by forcing the offending couple to recognize their
transgression through its dramatic enactment. The skimmington seeks
"in merriment" to reassert traditional gender behaviors that are naturalized in Elizabethan culture as divinely ordained; but it also deconstructs that "naturalization" by its foregrounding of what is a humanly
constructed cultural product—the displacement of gender roles in a
dramatic representation.[4]

Family Politics

The events of Plough Monday 1604 have an uncanny relation to
Shakespeare's *The Taming of the Shrew,* which might well be read as
a theatrical realization of such a community fantasy, the shaming and
subjection of a shrewish wife. The so-called induction opens with the

hostess railing at the drunken tinker Sly, and their interchange figures him as the inebriated tanner from Wetherden.[5] Sly is presented with two "dreams," the dream he is a lord, a fantasy that enacts traditional Elizabethan hierarchical and gender relations, and the "dream" of Petruchio taming Kate. The first fantasy is a series of artificially constructed power relationships figured first in class relations, then in terms of gender. The lord exhorts his serving men to offer Sly "low submissive reverence" and traditional lordly prerogatives and pursuits—music, painting, hand washing, rich apparel, hunting, and finally a theatrical entertainment. In the longer, more detailed speech that follows at Induction, 1.100ff., he exhorts his page to "bear himself with honourable action / Such as he hath observ'd in noble ladies / Unto their lords." Significantly, Sly is only convinced of his lordly identity when he is told of his "wife." His realization of this newly discovered self involves calling for the lady, demanding from her submission to his authority, and finally seeking to exert his new power through his husbandly sexual prerogative: "Madam, undress you and come now to bed" (Ind., 2.118). By enacting Sly's identity as a lord through his wife's social and sexual, if deferred, submission, the Induction suggests ironically how in this androcentric culture men depended on women to authorize their sexual and social masculine identities.[6] The Lord's fantasy takes the drunken Sly, who brawls with the hostess, and by means of a "play" brings him into line with traditional conceptions of gender relations. But in the Induction, these relationships of power and gender, which in Elizabethan treatises, sermons and homilies, and behavioral handbooks and the like were figured as natural and divinely ordained, are subverted by the metatheatrical foregrounding of such roles and relations as culturally constructed.

The analogy between the events at Wetherden and Shakespeare's play suggests a tempting homology between history and cultural artifacts. It figures patriarchy as a master narrative, the key to understanding certain historic events and dramatic plots. But as Louis Althusser's critique of historicism epigrammatically has it, "history is a process without a *telos* or a subject."[7] This Althusserian dictum repudiates such master narratives, but as Fredric Jameson points out, "What Althusser's own insistence on history as an absent cause makes clear, but what is missing from the formula as it is canonically worded, is that he does not at all draw the fashionable conclusion that because history is a text, the 'referent' does not exist . . . history is *not* a narrative, master or otherwise, but that, as an absent cause, it is inaccessible to us except in textual form, and that our approach to it and to the Real itself necessarily passes through its prior textualization, its narrativization in the political unconscious."[8] If we return to Nicholas Rosyer's complaint against his neighbors and consider its textualization, how it is made accessible to us through narrative, we can make several observations. We notice immediately that Rosyer's wife, the subject of the complaint, lacks the status of a subject. She is unnamed and referred to only as the "wief." Rosyer's testimony, in fact, begins with a defense not of his wife but of his patrimony, an account of his background and history in the village in terms of male lineage. His wife has no voice; she never speaks in the complaint at all. Her husband brings charges against his neighbors presumably to clear his name and to affirm his identity as patriarch, which the incident itself, from his wife's "abuse" to the transvestite skimmington, endangers.

From the account of this case, we also get a powerful sense of life in early modern England, the close proximity of neighbors and the way in which intimate sexual relations present a scene before an audience. Quarry and the neighbors recount Rosyer's attempted assertion of his sexual "prerogatives" over his wife and her vehement refusal: "she struck him several times, clawed his face and arms, spit at him and beat him out of bed." There is evidently no place in the late Elizabethan "sex/gender system"[9] for Rosyer's wife to complain of her husband's mistreatment, drunkenness, and abuse or even give voice to her point of view, her side of the story. The binary opposition between male and female in the Wetherden case and its figuration of patriarchy in early modern England generates the possible contradictions logically available to both terms: Rosyer speaks, his wife is silent; Rosyer is recognized as a subject before the law, his wife is solely its object; Rosyer's family must be defended against the insults of his neighbors, his wife has no family but has become merely a part of his. In turning to *The Taming of the Shrew*, our task is to articulate the particular sexual/political fantasy or, in Jameson's Althusserian formulation, the "libidinal apparatus" that the play projects as an imaginary resolution of contradictions that are never resolved in the Wetherden case, but which the formal structures of dramatic plot and character in Shakespeare's play present as seemingly reconciled.

A Shrew's History

Many readers of Shakespeare's *Shrew* have noted that both in the induction and the play language is an index of identity. Sly is convinced of his lordly identity by language, by the lord's obsequious words and recital of his false history. Significantly, when he believes himself a lord, his language changes and he begins to speak the blank verse of his retainers. But in the opening scene of the play proper, Shakespeare emphasizes not just the relationship between language and identity but between women and language, and between control over language and patriarchal power. Kate's linguistic protest is against the role in patriarchal culture to which women are assigned, that of wife and object of exchange in the circulation of male desire. Her very first words make this point aggressively: she asks of her father "I pray you, sir, is it your will / To make a stale of me amongst these mates?"[10] Punning on the meaning of "stale" as laughing-stock and prostitute, on "stalemate," and on "mate" as husband, Kate refuses her erotic destiny by exercising her linguistic willfulness. Her shrewishness, always associated with women's revolt in words, testifies to her exclusion from social and political power. Bianca, by contrast, is throughout the play associated with silence (1.1.70–71).[11]

Kate's prayer to her father is motivated by Gremio's threat "to cart her rather. She's too rough for me" (1.1.55). Although this line is usually glossed as "drive around in an open cart (a punishment for prostitutes)," the case of Nicholas Rosyer and his unnamed wife provides a more complex commentary. During the period from 1560 until the English Civil War, in which many historians have recognized a "crisis of order," the fear that women were rebelling against their traditional subservient role in patriarchal culture was widespread.[12] Popular works such as *The Two Angry Women of Abington* (1598), Middleton's *The Roaring Girl* (1611), *Hic Mulier, or The Man-Woman (1620)*, and Joseph Swetnam's *Arraignment of lewd, idle, froward and inconstant women,* which went through ten editions between 1616 and 1634, all testify to a preoccupation with rebellious women.[13]

What literary historians have recognized in late Elizabethan and Jacobean writers as a preoccupation with female rebellion and independence, social historians have also observed in historical records. The period was fraught with anxiety about rebellious women. David Underdown observes that "women scolding and brawling with their neighbours, single women refusing to enter service, wives dominating or even beating their husbands: all seem to surface more frequently than in the periods immediately before or afterwards. It will not go unnoticed that this is also the period during which witchcraft accusations reach their peak."[14] Underdown's account points out a preoccupation with women's rebellion through language. Although men were occasionally charged with scolding, it was predominantly a female offense usually associated with class as well as gender issues and revolt: "women who were poor, social outcasts, widows or otherwise lacking in the protection of a family . . . were the most common offenders."[15] Underdown points out that in the few examples after the Restoration, social disapproval shifts to "mismatched couples, sexual offenders, and eventually . . . husbands who beat their wives."[16] Punishment for such offenses and related ones involving "domineering" wives who "beat" or "abused" their husbands often involved public shaming or charivari of the sort employed at Wetherden. The accused woman or her surrogate was put in a scold's collar or ridden in a cart accompanied by a rough musical procession of villagers banging pots and pans.

Louis Montrose attributes the incidence of troubled gender relations to female rule since "all forms of public and domestic authority in Elizabethan England were vested in men: in fathers, husbands, masters, teachers, magistrates, lords. It was inevitable that the rule of a woman would generate peculiar tensions within such a 'patriarchal' society."[17] Instead of assigning the causes of such rebellion to the "pervasive cultural presence" of the Queen, historians point to the social and economic factors that contributed to these troubled gender relations. Underdown observes a breakdown of community in fast-growing urban centers and scattered pasture/dairy parishes where effective means of social control such as compact nucleated village centers, resident squires, and strong manorial institutions were weak or nonexistent. He observes the higher incidence of troubled gender relations in such communities as opposed to the arable parishes, which "tended to retain strong habits of neighborhood and cooperation." Both Montrose's reading of the Elizabethan sex-gender system in terms of "female rule" and Underdown's explanation for this proliferation of accusations of witchcraft, shrewishness, and husband domination are less important here than the clear connection between women's independent appropriation of discourse and a conceived threat to patriarchal authority contained through public shaming or spectacle—the ducking stool, usually called the cucking stool, or carting.[18]

From the outset of Shakespeare's play, Katherine's threat to male authority is posed through language; it is perceived as such by others and is linked to a claim larger than shrewishness—witchcraft—through the constant allusions to Katherine's kinship with the devil.[19] Control of women and particularly of Kate's revolt is from the outset attempted by inscribing women in a scopic economy.[20] Woman is represented as spectacle (Kate) or object to be desired and admired, a vision of beauty (Bianca). She is the site of visual pleasure, whether on the public stage, the village green, or the fantasy "cart" with which Hortensio threatens Kate. The threat of being made a spectacle, here by carting, or later in the wedding scene by Petruchio's "mad-brain rudesby," is an important aspect of shrew-taming.[21] Given the evidence of social history and of the play itself, discourse is power, both in Elizabethan and Jacobean England and in the fictional space of the *Shrew*.

The *Shrew* both demonstrated and produced the social facts of the patriarchal ideology that characterized Elizabethan England, but *representation* gives us a perspective on that patriarchal system that subverts its status as natural. The theatrically constructed frame in which Sly exercises patriarchal power and the dream in which Kate is tamed undermine the seemingly eternal nature of those structures by calling attention to the constructed character of the representation rather than veiling it through mimesis. The foregrounded female protagonist of the action and her powerful annexation of the traditionally male domain of discourse distance us from that system by exposing and displaying its contradictions. Representation undermines the ideology about women that the play presents and produces, both in the Induction and in the Kate/Petruchio plot: Sly disappears as lord, but Kate keeps talking.

The Price of Silence

At 2.1, in the spat between Bianca and Kate, the relationship between silence and women's place in the marriage market is made clear. Kate questions Bianca about her suitors, inquiring as to her preferences. Some critics have read her questions and her abuse of Bianca (in less than thirty lines, Kate binds her sister's hands behind her back, strikes her, and chases after her, calling for revenge) as revealing her secret desire for marriage and for the praise and recognition afforded her sister. Kate's behavior may invite such an interpretation, but another view persistently presents itself as well. In her questions and badgering, Kate makes clear the relationship between Bianca's sweet sobriety and her success with men. Kate's abuse may begin as a jest, but her feelings are aroused to a different and more serious pitch when her father enters, taking as usual Bianca's part against her sister.[22] Baptista emphasizes both Bianca's silence, "When did she cross thee with a bitter word?," and Katherine's link with the devil, "thou hilding of a devilish spirit" (2.1.28, 26). We should bear in mind here Underdown's observation that shrewishness is a class as well as gender issue—that women "lacking in the protection of a family . . . were the most common offenders."[23] Kate is motherless, and to some degree fatherless as well, for Baptista consistently rejects her and favors her obedient sister. Kate's threat that follows, "Her silence flouts me, and I'll be reveng'd" (2.1.29), is truer than we have heretofore recognized, for it is that silence that has insured Bianca's place in the male economy of desire and exchange to which Kate pointedly refers in her last lines:

> What, will you not suffer me? Nay, now I see
> She is your treasure, she must have a husband,
> I must dance barefoot on her wedding day,
> And, for your love to her lead apes in hell.
> (2.1.31–34)

Here we recognize the relationship between father and husband, in which woman is the mediating third term, a treasure the exchange of which assures patriarchal hegemony. Throughout the play Bianca is a treasure, a jewel, an object of desire and possession. Although much has been made of the animal analogies between Kate and beasts, the metaphorical death of the courtly imagery associated with Bianca has been ignored as too conventional, if not natural, to warrant comment.[24] What seems at issue here is not so much Kate's lack of a husband, or indeed her desire for a marriage partner, but rather her distaste at those folk customs that make her otherness, her place outside that patriarchal system, a public fact, a spectacle for all to see and mock.

In the battle of words between Kate and Petruchio at 2.1.182ff., it is Kate who gets the best of her suitor. She takes the lead through puns that allow her to criticize Petruchio and the patriarchal system of wooing and marriage. Her sexual puns make explicit to the audience not so much her secret preoccupation with sex and marriage but what is implicit in Petruchio's wooing—that marriage is a sexual exchange in which women are exploited for their use-value as producers. Significantly, Petruchio's language is linguistically similar to Kate's in its puns and wordplay. He also presents her, as many commentators have noted, with an imagined vision that makes her conform to the very order against which she rebels—he makes her a Bianca with words, shaping an identity for her that confirms the social expectations of the sex/gender system that informs the play. Their wooing can be interestingly compared with the next scene, also a wooing, between Bianca and her two suitors. Far from the imaginative use of language and linguistic play we find in Kate, Bianca repeats verbatim the Latin words Lucentio "construes" to reveal his identity and his love. Her revelation of her feelings through a repetition of the Latin lines he quotes from Ovid are as close as possible to the silence we have come to expect from her.

In the altercation over staying for the wedding feast after their marriage, Kate again claims the importance of language and her use of it to women's place and independence in the world. But here it is Petruchio who controls language, who has the final word, for he creates through words a situation to justify his actions—he claims to be rescuing Kate from thieves. More precisely, he claims she asks for that rescue. Kate's annexation of language does not work unless her audience, and particularly her husband, accepts what she says as independent rebellion. By deliberately misunderstanding and reinterpreting her words to suit his own ends, Petruchio effectively refuses her the freedom of speech identified in the play with women's independence. Such is his strategy throughout this central portion of the action, in their arrival at his house in the interchange with the tailor. Kate is figuratively killed with kindness, by her husband's rule over her not so much in material items—the withholding of food, clothing, and sleep—but the withholding of linguistic understanding. As the receiver of her messages, he simply refuses their meaning; since he also has material power to enforce his interpretations, it is his power over language that wins.

In the exchange between Petruchio and Kate with the tailor, Kate makes her strongest bid yet for linguistic freedom:

Why, sir, I trust I may have leave to speak,
And speak I will. I am no child, no babe.
Your betters have endur'd me say my mind,
And if you cannot, best you stop your ears.
My tongue will tell the anger of my heart,
Or else my heart conceaing it will break,
And rather than it shall, I will be free
Even to the uttermost, as I please, in words.
                                    (4.3.73–80)

When we next encounter Kate, however, on the journey to Padua, she finally admits to Petruchio: "What you will have it nam'd, even that it is, / And so it shall be so for Katherine" (4.5.21–22). On this journey Kate calls the sun the moon, an old man a budding virgin, and makes the world conform to the topsy-turvy of Petruchio's patriarchal whimsy. But we should look carefully at this scene before acquiescing in too easy a view of Kate's submission. Certainly she gives in to Petruchio's demands literally; but her playfulness and irony here are indisputable. As she says at 4.5.44–48:

Pardon, old father, my mistaking eyes,
That have been so bedazzled with the sun
That everything I look on seemeth green.
Now I perceive thou art a reverend father.
Pardon, I pray thee, for my mad mistaking.

Given Kate's talent for puns, we must understand her line, "bedazzled with the sun," as a pun on "son" and play with Petruchio's line earlier in the scene, "Now by my mother's son, and that's myself, / It shall be moon, or star, or what I list" (4.5.6–7). "Petruchio's bedazzlement" is exactly that, and Kate here makes clear the playfulness of their linguistic game. In his paper "Hysterical Phantasies and their Relation to Bi-Sexuality" (1908), Sigmund Freud observes that neurotic symptoms, particularly the hysterical symptom, have their origins in the daydreams of adolescence.[25] "In girls and women," Freud claims, "they are invariably of an erotic nature, in men they may be either erotic or ambitious."[26] A feminist characterological rereading of Freud might suggest that Kate's ambitious fantasies, which her culture allows her to express only in erotic directions, motivate her shrewishness.[27] Such behavior, which in a man would not be problematic, her family and peers interpret as "hysterical" or diabolic or both. Her "masculine" behavior saves her, at least for a time, from her feminine erotic destiny.

Freud goes on to claim that hysterical symptoms are always bisexual, "the expression of both a masculine and a feminine unconscious
sexual phantasy."[28] The example he gives is a patient who "pressed her
dress to her body with one hand (as the woman) while trying to tear
it off with the other (as the man)."[29] To continue our "analysis" in the
scene we are considering, we might claim that Kate's female masquerade obscures her continuing ambitious fantasies, now only manifest
in her puns and ironic wordplay that suggest the distance between
her character and the role she plays.[30] Even though she gives up her
shrewishness and acquiesces to Petruchio's whims, she persists in her
characteristic "masculine" linguistic exuberance while masquerading
as an obedient wife.[31]

Instead of using Freud to analyze Kate's character, a critical move
of debatable interpretive power, we might consider the Freudian text
instead as a reading of ideological or cultural patterns. The process
Freud describes is suggestive for analyzing the workings not of character but of Shakespeare's text itself. No speech in the play has been
more variously interpreted than Kate's final speech of women's submission. In a recent essay on the *Shrew*, John Bean has conveniently
assigned to the two prevailing views the terms "revisionist" for those
who would take Kate's speech as ironic and her subservience as pre-
tense, a way of living peaceably in patriarchal culture but with an
unregenerate spirit, and the "anti-revisionists" who argue that farce is
the play's governing genre, that Kate's response to Petruchio's taming
is that of an animal responding to "the devices of a skilled trainer."[32]
Bean himself argues convincingly for a compromise position that
admits the "background of depersonalizing farce unassimilated from
the play's fabliau sources," but it suggests that Kate's taming needs
to be seen in terms of romantic comedy, as a spontaneous change of
heart such as those of the later antic comedies "where characters lose
themselves in chaos and emerge, as if from a dream, liberated into
the bonds of love."[33] Bean rightly points out the liberal elements of
the final speech in which marriage is seen as a partnership as well as
a hierarchy, citing the humanist writers on marriage and juxtaposing
Kate's speech with the responding, and remarkably more misogynist,
lines in *The Taming of a Shrew* and other taming tales.[34]

Keeping in mind Bean's arguments for the content of the speech
and its place in the intersection of farce and romantic love plot, I
would like to turn instead to its significance as representation. What

we find is Katherine as a strong, energetic female protagonist represented before us addressing not the onstage male audience, only too aware of its articulation of patriarchal power, but Bianca and the Widow, associated with silence throughout the play and finally arriving by means, as Petruchio calls it, of Kate's "womanly persuasion" (5.2.120).

Unlike any other of Shakespeare's comedies, we have here represented not simply marriage, with the final curtain a veiled mystification of the sexual and social results of that ritual, but a view, however brief and condensed, of that marriage over time.[35] And what we see is not a quiet and submissive Kate but the same energetic and linguistically powerful Kate with which the play began. We know, then, in a way we never know about the other comedies, except perhaps *The Merchant of Venice,* and there our knowledge is complicated by Portia's male disguise, that Kate has continued to speak. She has not, of course, continued to speak her earlier language of revolt and anger. Instead she has adopted another strategy, a strategy that the French psychoanalyst Luce Irigaray calls mimeticism.[36] Irigaray argues that women are cut off from language by the patriarchal order in which they live, by their entry into the Symbolic, which the Father represents in a Freudian/Lacanian model.[37] Women's only possible relation to the dominant discourse is mimetic:

> To play with mimesis is . . . for a woman to try to recover the place of her exploitation by language, without allowing herself to be simply reduced to it. It is to resubmit herself . . . to ideas—notably about her—elaborated in and through a masculine logic, but to "bring out" by an effect of playful repetition what was to remain hidden: the recovery of a possible operation of the feminine in language. It is also to unveil the fact that if women mime so well they are not simply reabsorbed in this function. *They also remain elsewhere.*[38]

Whereas Irigaray goes on to locate this "elsewhere" in sexual pleasure (*jouissance*), Nancy Miller has elaborated on this notion of "mimeticism," describing it as a "form of emphasis: an italicized version of what passes for the neutral . . . Spoken or written, italics are a modality of intensity and stress; a way of marking what has already been said, of making a common text one's own."[39]

Joel Fineman has recently observed the difficulty in distinguishing between man's and woman's speech in the *Shrew* by demonstrating how the rhetorical strategies Kate deploys are like Petruchio's.[40] But

Kate's self-consciousness about the power of discourse, her punning and irony, and her techniques of linguistic masquerade are strategies of italics, mimetic strategies, in Irigaray's sense of mimeticism. Instead of figuring a gender-marked woman's speech, they deform language by subverting it, that is, by turning it inside out so that metaphors, puns, and other forms of wordplay manifest their veiled equivalences: the meaning of woman as treasure, of wooing as a civilized and acceptable disguise for sexual exploitation, of the objectification and exchange of women. Kate's having the last word contradicts the very sentiments she speaks; rather than resolve the play's action, her monologue simply displays the fundamental contradiction presented by a female dramatic protagonist, between woman as a sexually desirable, silent object and women of words, women with power over language who disrupt, or at least italicize, women's place and part in culture.

To dramatize action involving linguistically powerful women characters militates against patriarchal structures and evaluations of women in which their silence is most highly prized—which is why so many of Shakespeare's heroines, in order to maintain their status as desirable, must don male attire in order to speak: Rosalind, Portia, even the passive Viola. The conflict between the explicitly repressive content of Kate's speech and the implicit message of independence communicated by representing a powerful female protagonist speaking the play's longest speech at a moment of emphatic suspense is not unlike Freud's female patient who "pressed her dress to her body with one hand (as the woman) while trying to tear it off with the other (as the man)." We might even say that this conflict shares the bisexuality Freud claims for the hysterical symptom, that the text itself is sexually ambivalent, a view in keeping with the opposed readings of the play in which it is either conservative farce or subversive irony. Such a representation of gender, what I will call the "female dramatizable,"[41] is always at once patriarchally suspect and sexually ambivalent, clinging to Elizabethan patriarchal ideology and at the same time tearing it away by foregrounding or italicizing its constructed character.

Missing Frames and Female Spectacles

Kate's final speech is "an imaginary or formal solution to unresolvable social contradictions," but that appearance of resolution is an "ideological mirage."[42] On the level of plot, as many readers have noted, if one shrew is tamed two more reveal themselves. Bianca and the Widow refuse to do their husbands' bidding, thereby undoing the sense of closure Kate's "acquiescence" produces. By articulating the contradiction manifested in the scene's formal organization and its social "content"—between the "headstrong women," now Bianca and the Widow who refuse their duty, and Kate and her praise of women's submission—the seeming resolution of the play's ending is exploded and its *heterogeneity* rather than its unity is foregrounded. But can transgression of the law of women's silence be subversive? It has become a theoretical commonplace to argue that transgression presupposes norms or taboos. Therefore, the "female dramatizable" is perhaps no more than a release mechanism, a means of managing troubled gender relations. By transgressing the law of women's silence, but far from subverting it, the *Shrew* reconfirms the law, if we remember that Kate, Bianca, and the Widow remain objects of the audience's gaze, specular images, represented female bodies on display, as on the cucking stool or in the cart, the traditional punishments for prostitutes and scolds. Representation contains female rebellion. And because the play has no final framing scene, no return to Sly, it could be argued that its artifice is relaxed, that the final scene is experienced naturalistically. The missing frame allows the audience to forget that Petruchio's taming of Kate is presented as a fiction.

Yet even with its missing frame and containment of woman through spectacle, the *Shrew* finally deconstructs its own mimetic effect if we remember the bisexual aspect of the representation of women on the Elizabethan and Jacobean stage. Kate would have been played by a boy whose transvestism, like Thomas Quarry's in the Wetherden skimmington, emblematically embodied the sexual contradictions manifest both in the play and Elizabethan culture. The very indeterminateness of the actor's sexuality, of the woman/man's body, the supplementarity of its titillating homoerotic play (Sly's desire for the page boy disguised as a woman, Petruchio's "Come Kate, we'll to bed"), foregrounds its artifice and therefore subverts the play's patriarchal master narrative by exposing it as neither natural nor divinely ordained, but culturally constructed.

4

"AND WASH THE ETHIOP WHITE"

Femininity and the Monstrous

in *Othello*

Shakespear, who is accountable both to the Eyes *and to the* Ears, *And to convince the very heart of an Audience, shews that Desdemona was won by hearing* Othello *talk. . . . This was the Charm, this was the philtre, the love-powder, that took the Daughter of this Noble Venetian. This was sufficient to make the Black-amoor White, and reconcile all, tho' there had been a Cloven-foot into the bargain.*

—Thomas Rymer, *A Short View of Tragedy*

It would be something monstrous to conceive this beautiful Venetian girl falling in love with a veritable negro.

—Coleridge on Shakespeare

TO WASH AN ETHIOP WHITE" IS AN ANCIENT PROVERB used to express impossibility and bootless labor. Scholars speculate that it originated with Aesop, where the image of scrubbing an Ethiopian is used to demonstrate the power and permanence of nature. The proverb was common in Greek, and in Latin took the form "abluis Aethiopem: quid frustra" (you wash an Aethiopian: why the labor in vain). Figure 11, an emblem from Geoffrey Whitney's widely circulated emblem book, *A Choice of Emblemes* (Leyden, 1586), moralizes the proverb in the poem printed beneath the wood-cut.[1] The expression was proverbial in early modern England and commonplace on the English and Jacobean stage; in *The White Devil*, for example, the Moorish waiting woman Zanche promises Francisco coin and jewels, a dowry "should make that sunburnt proverbe false, / And wash the Ethiop white."[2] By the nineteenth century, the proverb is so familiar that it works as the underlying presupposition of the popular advertisement reproduced in Figure 12, which paradoxically inverts its meaning. Unlike the sixteenth-century emblem in which the Ethiop remains black despite the ministrations of the washerwomen, in the advertisement, a nineteenth-century Pear's Soap poster, the black

Æthiopem lauare.   57

L E A V E of with paine , the blackamore to skowre,
With washinge ofte, and wipinge more then due :
For thou shalt finde , that Nature is of powre,
Doe what thou canste, to keepe his former hue:
Thoughe with a forke, wee Nature thruste awaie,
Shee turnes againe , if wee withdrawe our hande:
And thoughe , wee ofte to conquer her assaie,
Yet all in vaine , shee turnes if still wee stande:
   Then euermore , in what thou doest assaie,
   Let reason rule , and doe the thinges thou maie.

Erasmus ex Luciano.
Ablue Æthiopem fru-
stra: quin desinis arte?
Haud unquæ efficies
nox sit ut atra , dies.
Horat. 1. Epist. 10.
Naturam expellas fur-
ca tamen usque ra-
surret.

——————— ——— *equusq,*
Nunquam ex degeneri fiet generosus asello,
Et nunquam ex stolido cordatus fiet ab arte.

                H   *Non*

Anulus in pict.
poesi.

Figure 11. Geoffrey Whitney, *A Choice of Emblemes*, 1586. Reprinted by permission of the Folger Shakespeare Library.

Figure 12. Pear's Soap advertisement, nineteenth century. From the collection of William G. McLoughlin.

baby has been scrubbed almost white. In the burgeoning consumer culture of nineteenth-century England, the man-made promises to reveal beneath black skin a hidden whiteness unimaginable to early modern man. In the modern period, difference is effaced and whiteness is the neutral term. So on a sign posted outside a Sussex inn called "The Labour in Vain," two men are represented "hard at work scrubbing a nigger [*sic*] till the white should gleam through."[3]

In the introduction to his widely used Arden edition of *Othello,* in circulation since 1958, when it was first published, and superseded only in 1997, when E. A. J. Honigmann's new edition finally appeared, M. R. Ridley offers the following answer to the long critical history that sought to refute Othello's blackness:

> To a great many people the word "negro" suggests at once the picture of what they would call a "nigger", the woolly hair, thick lips, round skull, blunt features, and burnt-cork blackness of the traditional nigger minstrel. Their subconscious generalization is as silly as that implied in Miss Preston's "the African race" or Coleridge's "veritable negro." There are more races than one in Africa, and that a man is black in colour is no

reason why he should, even to European eyes, look subhuman. One of the finest heads I have ever seen on any human being was that of a negro conductor on an American Pullman car. He had lips slightly thicker than an ordinary European's, and he had somewhat curly hair; for the rest he had a long head, a magnificent forehead, a keenly chiselled nose, rather sunken cheeks, and his expression was grave, dignified, and a trifle melancholy. He was coal-black, but he might have sat to a sculptor for a statue of Caesar.[4]

Ridley's implied "they" is troublesome. As scholars and teachers, we used his Arden edition of *Othello* for years and found ourselves implicated in his comfortable assumptions about "a great many people." Ridley affirms that Othello was black, but he hastens to add the adversative, "but." Othello was not a "veritable negro," he assures us, a type from vaudeville and the minstrel show, a figure of ridicule unworthy of tragedy who would evidently appear "subhuman" to European eyes, but a black who looks white and might have represented the most renowned general of the western tradition, Caesar.[5] What are we to make of a widely used scholarly edition of Shakespeare that, in the very act of debunking, canonizes the prejudices of Rymer and Coleridge? Can we shrug our shoulders, certain that Ridley's viewpoint represents a long ago past of American Pullman cars and dignified black conductors? Are such prejudices dismantled by the 1984 reprint, which represents on its cover a "veritable negro" of exactly the physiognomy Ridley assures us "a great many people" are wrong in imagining?

Much of the disgust Rymer, Coleridge, and other critics betray comes not from the fact of Othello's individual blackness but from the *relation* of that blackness to Desdemona's fair purity. Coleridge calls it "monstrous." Embedded in commentaries on the play that seek to ward off Othello's blackness is the fear of miscegenation, and particularly the white man's fear of the union of black man with white woman. Such commentators occupy the rhetorical position of Roderigo, Brabantio, and Iago who view the marriage of Othello and Desdemona as against all sense and nature: "I'll refer me to all things of sense, / . . . Whether a maid, so tender, fair, and happy, /. . . Would ever have (to incur a general mock) / Run from her guardage to the sooty bosom / Of such a thing as thou?" (1.2.64, 66, 69–71).

In *Othello,* the black Moor and the fair Desdemona are united in a marriage that all the other characters view as unthinkable. Shakespeare uses their assumption to generate the plot itself—Iago's ploy to string Roderigo along is his assurance that Desdemona could not, contrary to nature, long love a black man. Even his manipulation of Othello depends on the Moor's own prejudices against his blackness and belief that the fair Desdemona would prefer the white Cassio.

Miscegenation is an issue not only on the level of plot but also of language, for linked oppositions, especially of black and white and their cultural associations, characterize the play's discourse.[6] "Black ram" tups "white ewe"; "fair" Desdemona runs to Othello's "sooty bosom." The Duke mollifies Brabantio with "Your son-in-law is far more fair than black." Desdemona is described, in what for the Renaissance would have been an oxymoron, as a "fair devil" and as "fair paper" and a "goodly book" across the white pages of which Othello fears is written "whore." In the final scene Emilia exclaims in response to Othello's confession that he has killed Desdemona, "O, the more angel she, /And you the blacker devil!" Like the proverb "to wash an Ethiop white," Emilia's lines exemplify what I will term rhetorical miscegenation, for despite the semantics of antithesis, the chiasmus allies the opposing terms rhetorically.

In the Renaissance no other colors so clearly implied opposition or were so frequently used to denote polarization. As Winthrop Jordan points out in his monumental study *White over Black,* the meaning of *black* even before the sixteenth century, according to the *OED,* included "deeply stained with dirt, soiled, dirty, foul. . . . Having dark or deadly purposes, malignant; pertaining to or involving death, deadly, baneful, disastrous . . . iniquitous, atrocious, horrible, wicked . . . indicating disgrace, censure, liability to punishment, etc."[7] Of Jonson's *Masque of Blacknesse,* a preeminent example of the black/white opposition in the period, Stephen Orgel observes that it is "only necessary that the 'twelve *Nymphs, Negros*' be revealed—that we *see* them— for the 'antimasque' to have taken place"[8] *White* represented the opposite. The emphasis in *Othello* on Desdemona's fairness and purity, "that whiter skin of hers than snow / And smooth as monumental alabaster" (5.2.4–5), and the idealization of fair female beauty it implies— the entire apparatus of Petrarchanism —is usually said to point up the contrast between Desdemona and Othello. But I want to argue to the contrary that femininity is not opposed to blackness and monstrosity, as white is to black, but identified with the monstrous, an identification that makes miscegenation doubly fearful. The play is structured around a cultural aporia, miscegenation.

Femininity interrupts not only the characterological but also the critical discourse of the play. In his commentary, Ridley continues after the passage quoted above:

> To give an insult any point and barb it must have some relation to the facts. A woman may call a pale-complexioned rival "pasty" or "whey-faced," but it would be silly to call her swarthy . . . in the same way, "thick lips" would lose all its venom if it could not be recognizably applicable to Othello's mouth. (lii)

Ridley's justification of Othello's blackness and his reading of "thick lips" betray a woefully inadequate sense of irony: literary discourse often works by means of negative example, as in Shakespeare's vaunt "My mistress' eyes are nothing like the sun." But more important than Ridley's limitations as a reader of texts is how he illustrates his point about Othello's blackness: he evokes a cultural prejudice against women, their supposed cattiness in response to a rival. Femininity interrupts Ridley's commentary on Othello's blackness; pitting women against women, the critic displaces the struggle of white against black man onto a cultural femininity.

Miscegenation: Blacks and the Monstrous

Until the late sixteenth century, speculation about the cause of blackness depended on classical sources rather than experience or observation.[9] In the myth of Phaeton, for example, and Ptolemy's *Tetrabiblos,* Africans' blackness was explained by their proximity to the sun. With the publication in 1589 of the many travel accounts and geographies in Hakluyt's *Principal Navigations,* however, the rehearsal of this ancient topos, though often quoted, was usually countered by the observation that many peoples living equally close to the sun in the Indies and other parts of the New World were of olive complexion and thus disproved the ancients' latitudinal etiology. Myth and empirical observation collided.

In his *Discourse* (1578, repr. in Hakluyt, 1600), George Best, an English traveler, gives an early account of miscegenation and the causes of blackness:

I my selfe have seene an Ethiopian as blacke as a cole brought into England, who taking a faire English woman to wife, begat a sonne in all respects as blacke as the father was, although England were his native countrey, and an English woman his mother: whereby it seemeth this blacknes proceedeth rather of some natural infection of that man, which was so strong, that neither the nature of the Clime, neither the good complexion of the mother concurring, coulde any thing alter.[10]

Best's account of miscegnation is designed to refute the conventional latitudinal explanation, but it does much more. Not only does it emphasize the contrariety of black and white, "blacke as a cole" and "faire English woman,"[11] his repetitions also betray the Englishman's ethnocentric preoccupation with his native isle.[12]

Best also proffers an alternative explanation of blackness that he substitutes for the ancients' geographical theory: "this blacknes proceedeth rather of some natural infection of that man." Best's claim is more radical than his metaphor of disease implies because to assert that black and white were "naturally" different also posed a theological problem. If the union of black and white always results in black offspring, "in all respects as blacke as the father," then how can we account for the origin of blacks from our first parents? And so Best goes on to explain his claim by referring to Scripture and the story in Genesis of Noah and his three sons,

who all three being white, and their wives also, by course of nature should have begotten and brought foorth white children. But the envie of our great and continuall enemie the wicked Spirite is such, that as hee coulde not suffer our olde father Adam to live in the felicitie and Angelike state wherein hee was first created, but tempting him, sought and procured his mine and fall: so againe, finding at this flood none but a father and three sonnes living, hee so caused one of them to transgresse and disobey his father's commaundement, that after him all his posteritie shoulde bee accursed. The fact of disobedience was this: When Noe at the commandement of God had made the Arke and entered therein . . . hee straitely commaunded his sonnes and their wives, that they . . . should use continencie, and abstaine from carnall copulation with their wives. . . . Which good instructions and exhortations notwithstanding his wicked sonne Cham disobeyed, and being perswaded that the first childe borne after the flood (by right and Lawe of nature) should inherite and possesse all the dominions of the earth, hee contrary to his fathers commandement while they were yet in the Arke, used company with his wife, and craftily went about thereby to dis-inherite the off-spring of his other two brethren: for the which wicked and detestable fact, as an example for contempt of Almightie God, and disobedience of parents, God would a sonne should bee borne whose name was Chus, who not onely it selfe, but all his posteritie after him should bee so blacke and lothsome, that it might remaine a spectacle of disobedience to all the worlde. And of this blacke and cursed Chus came all these blacke Moores which are in Africa.[13]

Best's myth of a second fall is an extraordinarily rich rehearsal of early English social attitudes. In it are revealed the stock prejudices against blacks in Elizabethan and Jacobean culture: the link between blackness and the devil, the myth of black sexuality, the problem of black subjection to authority, here displaced onto obedience owed to the father and to God. Best's story passes "segregation off as natural — and as the very law of the origin." Derrida's words about apartheid are suggestive for understanding not only Best's *Discourse* but travel writing more generally:

> There's no racism without a language. The point is not that acts of racial violence are only words but rather that they have to have a word. Even though it offers the excuse of blood, color, birth — or, rather, because it uses this naturalist and sometimes creationist discourse — racism always betrays the perversion of man, the "talking animal."[14]

But Best's account also represents the specifically Elizabethan economic and social crisis that historians such as Lawrence Stone have described. Noah's son Cham disobeys his father's will because he is ambitious; he seeks to displace his older brothers in the hierarchy of inheritance. Best's account textualizes the problem of social mobility during the period and ironically, given Best's conservatism, challenges definitions of social identity based on birth. Best betrays fear of the social changes taking place in Elizabethan England, of "masterless men" and of challenges to traditional notions of order and degree. At a time when "elite identity gradually came to depend not on inherited or god-given absolute attributes, but on characteristics which could be acquired by human efforts," Best's account stands in an interesting transitional relation to such changes in the social formation.[15] Cham recognizes the authority of birthright, as does Best's own anxious parenthesis "(by righte and Lawe of nature)" but he seeks to enact the "Lawe of nature" through human effort, an effort duly punished by the ultimate authority, God.

Similarly Best's nationalism and fear of difference demarcate attitudes characteristic of the period. Even by 1578 the English had a considerable material investment in Africa: English explorers had begun to compete with Portuguese traders; John Hawkins had organized the first successful slave-trading venture between Africa and the West Indies in 1563. Best's is not just a fantasy about Africa and blackness but an enabling discourse that sustains a series of material and economic practices and interests. In England itself, by 1596, blacks were numerous enough to generate alarm. Elizabeth wrote to the Lord Mayor of London and to other towns and observed that "there are of late divers blackmoores brought into this realme, of which kinde of people there are allready to manie, consideringe howe God hath blessed this land with great increase of people of our own nation"; a week later she observed that "those kinde of people may be well spared in this realme, being so populous," and licensed a certain Casper van Senden, a merchant of Lubeck who had freed eighty-nine Englishmen imprisoned in Spain and Portugal, "to take up so much blackamoores here in this realme and to transport them into Spain and Portugal" for his expenses.[16] Five years later, in January 1601, van Senden was again licensed, this time to deport "the said kind of people . . . with all speed . . . out of this her majesty's realms."[17] Other travel accounts of the period display the intersection of ancient legends and myths about black Africa with contemporary experience, observation, and prejudice. Interspersed with descriptions of African tribal customs, language, and landscape were the legendary stories from Pliny and other classical sources, probably via Mandeville (whose popular *Travels* was included in the first [1589] edition of Hakluyt's *Principal Navigations)*, of the Anthropophagi who wore skins and ate human flesh, of people without heads or speech, of satyrs and Troglodytes who lived in caves and dens.[18] The African landscape was presented descriptively in terms of safe harbors, intense heat, and gigantic waterfalls, but also mythically, as traversed by flames and fire that reached as high as the moon, and as ringing with the sound of pipes, trumpets, and drums.[19] Always we find the link between blackness and the monstrous and particularly a monstrous sexuality. Early travelers describe women held in common and men "furnisht with such members as are after a sort burthensome unto them."[20] These accounts often bore no relation to African sexual habits, but they did confirm earlier discourses and representations of African sexuality found in Herodotus, Diodorus, and other classical authors.

The prejudices of the ancients were preserved into the fifteenth and sixteenth centuries: early cartographers ornamented maps with representations of naked black men bearing enormous sexual organs; Leo Africanus's *Historie of Africa* (1526), widely available in Latin in England and translated in 1600 by John Pory, claimed "negros" were "prone to Venery." Jean Bodin, in his widely read work of political philosophy *The Six Bookes of a Commonweale*, argues against slavery but nevertheless betrays the conventional prejudice about black sexuality when he claims:

> There be in mans bodie some members, I may not call them filthie (for that nothing can so be which is naturall) but yet so shamefull, as that no man except he be past all shame, can without blushing reveale or discover the same: and doe they [blacks] for that cease to be members of the whole bodie? [21]

Because of his organic conception of the state, Bodin's political theory does not permit a dualism, slavery for some, freedom for others. But he is so shamed by those members, and the Africans' custom of exposing them, that he dresses his prose in a series of parentheses and clauses that effectively obscure its meaning.

Such attitudes, both inherited from the past and reconstructed by contemporary historiographers, humanists, and travelers, were quickly assimilated into the drama and culture of early modern England.[22] In *Titus Andronicus,* for example, the lustful union of Aaron and Tamor resulted in a black baby called "a devil" in the play.[23] In *Tamar Cam* (1592) there is an entry of "Tartars, Geates, Amozins, Negars, ollive cullord moores, Canniballs, Hermaphrodites, Pigmes," company that testifies to the contemporary link between blackness and the monstrous. Similarly, Volpone's copulations resulting in his monstrous offspring, the fool, dwarf, and hermaphrodite, are accomplished with "beggars, gipseys and Jewes, and black moores." In Bacon's *New Atlantis* (1624), a holy hermit "desired to see the Spirit of Fornication; and there appeared to him a foul little Aethiop." Treatises on witchcraft and trials of the period often reported that the devil appeared to the possessed as a black man.[24] Finally, contemporary ballads and broadsides, the Renaissance equivalent of the news story, popularized monstrous births such as one recorded by the Stationers' Register (1580): a child, born at Fenstanton in Huntingdonshire, was described as "a monster with a black face, the Mouth and Eyes like a Lyon which was both Male and Female."[25]

Monstrous Desire in *Othello*

In *Renaissance Self-Fashioning* (1980), Stephen Greenblatt has argued persuasively that Othello submits to narrative self-fashioning, his own and Iago's. He demonstrates the congruence between their narratives and the ideological narratives of Renaissance culture, most powerfully the orthodox Christian attitude toward sexuality, and he shows how Iago and Othello are linked by shared, if dialectically opposed, cultural values about women and sexuality. Greenblatt quotes Kenneth Burke's claim that they are "consubstantial":

> Iago, to arouse Othello, must talk a language that Othello knows as well as he, a language implicit in the nature of Othello's love as the idealization of his private property in Desdemona. This language is the dialectical opposite of Othello's; but it so thoroughly shares a common ground with Othello's language that its insinuations are never for one moment irrelevant to Othello's thinking. Iago must be cautious in leading Othello to believe them as true: but Othello never for a moment doubts them as *values*.[26]

For Greenblatt, "identity depends upon a constant performance, as we have seen, of his [Othello's] 'story,' a loss of his own origins, an embrace and perpetual reiteration of the norms of another culture" (245).

What are Othello's lost origins? Greenblatt implies as somehow anterior to identity-as-performance an essential self, an ontological subjectivity, an Edenic moment of black identity prior to discourse, outside, in Derrida's phrase quoted earlier, "the perversion of man, the 'talking animal.'" Derrida's words about racism are also pertinent to a discussion of origins and permit the substitution of ontology for race: "there are no origins without a language." "Othello" doesn't lose "his own origins"; his only access to those origins is the exotic ascriptions of European colonial discourse. Othello's stories of slavery and adventure *are precisely* a rehearsal of his origins, from his exotic tales of monstrous races to the story of the handkerchief's genealogy in witchcraft and Sibylline prophecy. Othello charms by reiterating his origins even as he submits and embraces the dominant values of Venetian culture. His successful courtship of Desdemona suggests that those origins are not simply repressive but also enabling. Greenblatt is moving in his representation of Othello's submission to such cultural plots, but by focusing on Othello's ideological complicity, he effectively erases the other, which is constituted discursively in the play as both woman and black. Othello is both a speaking subject, a kind of George Best recounting his tales of conquest, and at the same time the object of his "Travellours historie" by virtue of his blackness, which originates with the very monstrous races he describes.[27]

Similarly he is both the representative and upholder of a rigorous sexual code that prohibits desire and defines it even within marriage as adulterous, as Greenblatt claims, and yet also the sign of a different, unbridled sexuality. Greenblatt effaces the profound paradox of the black Othello's embrace of Christian sexual mores: Othello is both monster and hero, and his own sexuality is appropriately indecipherable.[28] As the champion of Christian cultural codes, he assures the senators that his wish to take his bride with him to Cyprus is not "to please the palate of my appetite, / Nor to comply with heat, the young affects / In my defunct, and proper satisfaction" (1.3.262–64). He loves Desdemona "but to be free and bounteous of her mind" (265). Like Brabantio, Iago, and Roderigo, Othello perceives of his love and indeed his human, as opposed to bestial, identity as depending on property rights, on absolute ownership:

> O curse of marriage,
> That we can call these delicate creatures ours,
> And not their appetites! I had rather be a toad,
> And live upon the vapour in a dungeon,
> Than keep a corner in a thing I love,
> For others' uses . . .
> (3.3.271–76)

But opposed to the representation of Othello's participation in the play's dominant sex/gender system is a conventional representation of black sexuality evoked by other characters and by Othello himself in his traveler's tales and through his passionate action. The textual allusions to bestiality, lubriciousness, and the demonic have been often noted. Iago rouses Brabantio with "an old black ram / Is tupping your white ewe . . . / . . . the devil will make a grandsire of you"

(1.1.88–89, 91), and "you'll have your daughter cover'd with a Barbary horse; you'll have your nephews neigh to you; you'll have coursers for cousins, and gennets for germans" (110–13). "Your daughter and the Moor, are now making the beast with two backs" (115–16) and Desdemona is transported, according to Roderigo, "to the gross clasps of a lascivious Moor" (126). Not until the third scene is the Moor named, and the delay undoubtedly dramatizes Othello's blackness and the audience's shared prejudices, which are vividly conjured up by Iago's pictorial visions of carnal knowledge. To read Othello as congruent with the attitudes toward sexuality and femininity expressed in the play by the Venetians—Iago, Brabantio, Roderigo, and Cassio—and opposed to Desdemona's desire is to ignore the threatening sexuality of the other that divides the representation of Othello's character.[29] Othello internalizes alien cultural values, but the otherness that divides him from that culture and links him to the play's other marginality, femininity, remains in visual and verbal allusion.

For the white male characters of the play, the black man's power resides in his sexual difference from a white male norm. Their preoccupation with black sexuality is an eruption not of a normally repressed animal sexuality in the "civilized" white male but of the feared power and potency of a different and monstrous sexuality that threatens the white male sexual norm represented in the play most emphatically by Iago. For however evil Iago reveals himself to be, as Spivak pointed out, like the Vice in the medieval morality, or, we could add, the trickster/slave of Latin comedy, Iago enjoys a privileged relation with the audience.[30] He possesses what can be termed the discourse of knowledge in *Othello* and annexes not only the other characters but the resisting spectator as well into his world and its perspective. By virtue of his manipulative power and his superior knowledge and control over the action, which we share, we are implicated in his machinations and the cultural values they imply.[31] Iago is a cultural hyperbole; he does not oppose cultural norms so much as hyperbolize them.[32]

Before the English had wide experience of miscegenation, they seem to have believed, as George Best recounts, that the black man had the power to subjugate his partner's whiteness, to make both his "victim" and her offspring resemble him, to make them both black, a literal blackness in the case of a child, a metaphorical blackness in the case of a sexual partner. So in *Othello,* Desdemona becomes "thou black weed" (4.3.69) and the white pages of her "goodly book" are blackened by writing when Othello imagines "whore" inscribed across them. At 4.3, she explicitly identifies herself with her mother's maid Barbary, whose name connotes blackness. The union of Desdemona and Othello represents a sympathetic identification between femininity and the monstrous that offers a potentially subversive recognition of sexual and racial difference.

Both the male-dominated Venetian world of *Othello* and the criticism the play has generated have been dominated by a scopic economy that privileges sight, from the spectacular opposition of black and white to Othello's demands for ocular proof of Desdemona's infidelity. But Desdemona *hears* Othello and loves him, awed by his traveler's tales of the dangers he had passed, dangers that emphasize his link with monsters and marvels. Her responses to his tales are perceived as voracious—she "devours" his discourses with a "greedy ear," conflating the oral and aural, and his language betrays a masculine fear of a cultural femininity that is envisioned as a greedy mouth, never satisfied, always seeking increase, a point of view that Desdemona's response to their reunion at Cyprus reinforces.[33] Desdemona is presented in the play as a sexual subject who hears and desires, and that desire is punished because the nonspecular or nonphallic sexuality it displays is frightening and dangerous.[34] Instead of a specular imaginary, Desdemona's desire is represented in terms of an aural/oral libidinal economy that generates anxiety in Othello, as his account to the Senate of his courtship via fiction betrays.[35] Othello fears Desdemona's desire because it invokes his monstrous difference from the sex/race code he has adopted or, alternatively, allies her imagined monstrous sexual appetite with his own.

Thomas Rymer, a kind of critical Iago, claims the moral of *Othello* is first, "a caution to all Maidens of Quality how, without their parents' consent, they run away with Blackamoors," an instruction that he follows with the version of his Italian source, Cinthio: "Di non si accompagnare con huomo cui la natura & il cielo & il modo della vita disgiunge da noi."[36] Both Rymer and Cinthio reveal how Desdemona is punished for her desire: she *hears* Othello and desires him, and her desire is punished because it threatens a white male hegemony in which women cannot be desiring subjects. When Desdemona comes to tell her version of their wooing, she says: "I saw Othello's visage in his mind." The allusion here is certainly to her audience's prejudice against the black "visage" that both the senators and Shakespeare's audience see in Othello, but Desdemona "saw" his visage through hearing the tales he tells of his past, tales that, far from washing the Moor white, as her line seems to imply, emphatically affirm Othello's link with Africa and its legendary monstrous creatures. Rymer's moral points up the patriarchal and scopic assumptions of his culture, which are assumed as well in the play and most pointedly summed up by Brabantio's often quoted lines: "Look to her, Moor, have a quick eye to see: / She has deceiv'd her father, may do thee" (1.3.292–93). Fathers have the right to dispose of their daughters as they see fit, to whom they see fit, and disobedience against the father's law is merely a prelude to the descent into hell and blackness the play enacts, a fall, we might recall, Best's tale uncannily predicts. Desdemona's desire threatens the patriarchal privilege of disposing daughters and in the play world signals sexual duplicity and lust.

The irony, of course, is that Othello himself is the instrument of punishment; he enacts the moral Rymer and Cinthio point, both confirming cultural prejudice by his monstrous murder of Desdemona and punishing her desire, which transgresses the norms of the Elizabethan sex/race system. Both Othello and Desdemona deviate from the norms of the sex/race system in which they participate from the margins. Othello is not, in Cinthio's words, "da noi," one of "us," nor is Desdemona. Women depend for their class status on their affiliation with men—fathers, husbands, sons—and Desdemona forfeits that status and the protection it affords when she marries outside the categories her culture allows.[37] For her transgression, her desire of difference, she is punished not only in a loss of status but even of life. The woman's desire is punished, and ultimately its monstrous inspiration as well. As the object of Desdemona's illegitimate passion, Othello both figures monstrosity *and* at the same time represents the white male norms the play encodes through Iago, Roderigo, Brabantio.[38] Not surprisingly, Othello reveals at last a complicitous self-loathing, for blackness is as loathsome to him as to George Best, or any male character in the play, or ostensibly the audience.

At 4.1, Iago constructs a drama which Othello is instructed to interpret, a scene rich in its figurations of desire and the monstrous. Cast by Iago as eavesdropper and voyeur, Othello imagines and thus constitutes a sexual encounter and pleasure that excludes him, and a Desdemona as whore instead of fair angel. Cassio's mocking rehearsal of Bianca's love is not the sight/site of Desdemona's transgression, as Othello believes, but its representation; ironically this theatrical representation directed by Iago functions as effectively as would the real. Representation for Othello is transparent. The male gaze is privileged; it constructs a world that the drama plays out. The aptly and ironically named Bianca is a cypher for Desdemona, whose "blackened whiteness" she embodies. Plots of desire conventionally figure woman as the erotic object, but in *Othello* the iconic center of the spectacle is shifted from the woman to the monstrous Othello, whose blackness charms *and* threatens but ultimately fulfills the cultural prejudices it represents. Othello is both hero and outsider because he embodies not only the norms of male power and privilege represented by the white male hegemony that rules Venice, a world of prejudice, ambition, jealousy, and the denial of difference, but also the threatening power of the alien: Othello is a monster in the Renaissance sense of the word, a deformed creature like the hermaphrodites and other strange spectacles that so fascinated the early modern period. And *monstrum,* the word itself, figures both the creature and its movement into representation, for it meant as well a showing or demonstration, a *representation.*

Historical Contingency: Rereading *Othello*

Aphra Behn's description of her black protagonist Oroonoko (1688) is startling in its congruence with Ridley's portrait of the black Othello with which we began:

> His nose was rising and Roman, instead of African and flat: His Mouth the finest shaped that could be seen; far from those great turn'd Lips, which are so natural to the rest of the Negroes. The whole Proportion and air of his face was so nobly and exactly form'd, that bating his colour, there could be nothing in Nature more beautiful, agreeable and handsome.[39]

A black tragic hero of Othello's proportions, or Behn's noble Oroonoko, is only possible if black is really white, if features are "classical," that is European, and color is merely an unfortunate accident. By the late seventeenth century, the role and status of blacks in English society had changed, and the discourse of racism was fully established. No longer "spectacles of strangeness" and monstrosity who occupied unstable, exotic, and mythic ideological roles, they were slaves, situated in a growing capitalist economy that their exploited labor sustained. In the sixteenth and early seventeenth centuries, the slave trade in England was desultory and the status of blacks liminal rather than fixed. As Best's *Discourse* and the accounts of early voyagers illustrate, blacks occupied mythic roles rather than positions as mere chattel or economic linchpin. In Elizabethan and Jacobean England, blacks were not only servants: they owned property, paid taxes, went to church.[40] But with the establishment of the sugar industry in the Caribbean and the tobacco and cotton industries in America, the position of blacks changed and their value as slave labor was fully recognized and exploited. The Royal African Company, chartered in 1672, monopolized the African trade until 1698, when the rapid expansion of the colonies dependent on slave labor was so great that it was deprived of its exclusive rights and the market opened to competition. Newspapers of the late seventeenth century testify to a changed view of blacks—advertisements of slaves for sale, and more importantly, hue-and-cry notices seeking runaways who were often described as wearing collars emblazoned with their owners' arms, or with inscriptions such as one reported in the *London Gazette* (1688): "The Lady Bromfield's black, in Lincoln's Inn Fields."

By the late seventeenth century, Englishmen had come to realize the significance of the slave trade to the British economy. In 1746, M. Postlewayt put that realization forcefully into words: "The most approved Judges of the commercial Interests of these Kingdoms have ever been of Opinion, that our West-India and African trades are the most nationally beneficial of any we carry on . . . the daily Bread of the most considerable Part of our British Manufacturers, [is] owing primarily to the Labour of Negroes."[41] By the mid-eighteenth century, the *Gentleman's Magazine* claimed that there were some 20,000 blacks in London. Their increasing numbers led to growing prejudice and fear that they threatened the position of white working people. In pamphlets and the popular press, blacks were represented increasingly as caricatures, bestial, apelike, inhuman, stripped of the exotic or mythic discourses of the sixteenth and early seventeenth centuries. By the time of Rymer's attack on *Othello,* Shakespeare's heroic and tragic representation of a black man seemed unthinkable. In his "Short View of Tragedy" (1693), Rymer found Shakespeare's choice reprehensible, a transgression of both tragic and social decorum.[42] Rymer's attitude toward the "blackamoor" is historically predictable; more surprising, perhaps, is his critical slippage, like Ridley's some 250 years later, from blackness to femininity.[43]

Rymer notoriously claimed that the moral of *Othello* was "a warning to all good Wives that they look well to their Linnen" (221). He devotes the last pages of his attack to the "Tragedy of the Handkerchief," claiming that "had it been *Desdemona's* Garter, the Sagacious Moor might have smelt a Rat; but the handkerchief is so remote a trifle, no Booby on this side of *Mauritania* cou'd make any consequence from it. . . . Yet we find it entered into our Poets head to make a Tragedy of this *Trifle*" (251, 254). Rymer takes issue with Shakespeare's presentation of the handkerchief because he finds it too trifling a detail to sustain tragedy. His comment here reflects not only the changing generic expectations of neoclassicism but also Rymer's cultural prejudices against women, their supposed materiality and preoccupation with the trivial.[44] In the early modern period, the handkerchief was in fact a sign of wealth and status; by the early eighteenth century, however, it had become commonplace.[45] In *cinquecento* Venice, possession of a lady's handkerchief was considered proof of adultery and led to stringent punishments. In 1416, a certain Tomaso Querini received a stiff sentence of eighteen months in jail and a fine of 500 *lire di piccoli* for carrying out "many dishonesties" with Maria, wife of Roberto Bono. Records from the case describe Tomaso's crime as having

> presumed to follow the said lady and on this public street took from her hands a handkerchief, carrying it off with him. As a result of this deed the said Tomaso entered the home of Roberto many times during the day and night and committed many dishonesties with this lady with the highest dishonor for ser Roberto.[46]

Many critics and readers of the play have sought to save Shakespeare's handkerchief from Rymer's harsh judgment by demonstrating not its historical significance as a sign of adultery but its symbolic significance and meaning. Their efforts have been limited by their own historical boundaries and by reigning critical preoccupations and practices that too often seek to work out equations that restrict the richness of *handkerchief* as signifier. The handkerchief in *Othello* is what we might term a snowballing signifier, for as it passes from hand to hand, both literal and critical, it accumulates myriad associations and meanings.[47] It first appears simply as a love token given by Othello to Desdemona and therefore treasured by her; only later do we learn the details of its provenance and design. In the Renaissance, strawberries signified virtue or goodness but also hypocritical virtue as symbolized by the frequently occurring design and emblem of a strawberry plant with an adder hiding beneath its leaves.[48] This doubleness is, of course, appropriate for Othello's perception of Desdemona, for when the handkerchief is first given it represents her virtue and their chaste love, but it later becomes a sign, indeed a proof, of her unfaithfulness. Iago's description of the napkin as "spotted" constitutes for Othello a new meaning to the handkerchief—the strawberries become signs of Desdemona's deceit.[49]

In psychoanalytic terms, the handkerchief that Othello inherits from his mother and then gives to Desdemona has been read symptomatically as the fetishist's substitution for the mother's missing phallus. Like the shoe Freud's young boy substitutes "for the woman's (mother's) phallus which the little boy once believed in and does not wish to forego," the handkerchief is the fetish that endows "women with the attribute which makes them acceptable as sexual objects"—that is, makes them like men.[50] For Othello, it both conceals and reveals Desdemona's imperfection, her lack. But the psychoanalytic scenario is problematic because it privileges a male scopic drama, casting the woman as other, as a failed man, thereby effacing her difference and concealing her sexual specificity behind the fetish. The handkerchief in *Othello* does indeed figure a lack, but ironically it figures not simply the missing penis but the lack around which the play's dramatic action is structured, a desiring femininity that is described in the play as aberrant and "monstrous" or a "monster."[51] The handkerchief, with its associations with the mother, witchcraft, and the marvelous, represents the link between femininity and the monstrous that Othello's and Desdemona's union figures in the play. It figures a female sexual topography that is more than a sign of male possession, violated virginity, even deceit, and more than the fetishist's beloved object. It figures not only Desdemona's lack, as in the traditional psychoanalytic reading, but also her own sexual parts—the nipples, which incidentally are sometimes represented in the courtly love blazon as strawberries, lips, and even perhaps the clitoris, the berry of sexual pleasure nestled beneath phalanged leaves.[52]

The handkerchief, therefore, is significant not only historically as an indicator of class or transgression, or psychologically, because it signifies male fears of duplicity, consummation, and castration, but also politically precisely because it has become a *feminine* trifle. *Othello*'s tragic action revolves not around a heroic act or even object—a battle, as in *Antony and Cleopatra,* or kingship as in *Macbeth* and *King Lear* —but around a trifle, a feminine toy. Instead of relegating *Othello* to the critical category domestic tragedy, always implicitly or explicitly pejorative because of its focus on woman, jealousy, and a triangle, we can reread *Othello* from another perspective, also admittedly historically bound, that seeks to displace conventional interpretations by exposing the extraordinary fascination with and fear of racial and sexual difference that characterizes Elizabethan and Jacobean culture. Desdemona and Othello, woman and black man, are represented by discourses about femininity and blackness that managed and produced difference in early modern England.

Colonialism and Sexual Difference

Was Shakespeare a racist who condoned the negative image of blacks in his culture? Is Desdemona somehow guilty in her stubborn defense of Cassio and her admiring remark "Ludovico is a proper man"?[53] Or in a new critical vocabulary, in her "erotic submission, [which] conjoined with Iago's murderous cunning, far more effectively, if unintentionally, subverts her husband's carefully fashioned identity"?[54] Readers preoccupied with formal dramatic features claim that such questions are moot, that the questions themselves expose the limits of moral or political readings of texts because they raise the specter of intention or ignore the touted transcendence of history by art. But as much recent poststructuralist and/or political criticism has demonstrated, even highly formalist readings are political, inscribed in the discourses both of the period in which the work was produced and of those in which it is consumed. Or as Tony Bennett articulates this position, "The position which a text occupies within the relations of ideological class struggle at its originating moment of production is . . . no necessary indication of the positions which it may subsequently come to occupy in different historical and political contexts."[55] The task of a political criticism is not merely to expose or demystify the ideological discourses that organize literary texts but to *reconstitute* those texts, to reread canonical texts in noncanonical ways that reveal the contingency of so-called canonical readings, that disturb conventional interpretations and discover them as partisan, constructed, made rather than given, natural, and inevitable. Such strategies of reading are particularly necessary in drama because the dramatic immediacy of theatrical representation obscures the fact that the audience is watching a highly artificial enactment of what, in the case of *Othello,* a non-African and a man, Shakespeare, has made into a vision of blackness and femininity, of passion and desire in the other, those marginal groups that stand outside culture and simultaneously within it.

Shakespeare was certainly subject to the racist, sexist, and colonialist discourses of his time, but by making the black Othello a hero, and by making Desdemona's love for Othello, and her transgression of her society's norms for women in choosing him, sympathetic, Shakespeare's play stands in a contestatory relation to the hegemonic ideologies of race and gender in early modern England. Othello is, of course, the play's hero only within the terms of a white, elitist male ethos, and he suffers the generic "punishment" of tragedy, but he is nevertheless represented as heroic and tragic at a historical moment when the only role blacks played on stage was that of a villain of low status. The case of Desdemona is more complex because the fate she suffers is the conventional fate assigned to the desiring woman. Nevertheless, Shakespeare's representation of her as at once virtuous and desiring, and of her choice in love as heroic rather than demonic, dislocates the conventional ideology of gender that the play also enacts.

We need to read Shakespeare in ways that produce resistant readings, ways that contest the hegemonic forces the plays at the same time affirm. Our critical task is not merely to describe the formal parameters of a play, nor is it to make claims about Shakespeare's politics, conservative or subversive, but to reveal the discursive and dramatic evidence for such representations, and their counterparts in criticism, as representations.[56]

PORTIA'S RING

Gender, Sexuality, and Theories of Exchange
in *The Merchant of Venice*

The Traffic in Women

ACROSS DISCIPLINARY BOUNDARIES, TRANSHISTORICALLY, and in varied media, Western feminists have reproduced the paradigm of woman as object of exchange developed most influentially in anthropology.[1] In the French anthropologist Claude Lévi-Strauss's often cited formulation from *The Elementary Structures of Kinship:*

> The total relationship of exchange which constitutes marriage is not established between a man and a woman . . . but between two groups of men, and the woman figures as one of the objects in the exchange, not as one of the partners.[2]

The paradigm has been both productive and seductive, made available to many through Gayle Rubin's forceful and influential essay "The Traffic in Women: Notes on the 'Political Economy' of Sex," which named and analyzed the paradigm of woman as object of exchange.[3] The "traffic in women" is everywhere in feminist cultural analysis: in radical feminism, cultural feminism, Marxist feminisms, poststructuralist feminisms, in history, anthropology, art, literature, political theory, economics.[4]

In his *Essai sur le don* (1925), Marcel Mauss had argued that in primitive societies, exchange—giving, receiving, and reciprocating gifts—governed social intercourse. In the cultures Mauss described, "food, women, children, possessions, charms, land, labour, services, religious offices, rank" circulated in exchange.[5] Lévi-Strauss reworked Mauss's theory of the gift in the *Elementary Structures* by proposing that marriage is the most fundamental form of gift exchange, and women the most basic of gifts. He argues that incest taboos and other rules prohibiting sexual relations and marriage between family members ensure alliances and relationships among men:

> The prohibition of incest is less a rule prohibiting marriage with the mother, sister, or daughter, than a rule obliging the mother, sister, or daughter to be given to others. It is the supreme rule of the gift. (481)

For Lévi-Strauss, social life entails the exchange of women since culture depends upon the male bonds constituted by that traffic. Consequently he authorizes the exchange of women by presenting it rhetorically as decreed, ordained, eternal:

> In the matrimonial dialogue of men, woman is never purely what is spoken about; for if women in general represent a certain category of signs, destined to a certain kind of communication, each woman preserves a particular value arising from her talent, before and after marriage, for taking her part in a duet. In contrast to words, which have wholly become signs, each woman has remained at once a sign and a value. This explains why the relations between the sexes have preserved that affective richness, ardour, and mystery which doubtless originally permeated the entire universe of human communications. (496)

Once upon a time, then, in an anthropological Eden, there was an originary state of happy identity between word and thing; after the fall, words were no longer values as well as signs: "their signifying function . . . supplanted their character as values, [and] language, along with scientific civilization, has helped to impoverish perception and to strip it of its affective, aesthetic and magical implications" (496). Women, however, have somehow managed to preserve their value. They are objects, but something more than objects—*values* is Lévi-Strauss's term. Woman's value, for Lévi-Strauss, arises "from her talent, before and after marriage, for taking her part in a duet" (496).

In the late 1940s, in *The Second Sex,* perhaps the earliest example of feminist theory, Simone de Beauvoir demystified Lévi-Strauss's romantic "duet" by recognizing in his celebration of woman's mystery and magic qualities the production of woman "as the absolute Other," the eternal feminine, the binary always inferior, lacking, useful primarily in the Hegelian, or dialectical, sense in which subjectivity "can be posed only in being opposed":[6]

> Man defines woman not in herself but as relative to him. . . . She is defined and differentiated with reference to man and not he with reference to her; she is the incidental, the inessential as opposed to the essential. He is the Subject, he is the Absolute—she is the other. (16)

Anthropologists have challenged not the phallocentrism of Lévi-Strauss's claim that exogamous marriage and the exchange of women is a necessary condition for the formation of social groups and ultimately of culture, but his theory of kinship itself. Pierre Bourdieu, for example, adduces instances of parallel cousin marriage from nomadic and gatherer groups that refute the structuralist interpretation of kinship as a rule-governed *system,* arguing instead that kin relationships are social *practices* that produce and reproduce historically specific social relations. In the cultures Bourdieu examines, for example, women often take part in the choice of a spouse for their children: how marriages are made and what they do "depend on the aims or collective strategies of the group involved" and are not constitutive per se of male bonds or of culture.[7] But Bourdieu's ungendered social science vocabulary ("the collective strategies of the group involved") glosses over the significant fact that these aims and strategies inevitably allot women secondary status, for it is always the bride, and never the groom, who is an object of exchange among family groups and the means whereby social relations are reproduced. However they may disagree about the reasons for and results of kinship "rules" or "practices," in both Lévi-Strauss's structural anthropology and Bourdieu's functionalist analysis, women figure as capital, as objects of exchange among men.

But the "traffic in women" is neither a universal law on which culture depends, as Lévi-Strauss would have it, nor a means of producing and reproducing generalized "social relations," as Bourdieu claims, but a strategy for ensuring hierarchical gender relations. Since the pioneering work of de Beauvoir's *The Second Sex,* feminists have criticized the anthropological model by arguing that the exchange of women is neither necessary nor inevitable but produces and reproduces what Gayle Rubin has termed a "sex/gender system" in which the traffic in women is only part of an entire system of sexual access, genealogical statuses, lineage names and ancestors, rights and *people*—men, women and children—in concrete systems of social relationships. . . . "Exchange of women" is a shorthand for expressing that the social relations of a kinship system specify that men have certain rights over their female kin, and that women do not have the same rights either to themselves or to their male kin.[8]

The French psychoanalyst Luce Irigaray, in her rereading of Lévi-Strauss, recognizes the risk of reproducing what she seeks to contest. Rather than simply applying the exchange paradigm critically, she disrupts the grammar of the syntax of exchange by representing the anthropological case pushed to its logical end:

The exchanges which organize patriarchal societies take place, exclusively, between men. Women, signs, goods, currency, pass from man to man or risk—so it is claimed—slipping back into incestuous and exclusively endogamous relations that would paralyze all social and economic intercourse . . . the very possibility of the socio-cultural order would entail homosexuality. Homosexuality would be the law that regulates the socio-cultural economy.[9]

Irigaray takes Lévi-Strauss at his word but "with a difference" and in doing so distorts his argument so as to force her reader to recognize the logical implications of the anthropological paradigm. She makes that syntax ungrammatical in a culture of compulsory heterosexuality by acknowledging, in Eve Kosovsky Sedgwick's word, the "homosocial" character of patriarchal exchange. Sedgwick defines the homosocial as "the whole spectrum of bonds between men, including friendship, mentorship, rivalry, institutional subordination, homosexual genitality, and economic exchange—within which the various forms of the traffic in women take place."[10]

Feminist literary criticism has demonstrated women's objectification in countless texts from every period in literary history, but the traffic in women has figured with particular prominence in Renaissance studies, in part at least because of the complicity between anthropological paradigms and work in social history on women and the family in the early modern period. Lawrence Stone's description of the early modern family has been more often cited by feminist literary critics of Shakespeare than that of any other historian. Here is Stone's version of marriage in early modern England:

The accepted wisdom of the age was that marriage based on personal selection, and thus inevitably influenced by such ephemeral factors as sexual attraction or romantic love, was if anything less likely to produce lasting happiness than one arranged by more prudent and more mature heads. This view finds confirmation in anthropological studies of the many societies where love has not been regarded as a sound basis for marriage, and where one girl is as good as another, provided that she is a good housekeeper, a breeder and a willing sexual playmate.[11]

Here distanced amusement, authority-claiming generalization, and pseudoscientific diction work to assert the factual status of Stone's claims. With bemused detachment he describes "the wisdom of the age," suggesting his gentlemanly recognition that such notions are no longer wise but nevertheless managing to claim for his argument that such attitudes were widely held—by all sorts of people, and not just in England. His is not merely the argot of social science, but the cant of evolutionary biology—"personal selection," "factors," "sexual attraction"—all of which work to assert an indisputable "scientific" truth. Finally, there is the astonishing segue from the "wisdom of the age" concerning arranged marriages in the early modern period to woman as object, but the woman has become a "girl," at once maid, bitch, and lay. The choice of "girl" is particularly surprising since social historians, including Stone himself, have shown that the average age at marriage of Englishwomen was far from girlhood—their early twenties.[12] "Girl" depends on the anthropological context he invokes. Stone moves from describing a hegemonic ideology of elite marriage, in which the sex of the parties involved is appropriately unmarked,[13] to an ideologically suspect anthropology that conjures up visions of native girls paraded before men and chosen for their domestic and erotic talents. One is as good as another, provided she is clean, willing, and fertile.

Stone has, of course, been widely criticized by other historians, both for the interpretation of his "data" and for the claim he makes that his model, though based on evidence left by elite culture, trickled down to the "plebes" as he calls them. E. P. Thompson and Keith Wrightson have marshaled evidence for an opposing view, more nuanced and open to the vagaries of desire, but feminist critics of Shakespeare have continued to base their analysis of the sexual politics of early modern England on Stone's work.[14] As the most cursory glance at endnotes demonstrates, an introduction or opening chapter describing marriage and the family in early modern England heavily indebted to Stone is almost de rigueur.[15] Feminists substitute outrage or lament for Stone's pernicious scientism, but the anthropological model persists unchallenged. Whatever the *value* attributed to the exchange of women by Lévi-Strauss, de Beauvoir, Rubin, and the host of others who deploy the paradigm, the structure of exchange itself remains the same whether idealized as in Lévi-Strauss, scientized as in Stone, or debunked as in feminist analyses. Feminists criticize women's status as objects as oppressive and demeaning; they analyze strategies for disrupting the law of exchange; they demonstrate how women's object status precludes subjecthood; but the syntax of exchange itself remains unchallenged. The subject-object dichotomy persists untroubled: woman is property, goods, chattel, objectified, reified.

In an essay published in *Shakespeare Quarterly* in 1987 entitled "Portia's Ring: Unruly Women and Structures of Exchange in *The Merchant of Venice*," I read Shakespeare's play via feminist rereadings of Lévi-Strauss's paradigm of exchange. In what follows, I want to return to that argument, taking into account the critique of the exchange paradigm laid out above and, finally, in a brief epilogue, to consider the impact of recent work on gender and sexuality for reading Shakespeare's play.

Revisiting Portia's Ring

The Merchant of Venice would seem to offer an exemplary case of Levi-Strauss's exchange system and its feminist critique. The exchange of Portia from her father via the caskets to Bassanio is the ur-exchange upon which the main bond plot is based: it produces Bassanio's request for money from Antonio and in turn the bond between Antonio and Shylock. Though the disposition of Portia by her father's will, and the financial arrangements between Bassanio and Antonio that permit Bassanio's courtship, lead to heterosexual marriage, the traffic in women paradoxically promotes and secures homosocial relations between men. Read from within such a system, Portia's seeming centrality is a mystification, a pseudocenter, for woman in this series of transactions, to repeat Lévi-Strauss's phrase, "figures only as one of the objects in the exchange, not as one of the partners."[16]

In early modern England, among the elite at least, marriage was primarily a commercial transaction determined by questions of dowry, familial alliances, land ownership, and inheritance. Daughters were pawns in the political and social maneuvers of their families, particularly their male kin.[17] Marriage contracts and settlements, familiar letters and wills, conduct books and sermons alike recognize in marriage an economic transaction based on the exchange of gifts—women, cash, annuities, rents, land.[18] Divines preached sermons with such titles as "A Good Wife Gods Gift" and women were explicitly commodified, as in John Wing's exemplary exhortation in his treatise on marriage *The Crowne Conjugall, or The Spouse Royall* (1620) that men seek wives not in the devil's place—playhouses, May games, dance matches—but in God's house, since "all men love in merchandizing for any commodity, to goe as neere as they can, to such as *make the commodities themselves, and from those hands they do originally* come."[19] Wing not only calls women commodities; he also recognizes explicitly the male partnerships that were to be posited in Lévi-Strauss's paradigm.

The exchange of women and gifts that dominated kinship relations dominated power relations as well. Gift giving was a significant aspect of Elizabethan and Jacobean social intercourse, as demonstrated by royal prestation and patronage and by the New Year's gift roles, account books, and records of aristocratic families who vie with one another in their generosity to the monarch in quest of favor.[20] Not only the monarch and the aristocracy but also the gentry and the middling sort—all took part in these systems of exchange. Even the poorest families participated in such exchange systems: observers describe the custom in English villages of placing a basin in the church at weddings, into which guests placed gifts to help to establish the newly formed family in the community.[21] In the 1620s and 1630s, gift giving declined and signaled the alienation of the aristocracy, gentry, and urban elite from the Court.[22]

Commercial language describing love relationships common to Elizabethan love poetry and prominent in *The Merchant of Venice* displays not only the economic determinants of marriage in Elizabethan society but also England's economic climate more generally—its developing capitalist economy characterized by the growth and expansion of urban centers, particularly London; the rise of banking and over-seas trade; and industrial growth with its concomitant need for credit and large amounts of capital.[23] In *The Merchant of Venice,* act 3, scene 2, Portia offers her love to Bassanio in a speech that epitomizes the Elizabethan sex/gender system and its relation to political economy:

> You see me, Lord Bassanio, where I stand,
> Such as I am. Though for myself alone
> I would not be ambitious in my wish
> To wish myself much better, yet for you
> I would be trebled twenty times myself,
> A thousand times more fair, ten thousand times more rich,
> That only to stand high in your account
> I might in virtues, beauties, livings, friends
> Exceed account. But the full sum of me
> Is sum of something which, to term in gross,
> Is an unlessoned girl, unschooled, unpractised;
> Happy in this, she is not yet so old
> But she may learn; happier than this,
> She is not bred so dull but she can learn;
> Happiest of all is that her gentle spirit
> Commits itself to yours to be directed,
> As from her lord, her governor, her king.
> Myself and what is mine to you and yours
> Is now converted. But now I was the lord
> Of this fair mansion, master of my servants,
> Queen o'er myself; and even now, but now,
> This house, these servants, and this same myself
> Are yours, my lord's. I give them with this ring. . . .[24]

This speech begins with what we might term an affective paradox. Portia presents herself to Bassanio using the first person in an engagingly personal, if highly rhetorical, manner: "such as I am." But her account of herself, as my own dead metaphor suggests, illustrates the exchange between the erotic and the economic that characterizes the play's representation of human relations. The rhetorical distance created by the mercantile metaphor shifts the speech from her personal commitment to a more formal bond marked by the giving of her ring, and that move is signaled by the shift to the third person ("an unlessoned girl . . . she"). Portia objectifies herself and thereby suppresses her own agency in bestowing herself on Bassanio. The passives are striking—she casts herself grammatically in the role of object "to be directed"; she and all she owns "is . . . converted" to Bassanio by an unstated agent. Perhaps the most marked stylistic feature of these lines is the repeated use of "now," which signals both temporal shifts and, more importantly, a moment of conversion. The rhetorical balance of line 166 is arrested by the caesura and the "now" of line 167 which insists on the present moment of commitment to Bassanio. The "But now" that follows refers back in time, emphasizing Portia's prior role as "lord" of Belmont, a role that she yields to Bassanio with her vow "I give them with this ring"; the moment of fealty is underscored by the repeated "even now, but now" in line 169.

The governing analogy in Portia's speech is the Renaissance political commonplace that figures marriage and the family as a kingdom in small, a microcosm ruled over by the husband.[25] Portia's speech figures woman as microcosm to man's macrocosm and as subject to his sovereignty. Portia ratifies this prenuptial contract with Bassanio by pledging her ring, which here represents the codified, hierarchical relation of men and women in the Elizabethan sex/gender system in which a woman's husband is "her lord, her governor, her king."[26] The ring is a visual sign of her vow of love and submission to Bassanio; it is a representation of Portia's acceptance of Elizabethan marriage, which was characterized by women's subjection, their loss of legal rights, and their status as goods or chattel. It signifies her place in a rigidly defined hierarchy of male power and privilege, and her declaration of love at first seems to exemplify her acquiescence to woman's place in such a system. But Portia's declaration of love veers away in its final lines from the exchange system the preceding lines affirm. Having moved through past time to the present of Portia's pledge and gift of her ring, the speech ends in the future, with a projected loss and its aftermath, with Portia's "vantage to exclaim on" Bassanio:

> I give them with this ring,
> Which when you part from, lose, or give away,
> Let it presage the ruin of your love
> And be my vantage to exclaim on you.
> (3.2.171–74)

Here Portia is the gift giver; she gives more than Bassanio can ever reciprocate, first to him, then to Antonio, and finally to Venice itself in her actions in the trial, which allow the city to preserve both its law

and its precious Christian citizen. In giving more than can be recipro-
cated, Portia short-circuits the system of exchange and the male bonds
it creates, winning her husband away from the arms of Antonio.

Contemporary conduct books and advice about choosing a wife
illustrate the dangers of marriage to a woman of higher social status or
of greater wealth. Though by law such a marriage makes the husband
master of his wife and her goods, in practice contemporary sources
suggest unequal marriages often resulted in domination by the wife.
Some writers and Puritan divines even claimed that women purposely
married younger men, men of lower rank or of less wealth, so as to
rule them. Marriage handbooks and sermons all exhort women to sub-
mit to their husbands, regardless of disparity in rank or fortune, as
in this representative example from Daniel Tuvill's *St. Pauls Threefold
Cord* (1635):

> Yea, though there were never so great a disproportion betwixt them in
> state and condition; as say the wife were a Princesse, the husband but a
> pesant, she must be yet in conjugall respects as a hand-mayd unto him;
> he must not be as a servant unto her. . . . And this subjection is so neces-
> sary, that without it the world could not long subsist; yea nature herselfe
> would suddenly be dissolved.[27]

The vehemence and fear of chaos and disorder Tuvill betrays are characteristic and imply a growing need in the Stuart period to shore up
eroding class and gender hierarchies.

Bassanio's answer to Portia's pledge of love implicitly recognizes
such disparity and its effect by metaphorically making her the master:

> Madam, you have bereft me of all words.
> Only my blood speaks to you in my veins,
> And there is such confusion in my powers
> As after some oration fairly spoke
> By a beloved prince there doth appear
> Among the buzzing pleased multitude,
> Where every something being blent together
> Turns to a wild of nothing save of joy,
> Expressed and not expressed. But when this ring
> Parts from this finger, then parts life from hence.
> O, then be bold to say Bassanio's dead.
>
> (3.2.175–85)

Bassanio's heavily marked epic simile is anomalous in Shakespearean
comedy. It echoes the first and perhaps most famous Virgilian simile

of the *Aeneid* when Neptune's effect in quelling the storm inspired by Juno is compared to that of "a man remarkable / for righteousness and service" for whom the people "are silent and stand attentively; and he controls their passion by his words and cools their spirits" (*Aeneid* 1.151–53).[28] Shakespeare translates the Virgilian simile into his own romantic context in which the speaker's words, instead of having a quieting effect on heart and mind, create a Petrarchan paradox: blood that speaks, but a lover silenced. And in keeping with Petrarchan conventions, Bassanio's comparison figures Portia as dominating and distant—that is, as a prince. Renaissance rhetoricians such as Wilson and Puttenham define figurative language as *translation,* "an inuersion of sence by transport"—a kind of figurative exchange that disturbs normal communication and makes unexpected connections.[29] Poets use tropes so that "the hearer is ledde by cogitation vppon rehearsall of a Metaphore, and thinketh more by remembraunce of a worde translated, then is there expressely spoken: or els because the whole matter seemeth by a similitude to be opened."[30] Bassanio's political simile, with its Virgilian intertextual exchange, "disguises" Portia as a man and prefigures her masculine role in the trial scene where she ensures the Venetian republic by reconciling the principle of equity with the rigor of the law.

We should also remember that Portia, whom Bassanio earlier describes as "nothing undervalued / To Cato's daughter, Brutus' Portia" (1.1.165–66), is named after her classical ancestor who describes herself in *Julius Caesar* as "a woman well reputed, Cato's daughter. / Think you I am no stronger than my sex, / Being so fathered and so husbanded?" (2.1.295–97). That Portia was renowned in antiquity for sharing the political ideals of her father and husband, and Shakespeare represents her commitment to political action by her insistence, as Plutarch had recorded, on knowing of the plot to murder Caesar and by her taking part in the conference of Republicans at Antium. *The Merchant*'s Portia resembles her classical namesake and her figural persona ("beloved prince") by entering the male lists of law and politics. Far from simply demonstrating the Elizabethan sex/gender system, *The Merchant* short-circuits the exchange, mocking its authorized social structure and hierarchical gender relations.

For Portia's ring, we should remember, does not remain on Bassanio's finger, and *his* gift of the ring to Balthasar does indeed give Portia "vantage to exclaim." The gift of Portia's ring shifts the figurative ground of her speech from synecdoche, a figure in which the part stands for the whole, to metonymy, a figure of association or contiguity. Her lines first figure the ring as a part of her that she gives as a sign of the whole to Bassanio; in the final lines, however, the prefigured loss of the ring signals not substitution but contiguity, metonymic relations. By following the movements of her ring, we may discover something about how the play both enacts and interrogates Elizabethan structures of figural and sexual exchange. Objects, like words, change their meaning in different contexts; as things pass from hand to hand, they accumulate meanings from the process of exchange itself. Bassanio gives away his ring in payment for services rendered and in doing so transgresses his pledge to Portia. When it begins its metonymic travels from Bassanio to the young doctor, the ring picks up new meanings that contradict its status as a sign of male possession, fidelity, and values; it moves from Bassanio to Balthasar to Portia to Antonio and back to Bassanio again and the very multiplicity of exchanges undermines its prior signification. The ring also makes a figural progress; in Renaissance rhetorical terms it is transmuted, "which is, when a word hath a proper signification of the [*sic*] owne, and being referred to an other thing, hath an other meaning."[31] Portia's ring becomes a sign of hierarchy subverted by establishing contiguities in which the constituent parts have shifting sexual and syntactic positions. By opening out the metonymic chain to include Balthasar, Bassanio opens his marriage to what were for an Elizabethan audience forces of disorder: gender instability, equality between the sexes, cuckoldry, sodomy, all in opposition to the decorous world of Renaissance marriage represented by the love pledges in act 3, scene 2. Bassanio gives his ring to an "unruly woman," that is, to a woman who steps outside her role and function as subservient, a woman who dresses like a man, who embarks upon behavior ill suited to her "weaker" intellect, a woman who argues the law.

In her fine essay "Women on Top: Symbolic Sexual Inversion and Political Disorder in Early Modern Europe," Natalie Zemon Davis details the ways in which women's disorderliness manifested itself in England and Europe during this period. Davis observes that anthropologists generally agree that forms of sexual inversion—switches in sex roles, topsy-turvy, and images of the world turned upside down, "the topos of the woman on top"—

like other rites and ceremonies of reversal, are ultimately sources of order and stability in hierarchical society. They can clarify the structure by the process of reversing it. They can provide an expression of, and safety valve for, conflicts within the system. They can correct and relieve the system when it has become authoritarian. But, so it is argued, they do not question the basic order of the society itself. They can renew the system, but they cannot change it.[32]

Many feminist critics have agreed with such judgments in their readings of Shakespeare's comedies of sexual inversion. They argue that such play, usually in the service of courtship, is ultimately conservative, leading to conventional gender roles and patriarchal marriage.[33] Portia, we are told, in giving up her disguise and returning Bassanio's ring, returns to "unthreatening femininity."[34] But Davis herself disputes the interpretation of sexual inversion as simply a safety mechanism. She points out first that historians of early modern Europe are likely to find inversion and reversals less in prescribed rites than in popular festivities and carnival. Cultural play with the concept of the unruly woman, she argues, was a multivalent image which could *"undermine* as well as reinforce" (131) traditional hierarchical formations. Davis adduces examples of comic and festive inversion that carried over into political action, which not only provided release but also represented efforts or provided the means whereby the distribution of power in society was questioned and changed. And, I would add, inversion affects not only the distribution of power but also perhaps structures of exchange themselves that historically have ensured male hegemony and patriarchal power. Sexual inversion and play with the topos of the woman on top offered an alternative mode of conceiving family structure and gender behavior within that structure.

When Bassanio leaves for Venice to aid his friend, Portia evokes the conventional ideal of a Renaissance lady: she promises that "my maid Nerissa and myself meantime / Will live as maids and widows" (3.2.307–8); to Lorenzo she claims they will live in a monastery to fulfill a vow "to live in prayer and contemplation" (3.4.28), behavior that conforms to the Renaissance ideal of womanhood: chaste, silent, and obedient. Shakespeare evokes here the accepted codes of feminine behavior in his culture, thereby distancing the action from the codes of dramatic comedy that permit masculine disguise, female dominance, and linguistic power. Portia evokes the ideal of a proper Renaissance lady and then transgresses it; she becomes an unruly woman.

The common remedies for the weaker sex's disorderliness were, even among the humanists such as Vives, Erasmus, and More, religious training to make her modest and humble, education of a restricted kind designed not to inflame her imagination but to acquaint her with her moral duty and honest work of a sort appropriate to female capabilities. Transgression of the traditional expectations for women's behavior brought down wrath such as John Knox's *The First Blast of the Trvmpet against the Monstrvovs Regiment of Women* (1558):

> The holie ghoste doth manifestlie expresse, saying: I suffer not that woman vsurpe authoritie aboue man: he sayth not, I will not, that woman vsurpe authoritie aboue her husband, but he nameth man in gen-erall, taking frome her all power and authoritie, to speake, to reason, to interprete, or to teache, but principallie to rule or to iudge in the assem-blie of men . . . [A] woman promoted to sit in the seate of God, that is, to teache, to iudge, or to reigne aboue man, is a monstre in nature, con-tumelie to God, and a thing most repugnant to his will and ordinace.[35]

It might be argued that the excess of Knox's attack, directed specif-ically against Mary Tudor, reflects his own rather than widely held views. But even humanist writers sympathetic to the cause of women's education assume the propriety of Knox's claims, if not his rhetoric. They exclude women from the public arena and assume the necessity of their silence. Leonardo Bruni, for example, warns that "rhetoric in all its forms—public discussion, forensic argument, logical fence, and the like—lies absolutely outside the province of women."[36] When Portia takes off for Venice dressed as a man, she looses her tongue in public talk on subjects ill suited to the ladylike conduct she posits as a model and does exactly those things Knox and others violently attacked. She engages, that is, in productive labor reserved for men, and not insignificantly, in linguistic labor, in a profession the success-ful practice of which depended on a knowledge of history and prece-dent, on logic and reasoning, and on rhetoric, all areas of education traditionally denied to women.

Portia's manner of winning her case requires consideration. Her defense depends on a verbal quibble, a characteristic linguistic strat-egy of Shakespearean clowns that allows them to express ideologically subversive or contradictory attitudes or ideas. Indeed, in *The Merchant of Venice,* Launcelot Gobbo uses the quibble for just such purposes. His wordplay around the command to come to dinner at 3.5.48–50 and his earlier play with Jessica on damnation (3.5.4–7) give a double perspective to serious issues in the play, issues of social and Christian hierarchy and the like.[37] Portia and Launcelot Gobbo, woman and servant, are linked by this shared verbal strategy, which allows them seemingly at least to reconcile irreconcilable perspectives and to challenge the play's overall mimetic design. They represent in part marginal groups oppressed under the Elizabethan class/gender system but whose presence paradoxically is needed to ensure its maintenance. Their playful, quibbling misuse of language veils their subversive linguistic power. Portia's wise quibble saves the Venetian republic by enabling the Duke to follow the letter of the law *and* to save Antonio, to satisfy the opposing viewpoints represented by the Old and New law, by Shylock and Antonio. In another register, as Walter Cohen has pointed out, it unites the bourgeois values of self-interest with those of the traditional landed gentry, an imaginary literary solution to ideological conflicts manifest in late sixteenth-century England.[38] But Portia's linguistic play here and in the final scene, like Launcelot Gobbo's, resists the social, sexual and political system of which she is a part and provides a means for interrogating its distribution of power along gender lines.

The Merchant of Venice does not end with Portia's success in the courtroom; after her winning defense of Antonio, Portia asks Bassanio to return her ring, knowing, as her husband puts it, that "there's more depends on this than the value" (4.1.430). We know this ring symbolizes the bargain of faith in patriarchal marriage Portia and Bassanio have made in act 3, scene 2. By obeying Antonio's exhortation and giving his ring to Balthasar, Bassanio affirms homosocial bonds—the exchange of women, here represented by Portia's ring, sustains relations between men. But Balthasar is, of course, Portia in disguise (and Portia, we should not forget, was played by a boy, so that literally all the love relations in the play are homosocial). When Portia laughs at the thought of "old swearing / That they did give the rings away to men; / But we'll outface them, and outswear them too" (4.2.15–17), she keeps her promise. In losing their rings and breaking their promises to Portia and Nerissa, Bassanio and Graziano seem paradoxically to lose the male privileges the exchange of women and the rings ensured.

When in act 5 Portia returns her ring to her husband via Antonio, its multiple metonymic travels have changed it. The ring no longer represents the traditional relationship it figured in act 3, scene 2. On its figural as well as literal progress, it accumulates other meanings and associations: cuckoldry and thus female unruliness, female genitalia, woman's changeable nature and so-called animal temperament, her deceptiveness and potential subversion of the rules of possession and fidelity that ensure the male line.[39] By dressing up as a man and arguing the law, by imaginatively expressing her own sexuality with Balthasar—"I had it of him. Pardon me, Bassanio, / For by this ring the doctor lay with me" (5.1.258–59)—Portia refuses the role of subservient woman she played in act 3, scene 2.[40] Now her speech is filled with imperatives —"speak not so grossly . . . Read it . . . Unseal this letter" (5.1.266, 267, 275). Having expressly given over her house to Bassanio in act 3, scene 2, she says, "I have not yet / Entered my house" (5.1.272–73). She emphasizes her power and secret knowledge by giving Antonio the mysterious letter but refusing to reveal how she came by it: "You shall not know by what strange accident / I chanced on this letter" (5.1.278–79).

It is often said that act 5 of *The Merchant of Venice* is unusually harmonious even for Shakespearean comedy; certainly the world of usury, hatred, and aggression that characterizes Venice has receded.[41] But act 5 is far from presenting the harmonious view of love and marriage many have claimed, for even the idyllic opening dialogue between Jessica and Lorenzo is troubled by allusions to unhappy love and broken vows. Lorenzo mockingly calls Jessica a shrew and the play ends on an obscene pun on "ring" and a commonplace joke about female sexuality and cuckoldry, not on the idealized pledges of true love that characterize 3.2.50–60. Portia's verbal skills, her quibbles and play with words, her duplicitous representation of herself as an unlessoned girl who vows "to live in prayer and contemplation," even as she rules her household and prepares to argue the law, bring together contradictory attitudes and views towards women and their role and place both in drama and society. Bassanio accepts the oppositions that her play with language enacts: "sweet doctor, you shall be my bedfellow" (5.1.284), he says. But in an aside that scarcely requires a psychoanalytic gloss, Bassanio exclaims, "Why, I were best to cut my left hand off / And swear I lost the ring defending it" (5.1.177–78). Portia's unruliness of language and behavior exposes the male homosocial bond the exchange of women ensures, but it also multiplies the terms of sexual trafficking so as to disrupt those structures of exchange that ensure hierarchical gender relations and the figural hegemony of the microcosm/macrocosm analogy in Elizabethan marriage. Instead of being "directed, / As from her lord, her governor, her king" (3.2.164–65), Portia resumes her role as lord of Belmont: "Let us go in" (5.1.297), she commands. As Davis suggests, in the "little world of the family, with its conspicuous tension between intimacy and power, the larger matters of political and social order could find ready symbolization."[42] The sexual symbolism of transvestism, the transgression of traditional gender roles and the figural transgression of heterosexual relations, the multivalence of linguistic meanings in women's and clowns' speech, all interrogate and reveal contradictions in the Elizabethan sex/gender system in which women were commodities whose exchange both produced and reproduced hierarchical gender relations.

Other *Merchant* Rings

However powerful a hermeneutic device for reading Shakespeare's play, "the traffic in women" paradigm as it is currently used in feminist analysis is no longer tenable. Putting aside the very real risk of reinserting a victim's discourse by repeatedly reading woman as the object of male exchange, reading women as objects exchanged by male desiring subjects, or even as I have done above, reading Portia as derailing that system by acting as a subject herself, partakes of a degraded positivism that relies on an outmoded, humanist view of identity characterized by a metaphysics of presence.[43] It assumes an unproblematic subjectivity for "men" as desiring subjects and concomitantly assumes as directly accessible woman-as-object. It is as if there were two theoretical regimes uneasily conjoined in feminist analysis: one that recognizes and analyses the fragmentary, nonunitary subject in certain critical contexts; the other, governed by the exchange paradigm, that assumes untroubled, unified subjects exchanging women/objects. Contemporary theories of the subject and of the subject/object problem have rendered the "traffic in women" paradigm as it is currently used untenable.

Revisiting *The Merchant of Venice* at the current critical moment compels analysis of Portia's disruption of the syntax of exchange not by pointing to her agency, her unruliness in playing the man's part, but by considering Portia's transvestism as a central aspect of the performative character of gender in the play. As Judith Butler argues:

> That gender reality is created through sustained social performances means that the very notions of an essential sex and a true or abiding masculinity or femininity are also constituted as part of the strategy that conceals gender's performative character.[44]

And not only gender but also identity more generally as it is produced and traduced in the performance of class or status and degree, nationality, race, and sexuality. The play can no longer be read by isolating the category of gender from those other categories of difference "understood as historically contingent and relational rather than foundational concepts."[45] The exchange of women in *The Merchant of Venice,* after all, hinges upon the subjection of the body and property of the Jew, on the theft of Shylock's ring by Jessica and its circulation to one of Antonio's creditors in trade for a monkey. And Portia's part in the "traffic in women," far from simply enabling or promoting homosocial relations, robs Antonio of his beloved, a theft poignantly rendered in the trial scene when he pleads, "Bid her be judge / Whether Bassanio had not once a love" (4.1.273–74).[46] In the final scene, Antonio once again hazards his body on Bassanio's behalf:

> I once did lend my body for his wealth
> Which, but for him that had your husband's ring,
> Had quite miscarried. I dare be bound again,
> My soul upon the forfeit, that your lord
> Will never more break faith advisedly.
> (5.1.249–53)

Portia's response is "Give him this / And bid him keep it better than the other" (5.1.254–55). Here Antonio, not Portia, is the conduit, the channel, the passage that secures their heterosexual union. Portia's ring is here again transmuted, but here it figures the anal ring Antonio must forgo.

GHOSTWRITING
Hamlet and Claude Chabrol's *Ophélia*

A LONG SHOT OF A TYPICAL FRENCH MANOR HOUSE DRAPED in funereal black. The camera cuts to a close-up: the face of a corpse in a coffin; a reverse shot places us in the coffin itself, peering out first at the widow who approaches and lifts her heavy black veil; then at a young man, evidently her son, who steps to her side; finally at an older man who joins her on the other side. The coffin closes; the screen goes black for several seconds. The scene cuts to mourners bearing the coffin into a church. When the door closes and the shot fades again to black, the titles appear; so begins Chabrol's *Ophélia* (1961).

As the titles end we find ourselves outside the same church door. When it opens, however, instead of mourners, out walks a wedding party, with the widow on the arm of the older man seen earlier by her side at the coffin. The bridal couple are followed by the same group of people who attended the funeral, but in wedding rather than funereal garb. The last to emerge, slowly from the shadows inside the church, is the young man we saw beside the coffin in the opening shots. Only he is dressed exactly as before, in a dark suit, white shirt, and solid black tie.

This opening sequence is Chabrol's witty substitution of visual for verbal signs that expands into images a short dialogue between Hamlet and Horatio at the beginning of Shakespeare's *Hamlet*. In response to Hamlet's question "But what is your affair in Elsinore?" Horatio answers:

HORATIO. My lord, I come to see your father's funeral.
HAMLET. I prithee do not mock me, fellow student. I think it was to see
my mother's wedding.
HORATIO. Indeed, my lord, it followed hard upon.

(1.2.176–79)[1]

In repeating the *Hamlet* story, Chabrol observes the sequence of Shakespeare's play only for those narrative units that must happen in temporal order: the father's death and mother's remarriage; the "Murder of Gonzago" and subsequent conversation between mother and son; the deaths of Polonius (André) and Claudius (Adrien). Aside from these events, Chabrol repeats other elements of the text randomly, from meal scenes that satirize French bourgeois manners and parody the often remarked feeding imagery in Shakespeare's text, to a substitution of class satire and capitalist/labor disputes for the political dimension of Shakespeare's play.[2]

Despite multiple substitutions and correspondences, Chabrol's *Ophélia* is not an adaptation of *Hamlet*.[3] By substituting one class of signs for another, he reveals the structures of exchange and repetition that characterize parody and intertextuality, and he thereby undermines the entire enterprise of mimetic representation. *Ophélia* depends not simply on the original Shakespearean tragedy but also on its many versions and adaptations, from the Freud/Jones psychoanalytic interpretation to Olivier's 1948 film. It depends as well on the particular generic and stylistic characteristics of the French feature film of the early 1960s; on the idiosyncrasies of Chabrol's individual style—his preoccupation, for example, with Hitchcock; and finally on the responses and expectations of various viewers.[4] But I want to focus on what we might call amputation rather than adaptation, for Chabrol subtracts from Shakespeare's play not simply details but a major unit of plot from the earlier text.[5] In doing so, he reveals the structure of repetition on which even *Hamlet* depends but which is obscured in Shakespeare's text by a powerful diegetic element: the ghost of Hamlet's father.

In Shakespeare's play, the ghost of Hamlet's father motivates the prince's revenge. Though he is melancholy and distraught at the death of old Hamlet and the "most wicked speed" with which his mother remarries, only the ghost's tale of murder and adultery drives Hamlet to his antic disposition and its tragic consequences. The paternal ghost is absent from Chabrol's film, and not simply because our cultural expectations reject ghosts and require an interiorization of psychological phenomena. Instead of an appearance from the dead, at the moment Shakespeare's prince meets his father's specter, Chabrol's Yvan encounters a text in celluloid: Olivier's *Hamlet*.

While walking in his native village, Yvan pauses outside a local hall advertising Olivier's film. This chance encounter prompts Yvan to project the central situation of *Hamlet* onto his own circumstances and to believe he has discovered the murder of his father and the incest of his mother. In a whimsical transformation, the ghost of old Hamlet in Shakespeare's tragedy becomes in Chabrol's film not the Shakespearean original but a repetition of that text, Olivier's *Hamlet,* famous, if not notorious, for its strongly Freudian interpretation of the play.

We need to look carefully at the sequence in which Chabrol's Hamlet character comes to identify his circumstances with those of Shakespeare's prince. Yvan Lesurf's responses are a paradigm for those processes of identification between spectator and film that Christian Metz and other theoreticians have described and analyzed.[6] Yvan pauses before an advertising board posted outside the hall in which the film is being shown and looks at the publicity photographs one at a time. Instead of watching Yvan look, we gaze at them with him, for Chabrol superimposes Yvan's point of view upon that of the camera and spectators. The camera/Yvan looks first at the well-known dashing portrait of Olivier as Hamlet; then at the gravediggers scene; next at an early scene between Hamlet and Ophelia; then at Hamlet kissing his mother in their interview after the "Mousetrap"; finally, at the confrontation between Hamlet and Claudius after the death of Polonius. Then he is drawn back to the Olivier portrait with which the sequence began. Meanwhile he hears the film's soundtrack amplified from the village hall: the opening dialogue between Hamlet and Gertrude, in which she exhorts her son to give up mourning, and he condemns "seeming."

Metz describes three different instances of identification between spectator and film: identification with the representation of a person through the concepts of character and star; identification of particular persons, objects, or situations as specific or referential; and finally, that identification which he terms primary, an identification with the camera in which the spectator identifies himself as the viewing subject or "look."[7] For Metz, this primary identification is built into the very institution of the cinema, for by sharing the position of the camera, the spectator becomes the condition and measure of the knowable. Yvan is subject to all three kinds of identification. He identifies himself not only with the character of Hamlet but also with the star, Sir Laurence Olivier in his role as Hamlet. This identification is emphasized by the pause and return to the portrait of Olivier, and indeed by the very use of a film rather than the dramatic text. Though ordinarily this connection insures only empathy because the viewer remains aware that he watches a fiction, Yvan Lesurf believes himself not to be *like* Hamlet but *to be* Hamlet. Such identification, as many have noted, depends on the representation of the body as image—the character's body on the screen functions as a decoy and mooring for the identification process.[8]

In primary identification, the spectator identifies with his own "look" or point of view and consequently with the camera. Chabrol works out this identification wittily by having Yvan actually make a film projecting his interpretation of events as spectator onto the screen. This in turn forces others, specifically his mother and uncle, to identify with his "look," not so much in positional but in epistemological terms—his version of their actions becomes their own.

Of particular interest for our purposes, however, is the second type of identification Metz describes. In this scene, Yvan as spectator falls prey to that drive to recognize and translate what is represented into the already known. In a series of repetitions, Yvan identifies his circumstances, the already known, with the familiar story of Hamlet evoked by the stills from Olivier's film. To recognize is not only to know again, as its etymology implies; in psychoanalytic theory, recognition is linked to what Freud termed the compulsion to repeat (*Wiederholungszwang*). Yvan's recognition of the Hamlet story and his identification of it with his own circumstances is an excellent example. In his essay "The Uncanny," Freud claims that it is

> involuntary repetition which surrounds with an uncanny atmosphere what would otherwise be innocent enough, and forces upon us the idea of something fateful and unescapable where otherwise we would have spoken of "chance" only. For instance, we of course attach no importance to the event when we give up a coat and get a cloakroom ticket with the number, say 62; or when we find that our cabin on board ship

is numbered 62. But the impression is altered if two such events, each in itself indifferent, happen close together, if we come across the number 62 several times in a single day, or if we begin to notice that everything which has a number—addresses, hotel-rooms, compartments in railway trains—always has the same one, or one which at least contains the same figures. We do feel this to be "uncanny," and unless a man is utterly hardened and proof against the lure of superstition he will be tempted to ascribe a secret meaning to this obstinate recurrence of a number.[9]

Yvan Lesurf mourning his father's death and mother's remarriage is hardly "proof against the lure of superstition." By looking at the sequence of events from Yvan's encounter with Olivier's *Hamlet* to his decision to make a film, his parody of Hamlet's "Mousetrap," we can see the effect on Yvan of such "involuntary repetitions," uncanny, as Freud observes, not because of any specific content but simply because they recur.

The last words Yvan hears as he walks away from the village hall are Claudius's lines:

> your father lost a father,
> That father lost, lost his, and the survivor bound
> In filial obligation for some term
> To do obsequious sorrow.
>
> (1.2.89–92)

He recognizes in those words his own loss and projects his situation onto that of Hamlet. Next he walks past the edge of his village, turns back and sees the sign displaying its name: Erneles. We cut then to Yvan's room. In the condensation on his window he writes Erneles, and beneath it, Elseneur; he then carefully marks out each corresponding letter. From Yvan's point of view we have the third coincidence: the first is the death of his father and remarriage of his mother to her brother-in-law; the second is the showing of Olivier's *Hamlet* in the village; the third, the "uncanny" correspondence between Elseneur and Erneles. In the next scene, still in his room, but now with Lucy/Ophélia, the two make faces at a mirror in a series of reverse shots, each mimicking a historical figure. Finally, Yvan walks to a lamp, turns on the light beneath his face, and says, "Hamlet." Instead of allowing her a sequential turn, he holds her dark hair up to the light until the illumination makes it appear blond and says, "Ophélia." To Yvan, things *are* as they seem.

In the next sequence in a local café, a waitress walks in carrying a mousetrap holding a dead mouse. In mimetic terms, this is the final coincidence. Yvan tells his friend François his tale of murder and incest and claims to have proof of the crime. We know that proof consists of nothing more than these "uncanny" coincidences, "uncanny" because they repeat familiar elements from *Hamlet*. Yvan is driven by this series of coincidences to assume the role of Hamlet, to play at madness and to set a trap by making a film, here a dated murder melodrama instead of Shakespeare's Elizabethan fustian, to expose the crime. In the background soundtrack ominous rolling thunder creates a slightly comic effect because François hasn't any idea what Yvan is talking about. He sits, mouth hanging open in gestural *bêtise*, half-listening and rolling a cigarette.[10] Any power the series of coincidences might have of arousing our sense of the uncanny is undermined by Yvan's willfulness in recognizing such repetitions. As Freud remarks in his discussion of the uncanny in fiction, a ghost or any event that would be uncanny in real life becomes comic or loses its uncanniness if the author amuses himself at its expense.[11] Chabrol here takes such liberties with the Hamlet story, moving back and forth between tragedy and burlesque, that the effect is inevitably comic.

Chabrol's film obviously permits a rather straightforward psychoanalytic reading of Yvan's participation and response to these involuntary repetitions that would follow Freud's analysis of the Hoffman story "The Sandman," which he analyses in "The Uncanny." In Yvan's compulsion to repeat what we would then recognize as an Oedipus complex, motivated by the repressed drives Freud and Jones claimed motivated Hamlet. Yvan, like Hamlet, desires his mother; when his father dies he feels guilt, which then motivates him to idolize his dead father and to wish his uncle dead for usurping his father's/his role in the maternal bed. But as Jeffrey Mehlman has pointed out in his reading of Freud's essay, Freud himself tends to repress the real discovery of the *process* of repression by attempting to locate it in a particular object and event—in the penis and castration. Mehlman claims that the significance of Freud's discovery of repression is its *structure* of repetition rather than some referential object or moment in time.[12]

For Chabrol and any spectator, the sheer process of substitution or exchange expressed in *Ophélia*, and perhaps in *Hamlet* as well, the compulsion to repeat fictions and stories, is far more interesting than a return of the repressed castration complex and subsequent fixation on the father located as a particular moment of psychological development. This compulsion to repeat fictions is shared by character and director, for Yvan enacts it diegetically, and Chabrol in making his film. Yvan takes Hamlet's situation and lives out his own version. Chabrol's film is a sly and halfheartedly frightening parody of the entire enterprise of adaptation, or more broadly, ontology, for it interrogates, through its mise-en-abîme of vanishing texts and its emphatic camera presence, any theory of origins. After all, Shakespeare himself repeated his *Hamlet* from some unknown ur-*Hamlet* that formed part of a large body of legends and stories about the Danish royal line. Olivier repeated Shakespeare's text as read by Freud; Chabrol repeats Shakespeare's, Freud's, and Olivier's, at least. Compelled by Olivier's *Hamlet,* Yvan makes himself a text, and the mise-en-abîme created by a series of intertexts calls into question the entire process of adaptation.[13]

Instead of anxiety of influences, we might call Yvan's predicament the power of projection. Fiction, a representation of life, for him takes the place of life, bringing with it madness and death. Literature as mimesis is diabolic, for it represents an attempt to re-create the world.[14] Repetition is the formal cause of the film, and ghostwriting, we shall recall, is a form of repetition. A writer or artist produces a work from a story he is told which is then repeated by the storyteller as if it were his own. So here, Chabrol, himself repeating the *Hamlet* text, has Yvan repeat the Hamlet story as if it were *his* own. By doing so he makes manifest what is merely virtual in Shakespeare's and Olivier's *Hamlet*s, the structure of repetition or substitution that generates both texts, for in both, we should remember, the prince is also motivated to revenge by a story, the tale told by the ghost of Hamlet's father. In Shakespeare and Olivier, this important detail is forgotten, subsumed by the powerful dramatic presence of the ghost itself.[15]

In closing I want to consider the film's title, *Ophélia,* and that character's role in the text. The missing ghost of the father leaves room in Chabrol's film to develop the female character of Lucy/Ophélia. In Shakespeare's text, the prince is troubled by uncertainty about the ghost. Is it, he wonders, a manifestation of good or evil? Is his revenge just or wicked? In Shakespeare, Claudius confesses his crime, but in *Ophélia* the audience has no proof of any crime except for the diegetic series of coincidences. Lucy fills this gap, the space created by the lack of patriarchal power—Chabrol's missing ghost and Yvan's weak uncle, who is so different from Shakespeare's Claudius. Lucy/Ophélia judges Yvan's actions in the film and provides a perspective missing from Shakespeare whereby we are able to see them not as heroic revenge but obsessional neurosis.[16] Chabrol refuses Yvan the complex ambiguity with which Shakespeare endows his Hamlet.

In an ironic reversal that confirms Lucy's judgment, the Claudius figure, Adrien, poisons himself, driven to suicide by Yvan's behavior and accusations. As he dies he tells Yvan he has committed no crime and calls him "mon fils." But Chabrol's point is, of course, not a death-bed confession of paternity, or just a sick joke, but Yvan's crime.[17] By driving his uncle to suicide, Yvan commits symbolic patricide. In his *Outline of Psycho-analysis,* Freud says of the words of the oracle in *Oedipus Rex* that the coercive power of the oracle, which makes or should make the hero innocent, is a recognition of the inevitability of the fate that has condemned every son to live through the Oedipus complex.[18]

Perhaps instead of demonstrating the power of some specific repressed drive or complex, the oracle demonstrates the power of *words* that represent, of mimesis. Just as Freud sought to locate repression in a particular object or event, to find its referent, so we read fictions by identifying characters, plots, objects, and settings with referents in the world or with ourselves. We seek in fiction an equation; we need instead to recognize a continuous structure of substitution and exchange.

ENGLISHING THE OTHER

"Le tiers exclu" and Shakespeare's

Henry V

AT HIS DEPARTURE IN SEARCH OF A NORTHWEST PASSAGE, the English explorer Martin Frobisher was exhorted by Queen Elizabeth to bring back some of the native peoples he encountered on his voyage. Elizabeth betrayed her characteristic ambivalence toward colonial enterprise: she desired to see the "spectacle of strangeness" but at the same time ordered Frobisher not to compel the Indians against their wills. In his account of the voyage (1577), Frobisher reveals that despite Elizabeth's warning he laid hold of his captive forcibly. Worried about the well-being of his "strange and new prey," he also took a woman captive for his prisoner's comfort. Here is the account of that meeting:

> At their first encountring they beheld each the other very wistly a good space, without speech or word uttered, with great change of colour and countenance, as though it seemed the griefe and disdeine of their captivity had taken away the use of their tongues and utterance: the woman at the first very suddenly, as though she disdeined or regarded not the man, turned away, and began to sing as though she minded another matter: but being againe brought together, the man brake up the silence first, and with sterne and stayed countenance, began to tell a long solemne tale to the woman, whereunto she gave good hearing, and interrupted him nothing, till he had finished, and afterwards, being growen into more familiar acquaintance by speech, they were turned together, so that (I thinke) the one would hardly have lived without the comfort of the other. And for so much as we could perceive, albeit they lived continually together, yet they did never use as man & wife, though the woman spared not to doe

all necessary things that appertained to a good houswife indifferently for
them both, as in making cleane their Cabin, and every other thing that
appertained to his ease: for when he was seasicke, she would make him
cleane, she would kill and flea the dogs for their eating, and dresse his
meate. Only I thinke it worth the noting the continencie of them both:
for the man would never shift himselfe, except he had first caused the
woman to depart out of his cabin, and they both were most shamefast,
least any of their privie parts should be discovered, either of themselves,
or any other body.[1]

This remarkable description of the Eskimos' domestic relations is of
interest as much for what it reveals about the captors as for its description of the Eskimos themselves. The English found the Eskimos particularly troubling because they were both savage and civilized: they
wore sewn leather clothing, unlike their southern counterparts; they
"dressed" their meat, that is, prepared and cooked it; their complex-
ions were as white as those of many Englishmen. But they were also
savage: they sometimes ate raw flesh washed down, according to contemporary observers, with ox blood; they lived underground in caves
or burrows with holes for doors; they were nomads, "a dispersed and
wandering nation . . . without any certaine abode." Frobisher's account
demonstrates the English attitude; he and his men watch their captives as if they were animals in a cage.

But Frobisher not only constructs the alien; he fashions the Eskimos into an English man and wife. She is chaste, silent, and obedient,
blushing modestly at first sight of her fellow, listening in silence to
him speak, a good housewife in attending to "house" and "husband."
Frobisher marks the man as speaking first, in monologue, "with sterne
and stayed countenance," sublating the woman's initiative in breaking
silence with her phatic singing. The man is comically helpless, almost
pompous; the woman cares for him in sickness and prepares his food.
Both show what for the English sailors seems a surprising sexual con-
tinence and modesty: Frobisher is amazed that being "turned together
. . . they did never use as man & wife" and betrays his incredulity with
expressions of doubt—the qualifying "I think" and "for so much as we
could perceive." However willing the English are to see the strangeness of Eskimo customs—domiciliary, dietary, sartorial—heterosexual
relations are always the same. For the English explorer, gender—and
particularly womanhood—is a given of nature rather than a construct

of culture; it is transhistorical and transnational, to be encountered by Englishmen in their colonial travels the world over.

In Frobisher's account, ethnography is domesticated: he constructs the Eskimos' relations as an English marriage—domestic, naturalized, immanent. In doing so, he suppresses the Eskimos' strangeness not only for the Elizabethans but for modern readers of Renaissance texts as well, and thereby obscures the contingency of gender and sexuality. In his brilliant analysis of Renaissance culture and its response to the other, "Strange Things, Gross Terms, Curious Customs: The Rehearsal of Cultures in the Late Renaissance," Steven Mullaney casually remarks that Frobisher "brought an Eskimo couple back from his second voyage," though Frobisher's own account makes the status of the two Eskimos' relation perfectly clear.[2] Mullaney observes that "difference draws us to it; it promises pleasure and serves as an invitation to firsthand experience, otherwise known as colonization." But as Mullaney's elision of the Eskimos' relation suggests, the pleasures of sexual difference invite essentialist assumptions about gender and heterosexuality.

The early modern English fascination with the strange and alien has been widely documented. Explorers who returned from their voyages with native peoples often turned their captives to account, as Stephano and Trinculo plan to do with Caliban. Ostensibly brought back to be Christianized and to learn English language and customs so as to return one day to "civilize" their fellows, New World peoples were displayed like freaks and wild animals for viewers willing to pay a few pence for the sight. Ballads, almanacs, pamphlets, travelogues, and plays record not only the English interest in the other but the conflation of various discourses of difference—gender, race, class or degree, the nation-state—in representations of difference. In *Tamar Cam* (1592), for example, there is an entry of "Tartars, Geates, Amozins, Negars, ollive cullord moores, Canniballs, Hermaphrodites, Pigmes," a series that witnesses how the English set themselves off from their many others—sexual, racial, social. English culture defined itself in opposition to exotic others represented as monstrous but also in opposition to its near neighbors on which it had expansionist aims, the Welsh, the Irish, the Scots. As Mullaney observes, "Learning strange tongues or collecting strange things, rehearsing the words and ways of marginal or alien cultures, upholding idleness for a while— these are the activities of a culture in the process of extending its boundaries and reformulating itself."[3]

That extension of boundaries is often represented in drama linguistically, and nowhere more than in Shakespeare's *Henry V.* M. C. Bradbrook, C. L. Barber, Robert Weimann, and Steven Mullaney, Shakespeareans who approach the plays from widely varied perspectives, have all demonstrated how Shakespeare's language and stagecraft preserved or consumed the customs and voices of other cultures. The play is notable for what Bakhtin has called *heteroglossia,* its various voices or linguistic sociality.[4] According to Bakhtin, language is stratified not only into dialects in the linguistic sense but also "into languages that are socio-ideological: languages of social groups, 'professional' and 'generic' languages, languages of generations and so forth."[5]

Unlike the earlier plays in the tetralogy, the social voices of *Henry V* are represented not only in the taverns but on the battlefield and in the palace. Its wealth of dialects, its proverbs and folk sayings, are in the mouths not only of Bardolph, Pistol, and the Hostess but of respected soldiers of the "middling sort," and even the elite, as in the contest of proverbs between Orleans and the Constable of France. The linguist M. A. K. Halliday's distinction between dialect (language determined by who you are, your socioregional origins) and what he terms "register" (language determined by use and expressing the social division of labor) provides a useful schema for analyzing the way in which the play represents both social and gender difference linguistically.[6]

According to Halliday, register is affected by a number of variables including role relationships, social situations, and symbolic and ideological organization. Henry moves among a variety of speakers, situations, and modes of speech; he can vary his linguistic register according to context. Whereas the soldiers are limited by their dialects and by sociolects of degree, Henry is represented by a flexible linguistic register: he speaks with the voice of monarchical authority and the elite at one moment, with the voice of a common soldier at another. With his bishops, his nobles, and the French he speaks a highly rhetorical verse that indicates his status as king and is marked by mythological and scriptural allusion, the royal "we," the synecdochic figuration of the king's two bodies, and references to his genealogy and elite pastimes. With his soldiers on the field he speaks in another register, a prose of mercantile allusion, proverbial and colloquial.

Henry's linguistic flexibility and virtuosity enables him, unlike the other characters of the play, to move among and seemingly *to master* varied social groups. That seeming mastery is perhaps nowhere more prominent than in those speeches in which the king presents himself as constrained by "ceremony" rather than empowered by "place, degree, and form" and their appropriate rhetorics.[7] Paradoxically, perhaps, Henry's self-conscious manipulation of linguistic register is in part what undermines the play's glorification of the monarch and has prompted recent ironic readings.[8]

A dialectical speaker is quite different; his language limits his status, role and mobility. Fluellen, MacMorris, and Jamy all demonstrate not simply the variety of Englishmen on the battlefield at Agincourt and their unity under Henry, as has so often been noted, but speech and behavior governed by socioregional variables. An early modern illustration of the kind of linguistic determinism Halliday posits would be the annexation of Wales in 1536 that "permitted only English speakers to hold administrative office."[9] The nonelite, then, are presented as linguistically disadvantaged by dialect or, in the case of Princess Katharine, excluded from English altogether by her mother tongue.

The English lesson between the Princess and Alice at 3.4, the only scene in the play that takes place in a private, domestic space, powerfully represents Katharine's linguistic disadvantage. The dialogue locates and confines her not even to the comprehensible if comic dialect of the mother tongue spoken by the captains and soldiers but to a strange disfigured tongue and body. It is preceded by Henry's speech before the walls of Harfleur, often described as a generalized "disquietingly excessive evocation of suffering and violence," but in fact suffering and violence rhetorically enacted on the aged, the helpless, and especially on women—their bodies, the products of their bodies, and the ideological positions they occupy in the family and the commonwealth.[10] In these notorious lines, the expansionist aims of the nation-state are worked out on and through the woman's body. Henry speaks to the men of Harfleur by means of transactions in women: violation and the rape of "fair, fresh virgins" and the slaying of mothers' "flow'ring infants." The speech ends with a vision of familial destruction:

> look to see
> The blind and bloody soldier with foul hand

[Desire] the locks of your shrill-shrieking daughters;
Your fathers taken by the silver beards,
And their most reverend heads dash'd to the walls;
Your naked infants spitted upon pikes,
Whiles the mad mothers with their howls confus'd
Do break the clouds, as did the wives of Jewry
At Herod's bloody-hunting slaughtermen.

(3.23.33–41)[11]

In Henry's speech, the power of the English army is figured as aggressive violence against the weak, and particularly as sexual violence against women. In the dialogue between Katharine and Alice that follows, the "English" also conquer the woman's body. The bawdy of the lesson, the Princess's helpless rehearsal of gross terms, as Steven Mullaney calls it, confines woman discursively to the sexual sphere.[12] The "lesson" moves from sexually unmarked, if potentially eroticized, parts—the hand, fingers, nails, neck, elbow, chin—to sexually specific puns that name the sexual act and women's genitals. Katharine is dispersed or fragmented not through a visual description of her body as spectacle, as in the *blason* and its variants in Renaissance love poetry, but through an o/aural wordplay that dismembers her. Nancy Vickers suggests that this synecdochic mode of representing woman as a fragmented body was disseminated in Petrarch's *Rime Sparse*.[13] She outlines a history of such modes of representing woman and her body, from Latin love elegy to the novel and contemporary film. The most powerful theorization of this mode of representation has been articulated in contemporary film theory describing a fetishized female body, scattered, fragmented, and mastered—by a male gaze.[14] In drama, which lacks the mastering perspective of the look (cinematic or authorial), spoken language—and particularly the variable register—becomes the means of mastery, a linguistic command imposed not on, as in cinema or in Petrarch, "the silent image of woman still tied to her place as bearer of meaning," but on woman as speaker. The dialogue at 3.4 literally "Englishes" Katharine and her body, constituting her as a sexual object that, as the final scene demonstrates, will be disposed of in a sexual exchange, another form of communication that binds men to men, England to France.

The sexual exchange at act 5 is framed by Burgundy's speech representing France as a rank, wild, and overgrown garden (5.2.23–67).

Peace, personified as a poor, naked woman, has been chased from "our fertile France," and through a slippage in pronouns, France itself is feminized, a fitting figure for the following courtship scene resulting in the marriage of "England and fair France." Henry tells Burgundy quite clearly that "you must buy that Peace / With full accord to all our just demands" (5.2.70–71). Though most modern editions shift to lower case in Henry's response, thereby expunging the personification of Peace as a woman, the Folio extends the figure. Gender and the "traffic in women," as Gayle Rubin has dubbed it, have already a figurative presence before the wooing scene proper even begins.[15] Henry, called England in this scene in the Folio, continues, "Yet leave our cousin Katharine here with us: / She is our capital demand" (5.2.95–96).

Henry's wooing participates in a long tradition, dating at least from the troubadours, that conflates courtship and pedagogy: it stages an erotic education. Though the king begins by asking Katharine "to teach a soldier terms / Such as will enter at a lady's ear / And plead his love-suit to her gentle heart," she is his pupil throughout. Henry speaks the same prose to the princess he uses with his captains and regulars, his social inferiors. He talks bawdily of "leapfrog," of taking "the Turk by the beard," uses colloquialisms like "jackanapes," and refers to himself proverbially as the "king of good fellows." Eleven of his eighteen speeches addressed to her end with questions to which he prompts her responses. He enumerates the tasks "Kate" might put him to for her sake, only to refuse them and substitute his own. His refusal to use the conventional language of love and his self-presentation as a plain king who knows "no way to mince it in love" are strategies of mastery, for they represent Henry as sincere, plain-spoken, a man of feeling rather than empty forms. He renames her "Kate" and finally teaches her to lay aside French manners for English customs—specifically, the kiss. The wooing scene replays the conventional female erotic plot in which a sexual encounter transforms the female protagonist and ensures her destiny.[16] In *Henry V,* Henry systematically denies Katharine's difference—her French maidenhood—and fashions her instead into an English wife. He domesticates her difference, refashioning the other as the same. When Burgundy reenters, he asks, "My royal cousin, teach you your princess English? . . . Is she not apt?" At the end of this second language lesson, Katharine is not only "englished" but silenced as well by the witty banter at her expense between Henry and

Burgundy that excludes her from the dialogue.[17] When Henry asks the French king to "give me your daughter," he responds:

> Take her, fair son; and from her blood raise up
> Issue to me; that the contending kingdoms
> Of France and England, whose very shores look pale
> With envy of each other's happiness,
> May cease their hatred, and this dear conjunction
> Plant neighborhood and Christian-like accord
> In their sweet bosoms, that never war advance
> His bleeding sword 'twixt England and fair France.
>
> (5.2.366–73)

As this passage makes clear, the giving of Katharine to Henry in marriage ensures relations among men, or in Lévi-Strauss's often quoted formulation: "The total relationship of exchange which constitutes marriage is not established between a man and a woman, . . . but between two groups of men, and the woman figures only as one of the objects in the exchange, not as one of the partners."[18] For Lévi-Strauss, the exchange of women and the male bonds it constitutes are the origin of social life. Feminists have pointed out two related consequences of Lévi-Strauss's claims. First, Julia Kristeva has debunked the seeming centrality of woman as desired object: "site of occultation or valorization, woman will be a pseudo-center, a center latent or manifest that is blatantly exposed or modestly hidden . . . in which man seeks man and finds him."[19] Luce Irigaray has looked not at the woman in this system of exchange but at the male bonds it insures:

> The exchanges that organize patriarchal societies take place exclusively between men, . . . [and if] women, signs, goods, currency, pass from man to man or risk . . . slipping into incestuous and endogamous relations that would paralyze all social and economic intercourse, . . . [then] the very possibility of the socio-cultural order would entail homosexuality. Homosexuality would be the law that regulates the socio-cultural economy.[20]

For Irigaray, the traffic in women is revealed in its coarsest aspect, deromanticized, mercantile, hyperbolic. She eroticizes the ties between men Lévi-Strauss posits to point out a continuum—which she expresses through her pun "hom(m)osexualité"—that encompasses an entire array of relations among men from the homoerotic to the competitive to the commercial. Eve Kosofsky Sedgwick has appropriated the term "homosocial" from the social sciences to describe "the whole spectrum of bonds between men, including friendship, mentorship, rivalry, institutional subordination, homosexual genitality, and economic exchange—within which the various forms of the traffic in women take place."[21]

In contemporary analyses of systems of exchange, woman's status as object is hypostasized: she is goods, chattel, substance. The category of object, and conversely that of subject—the partners in the exchange (men)—is unquestioned, despite theoretical challenges to a unified subjectivity. Feminist literary readings of exchange systems are too frequently, to parody current literary parlance, always already read. But more disturbing, such readings may reinscribe the very sex/gender system they seek to expose or change. Such a crude confrontation between subject and object betrays a naive realism: the communication between men, what Sedgwick has called homosocial relations, does not always work smoothly but is often "pathological" in ways that disrupt the traffic in women.

In his essay on the Platonic dialogue, Michel Serres explores the "pathology of communication," in which what he terms noise or the phenomena of interference—stammerings, mispronunciations, regional accents, as well as forms of technical interference such as background noise, jamming, static—become obstacles to communication. He notes that Jakobson and other theoreticians of language have described dialogue as a sort of game in which the two interlocutors are united against phenomena of interference and confusion. In such a conception of dialogue, the interlocutors are in no way opposed, as in the traditional notion of dialectic, but

> are on the same side, tied together by a mutual interest: they battle together against noise. . . . *To hold a dialogue is to suppose a third man and to seek to exclude him;* a successful communication is the exclusion of the third man. The most profound dialectical problem is not the problem of the Other, who is only a variety—or a variation—of the Same, it is the problem of the third man. We might call this third man the *demon,* the prosopopoeia of noise.[22]

I want to call this third man a woman and to reconsider Serres's model of pathological communication in terms of sexual difference. Noise, in such a revision, the phenomena of interference, is not only dialects and mispronunciations, static and background noise but specificities, details, *differences.* Within a sex-gender system in which woman is the object of exchange, dialogue is homosocial, between men, and woman is the "tiers exclu" or what in a later extended meditation on this problem Serres calls "le parasite."[23] What makes Serres's model of the "tiers exclu" useful in a discussion of gender and systems of exchange is that it complicates the binary Same/Other that dominates analysis of sex/gender systems and recognizes the power of the excluded third.[24] For as Serres insists, "background noise is essential to communication"; the battle against the excluded third "is not always successful. In the aporetic dialogues, victory rests with the powers of noise" ("Platonic Dialogue," 67, 66). Katharine's speech, with its mispronunciations, consistently deflects Henry's questions and solicitations. In response to his request that she teach "a soldier terms / Such as will enter at a lady's ear / And plead his love-suit to her gentle heart" (5.2.99–101), Katharine responds, "I cannot speak your England." When the king asks "Do you like me, Kate?" she answers "Pardonnez-moi, I cannot tell wat is 'like me.'" When he plays on her response, saying, "An angel is like you, Kate, and you are like an angel," she must ask Alice "Que dit-il? que je suis semblable a les anges?" And at her "Oui, vraiment" and his "I said so, dear Katharine, and I must not blush to affirm it," she returns, "O bon Dieu! les langues des hommes sont pleines de tromperies" (115). Throughout the scene, Henry ends his speeches with questions: "What sayest thou then to my love?" and "Canst thou love me?" and Katharine responds equivocally "Is it possible dat I sould love de enemy of France?" "I cannot tell wat is dat" and "I cannot tell." Finally in response to his reiterated question "Wilt thou have me?" she responds, "Dat is as it shall please de roi mon père." Assured he is so pleased, she acquiesces only to allow "Den it sail also content me." Their dialogue represents a pathological communication in which phenomena of interference both thwart the exchange and at the same time enable it. Shakespeare, unlike his analogue, *The Famous Victories of Henry the Fifth,* represents Katharine at a linguistic disadvantage: she speaks not only French but a comically accented English and a similarly comical macaronic version of the two; but that very disadvantage becomes a strategy of equivocation and deflection.

Many readers have noted the troubling ironies generated by Henry's public justifications and private meditations and by his military threats and disguised sojourn among his common soldiers; but his relations with Katharine, which, after all, produce the play's sense of closure, have received scant attention. Since Dr. Johnson claimed that "the poet's matter failed him in the fifth act," critics have lamented the "comic" scenes and particularly the play's ending, describing it as an "anti-climax" and Henry's wooing as "ursine."[25] Readers who bother to justify the fifth act do so with the lame defense that the ideal hero must marry and act 5 is therefore the completion of Henry's character.[26] More often than not in recent "political" readings of the play, the scenes with Katharine are ignored or used to show that *Henry V* is a falling off from the earlier plays of the tetralogy. Mullaney, for example, suggests that the comic scenes exemplify Marx's "notorious" proposal "that the major events of history occur twice, once as tragedy, and again as farce"[27] and reiterates the well-worn claim that the language lesson was "borrowed" from French farce (though it certainly owes more to the popular and cheap French phrase books fashionable in socially mobile late sixteenth-century London).[28] Political readings tend to ignore the scenes altogether, thereby falling prey to the conventional assumptions of an outmoded political history that excludes social relations and gender from the domain of politics.[29]

Banishing the women's dialogue to the margins of critical discourse on *Henry V,* whether as a footnote to literary borrowing, a coda to the discussion of Falstaff and popular culture, or an absence in the "socio-political perspective of materialist criticism," is to erase gender as a historical category.[30] Gender is also the missing term in Bakhtin's enumeration of heteroglot voices.[31] Commentators have claimed that what Bakhtin terms "carnivalization" collapses hierarchic distinctions. Role reversals and the evocation of the body/bawdy are said to turn the world upside down, collapse distinctions between high culture and low, king and soldier, domination and submission. But the world turned upside down, the exchange of positions, absolute reversal, "the phase of overturning," is not enough. Reversal *preserves* the binary oppositions that ground sexual and social hierarchies: "the hierarchy of dual oppositions always reestablishes itself."[32] The disfiguring power of wordplay in the women's language lesson enables gender hierarchies, mastering the female body by dismembering it; but at the same time that very instability of linguistic meaning, the interference of noise, and the o/aural dispersal of the female body threaten linguistic mastery and successful communication not by means of reversal but through dissemination—of the body and of words.

CULTURAL CAPITAL'S
GOLD STANDARD
Shakespeare and the Critical Apostrophe
in Renaissance Studies

*that curious and mad public that cries continually for the new and original
while admiring only the tried and true*
— Gauguin, on painting

RECENT CRITIQUES OF NEW HISTORICISM AND CULTURAL poetics complain that for all their attention to noncanonical texts—historical, scientific, popular, written from the "margins"—Shakespeare and Milton remain the signal points of reference of most of these investigations. Typically, it is argued, such essays marshal and analyze a host of texts once considered "nonliterary"— diaries, cookbooks, anatomies, travelogues, court cases, pamphlets, wills, texts written by women—but the pay-off is analysis of a canonical author, more often than not, Shakespeare.[1] In what follows, I want to examine that critique and its assumptions, first, by considering carefully what constitutes "cultural capital" in the late twentieth-century United States academy, and then turning to a particular case that I shall use to exemplify the complex of issues at stake in these debates, *Timon of Athens,* a play that because it is "Shakespeare" is now always already canonical, and yet of all Shakespeare's plays, perhaps the most canonically problematic. That double status, *Timon's* dubious canonicity within Shakespeare studies coupled with the continuing canonical power of Shakespeare more generally within the schools and the culture at large, suggests the way in which the canon works through a logic of the supplement and not by way of, so to speak, a gold standard.

By the gold standard, I mean to invoke debates about coined and paper money that shaped political discourse in nineteenth-century America, debates that recent commentators have recognized as concerned with "symbolization in general, and hence not only with money but also with aesthetics. Symbolization in this context concerns the relationship between the substantial thing and its sign."[2] At stake in the gold-standard controversy and the logic of general equivalence that it presupposes is the referent— proponents of the gold standard, and to a lesser but shared degree, the silver money men, believed in the intrinsic value of precious metals, particularly gold, which "stood behind" paper money. Paper money, unlike gold, has no intrinsic value, only that which is bestowed by statutory alchemy, by act of Congress and the willingness of the society in which it is a medium of exchange to accept that denomination. As the history of political economy demonstrates, that value is never stable but changes over time, in different historical circumstances. Within debates about the canon, cultural conservatives argue on behalf of the intrinsic value of works of literature, for a sort of gold standard of cultural capital. Paper money men are like those cultural critics who challenge arguments on behalf of literature's intrinsic value and recognize instead the way in which a given text's or author's value as symbolic currency changes over time. When the new historicist or cultural materialist situates Shakespeare or, less frequently, Milton in relation to a host of texts not usually considered canonical, he or she recognizes not only the lesson that to be read or viewed, one must repeat, produce what is recognizable but never identical, the simulacrum that is not the copy, but also the way in which canonicity is always a question of rereading, that it is produced, not ontological, natural, innate.[3] The changing canonical fortunes of various authors and texts, including Shakespeare, via recent protocols of reading, criticism, and consumption show canonicity to be always retrospective, anachronistic, constructed through the various ways in which a text is endowed with value and made consumable at a particular cultural moment. In the final section of this essay I want to inflate *Timon*'s canonical value by reading it as a chapter in the history of early modern sexuality, to apostrophize, that is, to reanimate *Timon* in today's academy.

Before turning to *Timon,* however, I shall consider briefly the concept "cultural capital," which derives from the important work of the French sociologist/anthropologist Pierre Bourdieu. Bourdieu's work forms a part of the French movement that has been loosely termed post-Marxist because of its willingness to question classical Marxist accounts of capitalism, class, subjectivity, and domination. Bourdieu criticizes solely economic accounts of class formation and insists on the importance of what he terms symbolic capital. However, as the debates about the gold standard and recent work on symbolic economies demonstrate, economics has always been implicated in the processes of symbolization, and symbolization in the economic. Although commentators—new historicist and feminist alike—on the "canon debates" and new paradigms in Renaissance studies have appropriated the concept of "cultural capital" since the publication of Bourdieu's earliest discussions, John Guillory's *Cultural Capital: The Problem of Literary Canon Formation* has given it its recent currency in literary studies.[4]

Guillory opens his argument by stating boldly his claim that "the concept of cultural capital can provide the basis for a new historical account of both the process of canon formation and the immediate social conditions giving rise to the debate about the canon" (viii). Guillory challenges notions of canon formation organized on the model of *representation,* arguing that social conditions—class, not identity—determine the distribution of cultural resources. The canon, as Guillory observes, has always been subject to revision over time, even if those pressures that lead to canon revision are now represented as social and extrinsic rather than intrinsic and value-based. For example, Guillory, Gerald Graff, and others have shown how in the eighteenth and nineteenth centuries the move in the schools away from Greek and Latin culture to the vernacular, and from poetry to the novel, represented the formation of new forms of cultural capital. Guillory's chapter on Gray's "Elegy" and Wordsworth is a dazzling demonstration of the shift from the classical to the vernacular canon in response to the shifting hegemonic status of an emergent bourgeoisie. Subsequently Guillory analyzes Eliot, New Criticism, and de Man as toiling in the production of the "literary," a category that he claims is produced in order to ensure distinction and cultural hegemony.

Guillory assumes, then, that "literature" continues to represent cultural capital. I want to argue instead that mass cultural forms are fast superseding "literature" as cultural capital: even in the narrower confines of the academy, work on television, contemporary movies, popular musical forms such as rap, cultural icons—Elvis, Madonna, O. J. Simpson—refracted through the categorical grids of race, gender, sexuality, nationality, and (too infrequently) class, garners the highest enrollments and would seem to produce the highest economic rewards and prestige.[5] Just as the shift away from classical culture toward the vernacular has been historicized, so we need to historicize the shift in the late twentieth century toward mass cultural forms that are being constituted *in the schools* as symbolic capital. To return to Guillory's argument, economic analysis and historical specificity drop out as he turns to the recent history of literature and theory and rehearses what may be described as a nostalgic narrative of "high" cultural texts—literature—producing class distinctions. Historical and economic inquiry of the kind Guillory so painstakingly performs in the chapter on Gray needs to be undertaken in analyzing the status of literature as a contemporary form of cultural capital: publishing practices (what is in print and available for "consumption"), reading lists, syllabuses and course enrollments, period choices in graduate training, faculty compensation both across disciplines and in relation to the producers of other forms of symbolic capital, from coaches to entertainers, as well as a host of other factors challenge literature's assumed status as cultural capital. New forms of cultural capital with their own complex protocols of reception and interpretation are being produced through the institutionalization in the university of mass culture. Their enormous exchange value contrasts sharply with that of early modern canonical and noncanonical texts and their inordinate demands on today's reader, such as knowledge of Latin and classical culture, of early forms of English and of romance languages, of literary genres, of social and political history, of rhetoric and figuration. Let me be clear. My tone should not be heard as elegiac so much as hard-boiled: I am suggesting that we recognize the momentous shift in cultural practices and objects in which we are taking part, a shift as significant as was, for example, the advent of print culture in the early modern period.

And what of Shakespeare? Shakespeare has long been considered by some the gold standard in English studies, cultural capital of unquestioned value that stands behind other symbolic forms. In the schools, "the canon" is increasingly being reduced to a synecdoche—Shakespeare—a Shakespeare represented by a small and predictable series of plays deemed properly Shakespearean. If the cultural capital that was "literature," and that Guillory assumes in his analysis of de Man still confers distinction, has been superseded by mass cultural forms, and Shakespeare remains the signal reference point of "the canonical," then to complain as some have of bad faith on the part of the new historicists is to misunderstand how cultural capital works under late twentieth-century U.S. capitalism. The constriction of what is in print, of student and collegial interest in and knowledge of the larger tradition, much less of noncanonical authors of the early modern period, presses for the continued turn to Shakespeare, the *auctor rex* of a literary Jurassic Park. The new historicist, cultural materialist, or feminist turn to Shakespeare allows the contemporary critic working in the early modern period to be read, given the many forces that militate against the continued status of older canonical writers, much less noncanonical writers of earlier periods.

In his discussion of the importance of access to literacy, to the means of literary production and consumption through the regulation of reading and writing—in short, the educational system—in producing and revising what counts as canonical, Guillory poses a series of questions: "Who reads? What do they read? How do they read? In what social and institutional circumstances? Who writes? In what social and institutional contexts? For whom?" (18). Oh *Timon of Athens*! Who will read you? How will you be read? In what follows, I want to read and write about *Timon of Athens* in the institutional context of the academy and professional Shakespeare studies. In doing so, I will bear in mind the shifts in what constitutes cultural capital at the fin de siècle in order to produce *Timon of Athens* as such within the circumscribed limits of the university and the discursive topography of literary study in the 1990s.

Perverting the Canonical: An Apostrophe

Out of perverseness, I turn to perhaps the most dubiously canonical of Shakespeare's plays, to look at a text by a male, nonminority, canonical writer of the early modern period, a text that professional Shakespeareans barely afford the status of a Shakespearean play, to read it by *not* repeating what has become the canonical commentary about it, that it may have been collaborative and therefore not "authentically,

fully Shakespearean," that it has "unusual imperfections," is "unpleas-
ant," "incoherent," "unfinished."[6] *Timon*'s problematic canonical status is already gestured at in its peripatetic textual history. Although
first printed in the 1623 Folio, between *Romeo and Juliet* and *Julius
Caesar*, it apparently owes its inclusion to the copyright misfortunes
of *Troilus and Cressida*. In other words, the canonical status of *Timon*
seems already to have been troublesome in the seventeenth century.
Editors surmise that the spot was planned for *Troilus* because copies
of the Folio survive with the end of *Romeo* on one side of the leaf, and
the beginning of *Troilus* on the other. In addition, at the other end,
there is a gap in the pagination between *Timon* and *Julius Caesar*, a gap
that conforms to the difference in length between the printed texts of
Timon and *Troilus*. Frank Kermode ends his discussion of *Timon*'s textual fortunes by observing that "whether *Timon* would have been left
out altogether if that emergency had not arisen it is impossible to say
for certain."[7]

Although *Timon* has been largely ignored by critics until recently,
the play began to be reread and produced in the 1980s, presumably, it
is sometimes said, "because of its emphasis on an affluent and deca-
dent society."[8] Since Bradley, *Timon* has been characterized as unfinished, "weak, ill-constructed and confused," linked to *King Lear* either
as a failed first sketch, or alternatively as an after-vibration, with a
protagonist ridiculous rather than tragic.[9] Recently such judgments
have shifted as critical norms have changed. Readers have pointed to
Timon's topical relation to Jacobean gift giving at court and its links to
new forms of monetary exchange and credit specific to late sixteenth-
and early-seventeenth-century London. Readers have articulated that
historical context in terms of psychological and psychoanalytic structures— primary narcissism, fantasies of maternal power and castration.[10] To appropriate the title of an unpublished essay on *Timon of
Athens* by Barbara Correll, the poles of recent criticism might be allit-
eratively described as capitalism and castration.[11] But I want to read
Timon not in terms that would recuperate it to contemporary norma-
tive historicist or psychoanalytic protocols in Renaissance studies but
instead by way of different economies of figure and address.

Readers of *Timon of Athens* have often remarked that the play
begins with a *paragone*, the dialogue between the poet and the painter.[12]
Unlike a classic *paragone*, however, Shakespeare's poet and painter do

not in fact argue over the relative merits of their respective arts or even compete for Timon's patronage; instead they describe, discuss, and admire the work each has executed. Even a cursory look, for example, at the opening scene of Molière's *Le Bourgeois Gentilhomme,* in which the various masters of philosophy, music, dance, and fencing quarrel and brawl over whose art is best, shows how differently Shakespeare conceives of this scene and its function. More important than any implied debate among the arts is the initial invocation of poetry in the poet's first speech, with its odd figure initiating a rhetoric of apostrophe that comes to dominate the play, particularly in its "difficult" second half. In response to the painter's commonplace observation about how the world wears, the poet responds: "See, / Magic of bounty, all these spirits thy power / Hath conjur'd to attend!" (1.1.5–7).[13] The poet's imperative "see" initially seems to be addressed to the painter, with "magic of bounty" the object. See the magic of bounty, the poet seems to say to the painter. But in the second half of the line, the second-person "thy" shifts our understanding of the lines. "Magic of bounty" is a periphrastic epithet for Timon, an apostrophe summoning him to see the "spirits" that his generosity has conjured up, the swarm of dealers, artisans, and flatterers that surrounds his door awaiting his return. Barbara Johnson defines apostrophe as

> the direct address of an absent, dead, or inanimate being by a first person speaker. . . . Apostrophe is thus both direct and indirect: based etymologically on the notion of turning aside, of digressing from straight speech, it manipulates the I/Thou structure of *direct* address in an indirect, fictionalized way. The absent, dead, or inanimate entity addressed is thereby made present, animate, and anthropomorphic. Apostrophe is a form of ventriloquism through which the speaker throws voice, life, and human form into the addressee, turning its silence into mute responsiveness."[14]

Timon is not named at the outset of the play but is introduced in a periphrastic apostrophe suggesting the seemingly infinite, even supernatural quality of his generosity figured as "bounty." The word *bounty* or its forms is repeated fourteen more times in descriptions of Timon; the word derives from the Old French *bontet,* meaning goodness in persons, virtue, or high estate. Interestingly, the second meaning is "warlike prowess," which would seem to adumbrate the later obscure allusion, at 4.3.95–96, to Timon's "great deeds, when neighbour states, / But for thy sword and fortune, trod upon them [i.e., the Athenians]."

The third meaning of *bounty* is related to things—good quality or property. Finally, *bounty* means an act of kindness or good turn, a kindness that can also be shown through giving and liberality; *bounty,* in this final sense, which is certainly the primary sense here and in the play generally, is usually attributed to God or to the great or wealthy who have power to give liberally and lavishly. In the opening apostrophe, the poet not only introduces Timon; he also tells Timon what otherwise he could not outside the linguistic figure of apostrophe, namely, that the "spirits" he conjures up are merely there for rewards.

Many readers have commented on Timon as a gift giver and on the topical suggestiveness of his generosity when considered in relation to early modern gift culture. Although in act 1 we see Timon release Ventidius from prison by paying off his creditors and dower his manservant Lucilius, we know about Timon's material generosity more by what is said of him, and by the enumeration of his favors when he sends his servants for returns in act 3, than by seeing that generosity enacted. In fact, what Timon gives most generously, even in the first half of the play when he has property to give, is words; he never handles money, rarely handles a gift. We never see him engaged in the work of exchange, although the play would perhaps allow him to take up the proffered jewel in act 1, scene 1. Instead, Timon's gift giving is linguistic, performative; saying is doing. He gives by means of words: "I'll pay the debt" (1.1.106); "I will send his ransom" (108); "I'll counterpoise" (148); "you shall find I like it. Wait attendance / Till you hear further from me" (164–65); "I gave it freely ever" (1.2.10). Flavius's aside in act 1, scene 2 calls attention to a disjunction between the material and the linguistic:

> He [Timon] commands us to provide, and give great gifts,
> And all out of an empty coffer;
> Nor will he know his purse, or yield me this,
> To show him what a beggar his heart is,
> Being of no power to make his wishes good.
> His promises fly so beyond his state
> That what he speaks is all in debt; he owes for ev'ry word.
> (1.2.190–96)

When Timon offers his bay courser to a friend because that friend has praised it, he gives it saying, "You may take my word" (1.2.212). But perhaps the most emphatic example of the displacement of things by words is Flavius's comment, "O my good lord, the world is but a word: / Were it all yours, to give it in a breath, / How quickly were it gone!" (2.2.156–58).

Viewed from this perspective, the two "halves" of the play are not as opposed as the criticism has usually represented them; in the play's second half, we must remember, Timon continues giving. He continues his "magic of bounty," which conjures up spirits through the "performative" linguistic figure of apostrophe. Timon spews words, lavishing them as liberally as he has lavished gifts earlier, calling upon the gods, the heavens, the earth, apostrophizing the city walls, Athenian matrons, slaves, fools, bankrupts, servants, masters, even cold sciatica with his impassioned, misanthropic poetic gifts. To apostrophize is to "will" a state of affairs; for Barbara Johnson and Jonathan Culler the apostrophe figures the performativity of language not so much in the technical Austinian sense, although such an argument could certainly be made, but in the sense of language as constitutive.[15] Timon employs the apostrophe because he is a visionary poet engaged in a dialogue with the universe:

> O thou wall
> That girdles in those wolves, dive in the earth
> And fence not Athens! Matrons, turn incontinent!
> Obedience fail in children! Slaves and fools,
> Pluck the grave wrinkled senate from the bench,
> And minister in their steads! To general filths
> Convert, o' th' instant, green virginity!
> Do 't in your parents' eyes! Bankrupts, hold fast;
> Rather than render back, out with your knives,
> And cut your trusters' throats! Bound servants, steal!
> Large-handed robbers your grave masters are,
> And pill by law. Maid, to thy master's bed;
> Thy mistress is o' th' brothel! Son of sixteen,
> Pluck the lin'd crutch from thy old limping sire;
> With it beat out his brains! Piety and fear,
> Religion to the gods, peace, justice, truth,
> Domestic awe, night-rest and neighbourhood,
> Instruction, manners, mysteries and trades,
> Degrees, observances, customs and laws,
> Decline to your confounding contraries;
> And yet confusion live!
>
> (4.1.1–21)

Timon's impossible imperatives preempt the place of the *you* in the I/Thou structure of direct address and thereby enact what the lines demand—the annihilation of the *you,* the Athenians whom Timon so abhors.[16] The apostrophes in this notorious diatribe animate the inanimate by constituting death and destruction through language: incontinence, disobedience, treason, fornication, pillage, murder, parricide, plague, confusion.

In *Symbolic Economies: After Marx and Freud,* Jean-Joseph Goux analyzes "the intersections and conceptual parallels" (1) among and between semiotics, structural psychoanalysis, and political economy, particularly what he terms "the notion of the *general equivalent*" (3). For Goux, after Marx, gold is that general equivalent, the measuring object, the "metaphor for the transcendental guarantee of meaning" (103), the referential "gold standard." Goux analyzes three functions of gold: as a form of the imaginary or the ideal, as a *measure of values;* as a symbolic form in its function as a circulating medium or instrument; and as a real form of payment, no longer an image, but "as real money, as cold, hard cash" (48). In *Timon,* gold works in all three capacities; it is an ideal measure, a form of the imaginary, a function highlighted by the notorious confusion of numbers—the five, fifty, and five hundred talents.[17] That reckoning disorder merely serves to emphasize the idealized status of gold, its role as excess, "pure superfluity, excess par excellence" (Goux, 28). Gold also functions in the second sense as a symbolic form or instrument—as jewels and the bay courser—in the form of the gift that stands in for gold. Finally, in the opening scene it circulates as cold, hard cash to make Lucilius equivalent to the daughter of the old Athenian, and to pay Ventidius's debts and thereby release him from prison; later in the play, it enables Alcibiades to pay his soldiers and wage war against Athens. The homology that Goux explores between the economic and the linguistic is foregrounded in act 4, scene 3 when Timon, in a famously antipastoral moment, digs for roots and instead finds gold, gold that is summoned from the earth in the form of the apostrophe:

> . . . Earth, yield me roots.
> Who seeks for better of thee, sauce his palate
> With thy most operant poison. What is here?
> Gold? Yellow, glittering, precious gold?
> No, gods, I am no idle votarist.
> Roots, you clear heavens! Thus much of this will make
> Black, white; foul, fair; wrong, right;
> Base, noble; old, young; coward, valiant.

> Ha, you gods! Why this? What this, you gods? Why, this
> Will lug your priests and servants from your sides,
> Pluck stout men's pillows from below their heads.
> This yellow slave
> Will knit and break religions, bless th' accurs'd,
> Make the hoar leprosy ador'd, place thieves,
> And give them title, knee and approbation
> With senators on the bench. This is it
> That makes the wappen'd widow wed again:
> She whom the spital-house and ulcerous sores
> Would cast the gorge at, this embalms and spices
> To th'April day again. Come, damn'd earth,
> Thou common whore of mankind, that puts odds
> Among the rout of nations, I will make thee
> Do thy right nature.
>
> (4.3.23–45)

Conventionally these lines, like Volpone's at the opening of Jonson's play, are glossed in terms of the reversible world; gold turns the world upside down, reverses the values of family, state, nature.

I want instead to focus on the figure of address itself, apostrophe's power to animate—the earth, the gods, roots, finally gold itself:

> *Timon.* . . . O thou sweet king-killer, and dear divorce
> 'twixt natural son and sire, thou bright defiler
> Of Hymen's purest bed, thou valiant Mars,
> Thou ever young, fresh, loved and delicate wooer,
> Whose blush doth thaw the consecrated snow
> That lies on Dian's lap! thou visible god,
> That sold'rest close impossibilities,
> And mak'st them kiss; that speak'st with every tongue,
> To every purpose! O thou touch of hearts,
> Think thy slave Man rebels, and by thy virtue
> Set them into confounding odds, that beasts
> May have the world in empire!
>
> (4.3.384–95)

Unlike most tropes, as Jonathan Culler points out, apostrophe tropes not on the meaning of a word but on the circuit or situation of communication itself—apostrophe is a trope of reciprocity and giving— it animates, gives life, bestows qualities, agency; but it may also "complicate or disrupt the circuit of communication, raising questions about who is the addressee" (135). As such, apostrophe is a preeminently suitable trope for *Timon;* it is the "gold" of the play in its powers of performance and address. Apostrophe may also be the preeminent critical trope of academic discourse. Stephen Greenblatt famously opens his book on Shakespeare with the gnomic utterance "I began with the desire to speak with the dead"; in other words, with the desire, we might say, for apostrophe: "My own voice was the voice of the dead, for the dead had contrived to leave textual traces of themselves, and those traces make themselves heard in the voices of the living."[18] Criticism is always in some sense an act of apostrophe.

Early in his discussion of the canon debates, John Guillory points out that consumption is determined by the knowledge required to read historical works; but cultural capital within the university, however dependent on *knowledge* produced in the schools, is also disabled by the limits of that knowledge, by the canons of reading and gate-keeping protocols that keep the dead from speaking, that inhibit the critical apostrophe. Oh Plutarch! Speak what cannot be spoken. Speak the love that dares not speak its name! Shakespeareans have been almost unanimous in their judgment that Plutarch's *Lives* is not important to *Timon.*[19] Although Kenneth Muir admits the playwright used Plutarch "somewhat perfunctorily for the scenes in which Alcibiades appears" and mentions Shakespeare's use of the Life of Antonius in the portrayal of Timon, he emphasizes "the anonymous *Timon.*"[20] T. J. B. Spencer, in *Shakespeare's Plutarch,* does not include the Life of Alcibiades;[21] in *Plutarch Revisited* David Green tells us that Shakespeare's use of Plutarch in *Timon* is "slight" and that the play is not only "unfinished" but "inferior Shakespeare."[22] Geoffrey Bullough discounts Plutarch in his review of *Timon's* sources, stating that Shakespeare uses the Life of Alcibiades although "but slightly and emphasizes instead Lucian and the anonymous academic *Timon.*"[23] Why the continuing critical censure of *Timon?* Why the determination to read the play through Lucian and the Dyce manuscript *Timon* and not through Plutarch?[24] Can we animate Plutarch, make him speak, and in an act of critical apostrophe, animate a different *Timon of Athens?*

Plutarch is suggestive for our understanding of many aspects of the play. In both the Life of Marcus Antonius (Plutarch 4:290–360) and the Life of Alcibiades (1:346–89), Timon the misanthrope warmly commends Alcibiades' power and wishes the Athenians "undone."[25] The Life of Alcibiades contributes the name of the whore Timandra.

It recounts Alcibiades' intervention to save a friend in an incident suggestive of the strange scene (3.5) in which Alcibiades petitions on behalf of "a friend of mine" whose "hot blood / Hath stepp'd into the law" (3.5.11–13), a man "of comely virtues" (15). But more important than these isolated parallels is the characterization of Alcibiades and his homoerotic attachments. In North's translation of the Life of Marcus Antonius we learn that Timon was mocked by the Athenians, who called him "a vyper, and malicious man unto mankind, to shunne all other mens companies, but the companie of young Alcibiades, a bolde and insolent youth, whom he woulde greatly feast, and make much of, and kissed him very gladly" (Plutarch 4:348). The Life of Alcibiades begins with a description of his physical beauty, his lisping speech; it recounts his relationships with male suitors, particularly Socrates, and remarks on his propensity to dress in long, sweeping robes. The Life tells of Alcibiades' dream at the time of his death, in which he was made up and dressed in women's clothes. These aspects are emphasized as fully as is Alcibiades' ambitious involvement in Athenian politics and the Peloponnesian War. Alcibiades is presented as subject to flattery, blandishment, extravagance, and as often saved by Socrates, with whom it is twice repeated that he often shared his tent. North's Plutarch emphasizes Alcibiades' beauty and his "familliar friendshippe with Socrates": they played together, wrestled, and lodged together in the war (350). North includes Thucydides' reputed characterization of Alcibiades as "incontinent of bodie, and dissolute of life" (352). The Life ends with the protagonist's death following a transvestite dream. Is the refusal on the part of critics to animate Plutarch's Life a turning away from its homoeroticism, from its account of same-sex relations and desire that potentially changes our reading of *Timon?* Is *Timon* deemed an embryonic or, alternatively, a failed *King Lear* because it lacks a heterosexual familial attachment? Does Bullough's portrayal of Alcibiades as a womanizer and a prodigal, and his emphasis on Lucian and the Dyce manuscript *Timon,* in which the protagonist falls in love with and marries a woman, Callimela, rather than on Plutarch, represent a turning away from the play's avowed homoeroticism? Does Plutarch's Life suggest a different reading of male friendship in the play, a different understanding of the emotional power of Timon's disappointment at his friends' betrayal, a different understanding of what it means to be without "gold"?

It has been often remarked that *Timon* is unusual, even among Shakespeare's antique plays, in the intensity of its focus on homosocial relations and its exclusion of women. There are virtually no female characters, only the fleeting, almost speechless entrance of the masquing Amazons at the banquet in act 1, scene 2, who arrive only to be banished immediately by Timon, and the exchange in act 4 with Timandra and Phrynia, whom Timon terms, after Plutarch, Alcibiades' whores. In that second exchange, Timandra asks Alcibiades about Timon: "Is this th'Athenian minion whom the world / Voic'd so regardfully?" (4.3.82–83). *Minion* meant not only a specially favored or beloved one, the idol of a people or community, but, of course, also a sexual favorite, a wanton, a darling, a conflation of meanings that suggests a different attention to the presentation of male friendship in the play, an attention that takes into account Alan Bray's important challenge to the assumed distinction between male friendship and sodomy in the early modern period. Readers have often noted that Timon's investment in his male friends and his sharp misanthropy in the second half are prompted not so much by his loss of status or property as by his loss of friends, a loss symbolized by his vanished gold. Jody Greene has recently read *Timon* and its presentation of male friendship and clientage via sodomy as it has begun to be analyzed in reference to early modern England by Alan Bray and Jonathan Goldberg.[26] Greene's reading of the play's language of orality and spending is powerful, if occasionally anachronistic, but critics of *Timon* have generally evaded the play's insistent homoeroticism.

That Alcibiades was understood in the early modern period to symbolize homoerotic relations is not in doubt.[27] In the January eclogue of Spenser's *Shepheardes Calender*, E. K.'s gloss on Colin Clout's relation with Hobbinol describes Hobbinol as Colin Clout's "most familiar freend," alludes to the "sauour of disorderly loue, which the learned call paederastice," exemplified by Socrates and Alcibiades, and protests that the philosopher loved Alcibiades' soul: "And so is paederastice much to be praeferred before gynerastice."[28] E. K. goes on to demur that he does not defend "execrable and horrible sinnes of forbidden and vnlawful fleshlinesse," but the association of Alcibiades with homoerotic love is clear (423). In Marlowe's *Edward II* the association is even more emphatic. There Mortimer Senior admonishes his nephew to allow Edward his favorite since

> The mightiest kings have had their minions,
> Great Alexander loved Hephaestion,
> The conquering Hercules for Hylas wept,
> And for Patroclus stern Achilles drooped;
> And not kings only, but the wisest men:
> The Roman Tully loved Octavius,
> Grave Socrates, wild Alcibiades . . .
>   (1.4.390–96)[29]

Socrates and Alcibiades are the final dyad in a series of classical parallels representing same-sex love. Kings must have their minions whatever they cost.

In *Timon* gold is the necessary instrument of "friends." Even the loyal Flavius, whose speeches throughout the play foreground the indistinguishable languages of desire, friendship, and service, promises to "serve his mind, with my best will; / Whilst I have gold" (4.2.50–51). Gold is at once the imaginary form of love and loyalty and the signifier of the death of love and friendship. In his discussion of what he terms a general *"logic of the symbolization process"* (24), Jean-Joseph Goux analyzes not only the intersection of semiotic and monetary economies but the way in which

> all processes of exchange and valuation encountered in economic practice set up mechanisms in relation to what I am inclined to term a *symbology,* which is in no way restricted to the economic domain. This symbology entails a system, a mode of symbolizing, which also applies to signifying processes in which are implicated the constitution of the subject, the use of language, the status of objects of desire—the various overlapping systems of the imaginary, the signifying, the real." (113)

Goux's final sentence points clearly to Lacanian psychoanalysis and specifically to Lacan's *"equivalence function of the phallus."*[30] Timon's gold stands in for the phallus, but not only the phallus as absence, castration, or fear of feminine or maternal power. Timon's *"'phallic standard'"* (Goux 23; quoting *Ecrits*) adumbrates a different *sexual* narrative in which the absence of women is simply that, the absence of women. *Timon's* world of male/male love and passionate friendship speaks through Plutarch and the "wild" figure of Alcibiades, whose relation with Timon and his phallic, golden gifts adumbrates another view of Jacobean gift giving.

CHARACTERY

Characterie, an Arte of Shorte, Swifte, and Secrete Writing

—Timothy Bright, 1588

T LEAST SINCE THE THIRTIES, WHEN L. C. KNIGHTS published his wittily titled essay "How Many Children Had Lady Macbeth?," the study of Shakespearean character has been concerned to debunk the naive inclination to talk or write about characters as if they were real people with human personalities.[1] Here is Harry Berger Jr.'s powerful articulation of this position:

> Speakers are the effects rather than the causes of their language and our interpretation: in the unperformed Shakespeare text there are no characters, no persons, no bodies, no interiorities; there are only dramatis personae, the masks through which the text speaks. . . . Speakers don't have bodies, age, insomnia, corpulence, or illness unless and until they mention them. . . . Speakers don't have childhoods unless and until they mention them.[2]

Berger emphasizes his point by refusing even to use the word *character*, a term to which I will return. Instead he refers to speakers, to the dramatis personae of the plays, a reminder that Shakespeare and his contemporaries called such speakers *persons*, not characters, from the Latin *persona* or mask.

Yet in his sprawling, repetitive, self-indulgent, and self-satisfied *Shakespeare: The Invention of the Human*, Harold Bloom professes, as his subtitle advertises, that "our ideas as to what makes the self authentically human owe more to Shakespeare than ought to be possible."³ "Personality, in our sense," he pontificates, "is a Shakespearean invention, and is not only Shakespeare's greatest originality but also authentic cause of his perpetual pervasiveness" (4). "Falstaff and Hamlet are the invention of the human, the inauguration of personality as we have come to recognize it" (4). "Shakespeare's uncanny power in the rendering of personality is," he hazards, "perhaps beyond explanation" (6). In Bloom's bardolatrous universe, Shakespeare figures not only modern psychology but the heavens, outer space, even the divine: "He is a system of northern lights, an aurora borealis visible where most of us will never go. Libraries and playhouses (and cinemas) cannot contain him; he has become a spirit or 'spell of light,' almost too vast to apprehend" (3). For Bloom, who made his literary reputation with *The Anxiety of Influence*, in which he argued that literary production is the result of a continual Freudian *agon* between poets and their precursors, "the representation of human character and personality remains always the supreme literary value"; Shakespeare, he tells us, is its "mortal god," its "magister ludi" (3–4, 11).

These citations, however egregious, offer a fair sampling of this book's interminable 745 pages and in themselves might raise the question of why respond seriously to such a recital? Yet until the recent appearance of Stephen Greenblatt's literary biography of Shakespeare, *Will in the World: How Shakespeare Became Shakespeare*, Bloom's *Shakespeare: The Invention of the Human* has been more widely publicized and reviewed than any Shakespeare book to appear in decades; it is being bought not only by college and university libraries but in secondary schools, private lending libraries that cater to the so-called common reader, and, most worrisome, by unlessoned students of Shakespeare peopling our classrooms. It has been translated into Spanish and seems to have received more reviews on amazon.com than any other book on Shakespeare. In short, Bloom's polemical book, which might perhaps have been merely preposterous, a feeble end to a serious scholarly career, is instead hazardous in its vatic pretensions and pronouncements that have been embraced by a reactionary, anti-intellectual, middle-brow cultural establishment in the United States.

Professional Shakespeareans have colluded in this process—witness James Shapiro's inexplicably generous review in the *New York Times Book Review*.⁴ Inexplicable because from his opening pages, Bloom attacks exactly the sort of work Shapiro does and what Bloom complains "now passes as readings of Shakespeare" (xviii). Wholeheartedly embracing and perpetuating a long tradition of Anglo-American pragmatism, Bloom dubs the criticism he deplores "French Shakespeare," which he claims unfolds as follows: "The procedure is to begin with a political stance all your own, far out and away from Shakespeare's plays, and then . . . locate some marginal bit of English Renaissance social history that seems to sustain your stance. Social fragment in hand, you move in on the poor play" (9). No matter that the practice that Bloom describes metaphorically as somewhere between a hunt and an assault owes more to Raymond Williams, Clifford Geertz, and Stephen Greenblatt than to French "theory." No matter that new historicist approaches have not by and large been adopted by French critics and commentators working on Shakespeare. And no matter that Bloom paradoxically includes examples of the very criticism he here excoriates in the popular collections of critical essays on Shakespeare that cite Bloom as editor and that his publishers glossily, and no doubt lucratively, peddle.

Bloom goes on to complain that nowadays critics maintain that "Shakespeare did not write Shakespeare, his plays were written by the social, political and economic energies of his age," a posture that seems peculiar in that it raises, while at the same time ignoring, the long-standing debate about Shakespearean authorship. Bloom seems not to recognize that the sad state of affairs he decries began as a reaction to the putative deracination of New Criticism and has developed recently in response to new work on collaborative writing and printing practices in early modern England. For Bloom, it is apparently a French plot: "Certain more or less recent Parisian speculators have convinced many (if not most) academic critics that there are no authors anyway" (16). Conflating poststructuralist theory with new historicism, and with what have come to be called the new textual or bibliographical studies, Bloom derides what he ungrammatically describes as "Resentment"—those critics who value theory over the "literature itself" (9).

In what follows, I want to address the questions Bloom's book raises in the context of his phrase "literature itself." What was "personality" or "character" for Shakespeare? Who is this putative critic who begins, as Bloom complains, "with a political stance all your own, far out and away from Shakespeare's plays"? And who is it who values theory over the "literature itself"? To address these questions, we need to begin by considering the word *character* and its uses in Shakespeare; for this I turn to the *OED*, a book of which, happily, Bloom approves, since he assures us that this compendium of historical usage "is made in [Shakespeare's] image" (10). The word *character* comes, as has been often noted, from the Greek χαρακτήρ, meaning an instrument for marking or engraving, a stamp or impress, or perhaps from its verbal form, χαράττ-ειν, meaning to sharpen, to cut furrows in or to engrave. The word appears in Middle English as *caracter(e)*, seemingly from the French *caractère*. As the *OED* explains, the word "was further assimilated [to English] in [the] 16th c. by (fictitious) spelling with *ch*." A *character* is a graphic sign or symbol, writing, a letter of the alphabet, a printed letter, handwriting. Shakespeare's usage, and that of his contemporaries, conforms to these meanings: *character* means a mark or *marque*—a term that since the late sixties, of course, also invokes poststructuralist meaning and play.

The figurative notion of character as trait or feature dates from the early seventeenth century. But Bloom's notion of character as an aggregate of distinctive features, as a *personality*, or, again as the *OED* defines it, *character* as a "person regarded in the abstract as the possessor of specified qualities; a personage, a personality," seems to have come into active usage only in the late seventeenth and eighteenth centuries. The *OED* also offers the definition "individuality impressed by nature and habit on man or nation," with a usage from the mid-seventeenth century, but early examples related to this meaning always entail the specificity of the literary genre of the character as inaugurated by Theophrastus.[5] Classical precedent aside, the "character" as practiced in England by Bishop Hall, John Earle, Thomas Overbury, and in France by La Bruyère and others, seems to be specific to the seventeenth century. These were books made up of short satirical entries describing types of persons: perhaps the best known early example is Overbury's "A Wife," first published in 1614. It went through a number of editions and was quickly supplemented by additional characters including, among many others, "A Pedant," "An excellent Actor," and "A French Cook," whom Overbury maintains is an enemy of beef and mutton who "does not feed the belly but the Palate."[6]

Dryden appears to have first used the word *character* with reference to "a personality invested with distinctive attributes and qualities, by a novelist or dramatist"; and "the personality or 'part' assumed by an actor on the stage" (*OED*). In his preface to *Troilus and Cressida, or, Truth found too late* (1679), Dryden writes,

> A character, or that which distinguishes one man from all others, cannot be suppos'd to consist of one particular Virtue, or Vice, or passion only; but 't is a composition of qualities which are not contrary to one another in the same person: thus the same man may be liberal and valiant, but not liberal and covetous; so in a Comical character, or humour, (which is an inclination to this, or that particular folly) Falstaff is a lyar, and a coward, a Glutton, and a Buffon, because all these qualities may agree in the same man.[7]

As we see in this passage, Dryden's use of *character* already links it with Shakespeare's Falstaff and at the same time with character as humor or type. Dryden seems to have taken this usage of the word *character* as "that which distinguishes one man from all others" from the French as he did so many technical literary terms.[8] There is a certain irony, then, given Bloom's disparagement of the French, that the word *character* as he uses it, and the novelistic, rounded, character-with-an-interior-life he credits Shakespeare with inventing, were appropriated from French usage.

Jonathan Goldberg has insisted on the implications of the often noted early modern meaning of *character* as mark, letter, or writing for analyzing and discussing Shakespearean character in his "Shakespearian Characters: The Generation of Silvia."[9] There he reads *Two Gentlemen of Verona* to speculate:

> What's in a name? For Silvia, it is her destiny (already written in the *silva* tradition) and her destination. . . . In a word, her name is a genealogy, and in the play in which she appears, her generation is the generation of the letter—literally and figuratively. Silvia moves through a chain of signifiers to arrive (in the final scene of the play) in the place her name determines, the woods. There only the letter speaks, and the character falls silent. (68)

Goldberg goes on to play with both the Derridean and Lacanian character of the play's sylvan characters/letters and to argue that "the being of characters is their textuality" (77), that characters "are not veils to be penetrated but surfaces to be read and reread" (86). He ends with reflections on perhaps the most oft-cited exemplum of "the supposed interiority of the Shakespearian character," *Hamlet* (98). Hamlet's mind, he reminds us, is a book, a locus of *copia,* a scene of writing, of

impression. Harry Berger Jr., as we have seen, has also written tren-
chantly on character as language, as the effects of language rather than
persons imagined as "prior to and independent of the plays in which
they appear and as speaking a language that reflects this experiential
and psychological history."[10] Following Random Cloud, Margreta de
Grazia and Peter Stallybrass have pointed out that the very tradition
of affixing a list of dramatis personae to precede a Shakespearean play,
"which suggests that characters precede their speeches," dates from
Rowe's edition of Shakespeare in 1709 and is thus contemporaneous
with the meaning of character as a part assumed by an actor we find
in Dryden and throughout the eighteenth century.[11] Pope, who follows
Rowe in this editing practice, seems first to have used the word *character* with reference to Shakespeare in the sense, even the rhetoric, in
which Bloom uses it. In the prefatory remarks to his edition of Shakespeare, Pope opines, "Every single character in *Shakespear* is as much
an Individual, as those in Life itself."[12]

But as most critics and commentators acknowledge, the psy-
chologizing of Shakespearean character was codified in Maurice Morgann's *Essay on the Dramatic Character of Sir John Falstaff* (1777) and
probably culminates in A. C. Bradley's *Shakespearean Tragedy*, published in 1904 and, not coincidentally, roughly contemporaneous with
The Interpretation of Dreams in which Freud first outlines the Oedipal complex by reading *Hamlet*.[13] Morgann's essay is only one example
of what David A. Brewer has recently termed the "afterlife of character," the "peculiar, yet compelling logic which links detachability, character migration, and a virtual community" united around a character
perceived as "our mutual friend." Characters, he argues, with Falstaff
being a prime example, are often imagined "as existing prior to and
apart from his originary texts."[14] Brewer goes on to describe numerous eighteenth-century examples in which characters are detached
from their originary texts and thrust into "entirely new adventures."
He considers, for example, George Saville Carey's *Shakespeare's Jubilee,
A Masque* in which Falstaff is "'charm-called from his quiet grave' in
order to attend the 1769 Stratford Jubilee," the bicentennial celebration of Shakespeare's birth. There is also William Kenrick's *Falstaff's
Wedding*, the plot of which fills the temporal and diegetic gap between
the end of *2 Henry IV* and *Henry V*. In Kenrick's play, the traitors
Scrope and Cambridge plot to depose Hal and install Mortimer on the

throne. They hire the banished Falstaff to murder the king at Southampton, where, as Brewer neatly summarizes the plot, "the English are assembling to invade France in the campaign that will culminate at Agincourt. . . . And amid all this, as Kenrick's title suggests, Falstaff is scheming to marry Dame Ursula as a means of weaseling out of his £500 debt" (Brewer, 87–88). Brewer argues that such "imaginative expansions," as he terms them, demonstrate that the current critical consensus, that characters are not real people but effects of language, is wrongheaded.

Yet what Brewer's examples demonstrate is not that Falstaff is a real personality or "the invention of the human" but that literary character begets literary character, that character is a formal device that can be repeated in new imaginative contexts—which is what the genre of the character, after all, is all about. Evidence for this view is provided by a number of seventeenth-century allusions to Falstaff that are concerned to defend the historical figures after which he is named from the imputations attributed to them by conflation with Shakespeare's fat, cowardly knight. As is well known, Falstaff was originally called Oldcastle, but the Cobham family, descendents of the historical Sir John Oldcastle, who had served ably under both Henry IV and Henry V before dying a Lollard martyr, took offense at Shakespeare's naming his character after their ancestor. Shakespeare subsequently rechristened his character Falstaff, whose name evokes yet another historical figure, the soldier Sir John Fastolfe who fought with Henry V at Agincourt. In the dedicatory letter to his *The Legend and Defence of the Noble Knight and Martyr Sir Jhon Oldcastle,* usually dated 1625, Richard James writes that "Sr Iohn Oldcastel apperes to have binne a man of valour and vertue" and that "Sir Jhon Falstophe [was] a man not inferior of Vertue, though not so famous in pietie as the other."[15] In response to questions James represents as posed by "a young Gentle Lady" and reader of Shakespeare, he dismisses Falstaff's portrayal as "one of those humours and mistakes for which Plato banisht all poets out of his commonwealth" (*Shakespeare Allusion-Book*, 330). Contemporaries at least clearly distinguished the dramatic character of Falstaff from the "real" persons whose names Shakespeare borrowed.

Of the thirty-nine uses of *character* or its forms by Shakespeare throughout the plays and sonnets, none denotes or connotes, suggests or implies personality, individuality, or character as Bloom uses the terms. Perhaps the best-known Shakespearean instance is from *Twelfth Night,* Viola's words to the Captain, "of thee / I will believe thou hast a mind that suits / With this thy fair and outward character" (1.1.49–51). The lines resolutely identify character not with inwardness but with that which is displayed, marked, or impressed outside: the captain's appearance and "fair behavior."[16] *Character,* then, in Bloom's usage, is not Shakespearean. It is what we would call a "term of art" or critical analysis used to study the plays, just like those other terms of critical analysis Bloom criticizes such as gender, class, or race.[17] In short, *character,* in Bloom's usage, is *theoretical* and his attack on "Theory" in the academy and among critics and readers of Shakespeare is disingenuous at best. My point is not to deny the achievement of Shakespearean characterization: Shakespeare's rhetoric of inwardness can, has been, and will continue to be deservedly analyzed, studied, read, and interpreted.[18] Rather, it is to debunk Bloom's claims to be saving Shakespeare from the forces of evil and to expose his assumptions about genius, his solipsistic devaluation of language, and his anti-intellectual claim that Shakespeare's achievement "is perhaps without explanation."

Shakespeare only once uses the word *character* not to mean mark or writing. In *Coriolanus* 5.4.16–24, Menenius, speaking to the tribune Sicinius, says:

> The tartness of his face sours grapes. When he walks, he moves like an engine, and the ground shrinks before his treading. He is able to pierce a corslet with his eye, talks like a knell, and his hum is a battery. He sits in his state as a thing made for Alexander. What he bids be done is finish'd with his bidding. He wants nothing of a god but eternity and a heaven to throne in.[19]

Sicinius responds, "Yes, mercy, if you report him truly," to which Menenius replies, "I paint him in the character" (26). Philip Brockbank in the Arden edition glosses Menenius's phrase "in the character" to mean "to the life, as he is," but Menenius's description with its apt similes likening Coriolanus's stride to an engine of war, perhaps a battering ram or catapult or even simply a piece of ordnance; his eye to a spear; and his voice to a knell, which means both a resounding blow and the sound made by a bell that often announces death, is a generic *character.* It announces its genre through its formal features: its brevity, its seriality together with its asymmetry of form, its omission of syntactic ligatures, and the repeated "he," which Morris Croll in his study of seventeenth-century prose style observes as "so conspicuous a mannerism that it may serve to conceal what is after all the more significant feature of the 'character' style, namely, the constant variation and contrast of form in members that begin in this formulistic manner."[20] That asymmetry is also sometimes obscured by the character's misleading use of "and," as in "he moves like an engine *and* the ground shrinks before his treading." Generally dated 1608, *Coriolanus* is contemporaneous with Joseph Hall's *Characters of Virtues and Vices,* which seems to have initiated the English vogue for character writing that flourished throughout the seventeenth century.[21] Hall claims to follow Theophrastus, who "draw[s] out the true lineaments of every vertue and vice, so lively, that who saw the medals, might know the face: which Art they significantly tearmed Charactery." The genre of the character, with its emphasis on drawing and portraiture, engraving and coining, depends on the root meaning of *character* and its early modern usage as inscription, impression, engraving, marking.[22] The character offers a typological approach to the representation of subjectivity—characteristically it eschews inwardness and psychological speculation: its formal features—brevity and the frequent use of the scheme "he is, he does, he acts," as outlined earlier, offer observation from the outside, not interiority. As one commentator on the genre observes, "'Characters' are not concerned with complex, many-sided personalities; they are always selective and exaggerated."[23] Coriolanus's character drawn by Menenius as roughly a cross between a god and some piece of new technological weaponry, a war machine, exemplifies the generic character in its insistence on his valor to the exclusion of all else, in its pushing that quality to an extreme.

Coriolanus's character has been excoriated by generations of Shakespeareans: he is an "iron, mechanical warrior," a "human war machine," (Traversi) who lacks "maturity," (Knights), "a distant and rigid hero" at once filled with "hungry and mutinous forces" and "mantled in his self-sufficiency" (Adelman), "a killer" (Kuzner) with "hyperbolically warlike physical traits" (Kahn) and with "the self-sufficiency of a god" (Cantor).[24] Coriolanus shares much with Hall's character "Of a Valiant man," both formally in Menenius's character with its repeated "he" and its asymmetry, but also substantively: "he had rather have his bloud seene than his back; and disdaines life upon base conditions"; or, "He talks little, and brags lesse; and loves rather the silent language of the hand" (154). But unlike Coriolanus, Hall's "Valiant man" is a moralized warrior who "subdues his passions to reason," subjects himself to God, and "commands without tyranny and imperiousness" (154). In Coriolanus, valor vanquishes all else; it is the ruling extreme of his character.

The suffix *ery* added to *character* in my title was a typical Middle English form that first occurs in words adopted from French and later comes to be used extensively as an English formative: many of the French *er* words to which the suffix is added designate persons according to their occupation; *ery* denotes the class of goods in which that person deals, the place where those goods are produced, or the art or practice itself. Think of draper/drapery, baker/bakery, archer/archery, and brewer/brewery. Often the suffix denotes classes of goods as in pottery, crockery, machinery, even scenery. Again, as the *OED* puts it, "often the force of the suffix is 'that which is characteristic of, all that is connected with'" and then adds, "in most cases with contemptuous implication": here the examples are knavery and popery, which the *OED* terms coinages of "jocular nonce words." And we can add many more fitting, modern examples, perhaps most notable for our purposes, *bardolatry*. Formed on Shaw's contemptuous, jocular nonce word *bardolator*, *bardolatry* just missed inclusion in the then appearing early volumes of the *New English Dictionary*. The word had to wait for the first published Supplement of the dictionary in 1933.[25] *Charactery* would seem to be a formation to indicate "that which is characteristic of, all that is connected with" the character—with writing, marking, and the letter. Shakespeare uses it twice, first in *Julius Caesar* at 2.1.308 when Brutus promises Portia he will reveal to her "the secrets of my heart. / All my engagements I will construe to thee, / All the charactery of my sad brows," where the sense is literally graphic—his heart's secrets are secretly charactered in his sad brows.

The other usage is in *The Merry Wives of Windsor* at the moment of Falstaff's punishment, his lesson, when Mrs. Quickly exhorts the fairies to write the motto of the Garter, *honi soit qui mal y pense,* in flowers: "Fairies use flow'rs for their charactery." No play of Shakespeare's is for Bloom slighter than *Merry Wives*. His discussion of the comedy consists of assertions that "the hero-villain of *The Merry Wives of Windsor* is a nameless impostor masquerading as the great

Sir John Falstaff" (315). For Bloom, Falstaff, more than any other of Shakespeare's characters, epitomizes the playwright's "invention of the human." Bloom loves Falstaff, as he repeatedly asserts (271 passim), but only the Falstaff of the *Henry IV* plays; Falstaff "*is* Shakespeare's wit at its very limits" (273); he is the "Socrates of Eastcheap" (275). Bloom is so besotted that he is willing to imagine the craven Falstaff as, in his words, "a veteran warrior, now set against the chivalric code of honor" (277). "Sir John has genius, more of Shakespeare's own genius than any other character save Hamlet" (284). In Bloom's contest between Falstaff and Hamlet, "Falstaff has priority . . . [for] not to appreciate his personal largeness, which surpasses even his sublime girth, would be to miss the greatest of Shakespearean originalities: the invention of the human" (290). Bloom is indignant, therefore, at what he terms Shakespeare's capitulation to commerce in diminishing Falstaff in *Merry Wives,* but he is certain there is an explanation, a hermeneutic secret: "Shakespeare in his deepest inwardness harbored anxieties and resentments that he rarely allowed expression" (318). In his urgent need to reject the "false Falstaff," Bloom finds himself even keeping company with execrated feminist critics and reading the play as a "castration pageant" (318). Shakespeare punishes the pseudo-Falstaff, we are assured, "as a surrogate for himself," and Bloom concludes his chapter on the play portentously: "Shakespeare himself is warding off personal horror by scapegoating the false Falstaff in this weak play" (318).

Yet one other meaning of *charactery* is indicated in my epigraph taken from the title of Timothy Bright's *Characterie, an Arte of Shorte, Swifte, and Secrete Writing. Charactery* means cipher or code, writing that hides a secret, a hermeneutic secret. So, for example, in defining character, Overbury in his brief "What a character is" calls it "an Egyptian Hierogliphicke . . . in little comprehending much."[26] Bloom's *Shakespeare: The Invention of the Human* is not about Shakespearean character but *charactery,* a secret code, unfortunately for his readers a *long*hand in which he writes not Shakespeare but himself. In his "Coda," Bloom sums up his attack on "our current demystifications" and *nouveaux* historicizers, as he terms them (725) by saying with evident false modesty, that "to accuse Shakespeare of having invented . . . Harold Bloom is . . . to see that Bloom [is] a parody of Falstaff" (725). Given the series of displacements repeated endlessly throughout this book, Bloom's paean to Falstaff cum Shakespeare is a paean not to Shakespearean character but to himself as Falstaff as Shakespeare. *Charactery,* I repeat, a jocular nonce word with contemptuous implication.

The danger of Bloom's Shakespeare book is not simply its narcissism but its diminishment of Shakespeare's dramatic achievement to a selfish individualism in which personality and personhood—the liberal post-Enlightenment subject that Bloom dubs the human—dominates all. It is a return to Bradley's claim that Shakespearean tragedy "is pre-eminently the story of one person, the 'hero,' or at most two, the 'hero' and 'heroine'" and, despite his repeated claims to the contrary, it is a turning away from aesthetic value and from formal and artistic achievement. Not just "French Shakespeare" and "Parisian speculators" have argued that Shakespearean character is an effect of language; from L. C. Knights's article "How Many Children Had Lady Macbeth?" with which we began, to Arthur Sewell's insistence that Shakespeare distills "personality into style" and Wolfgang Clemen's study of the soliloquies in the 1950s, to the work of Harry Berger Jr., Jonathan Goldberg, Margreta de Grazia, and Peter Stallybrass quoted earlier, readers and critics of Shakespeare have looked to his language to understand his characters.[27] In an essay titled "The Question of Character in Shakespeare" that appeared in 1959, L. C. Knights confidently announced that the contemporary reader of Shakespeare, thanks to "critical work done in the last quarter century . . . is likely to take for granted that the essential structure of the plays is to be sought in the poetry rather than in the more easily extractable elements of 'plot' and 'character.'"[28] We would do well to remember that admonition.

SARTORIAL ECONOMIES
AND SUITABLE STYLE

The Anonymous *Woodstock* and

Shakespeare's *Richard II*

RICHARD II'S DECISION AT ACT I, SCENE 4 OF SHAKESPEARE'S play to go "in person to this war" is framed by two moments in which clothing plays an important symbolic role. First, the king recounts how Bolingbroke leaves London to banishment abroad courting the common people, "wooing poor craftsmen with the craft of smiles" and doffing "his bonnet to an oysterwench" as if he were "our subjects next degree in hope."[1] Bolingbroke's doffed bonnet points up clothing's role in showing deference and status in social relations. In doffing his cap to a street seller, Bolingbroke reverses conventional status hierarchies. Second, as commentators always note, when Bushy enters announcing that Gaunt is grievous sick, Richard wishes him quickly dead in order to finance "these Irish wars." But the specificity of his words is rarely noted: "the lining of his coffers shall make coats / To deck our soldiers for these Irish wars" (60–61).[2] Coats and coffers, alliteration and syntactical symmetry draw attention to the cost of clothing in early modern England. The metaphor for Gaunt's wealth—the lining of his coffers—extends the sartorial image since the first meaning of "lining" is "the stuff with which garments are lined; the inner or under surface of material stitched into coat, robe, hat, etc. for protection or warmth," a meaning in use at least since the beginning of the fifteenth century.

Richard's soldiers are in need of coats, as the poor so frequently were in Richard's day, and as they were in England in the sixteenth and seventeenth centuries. At act 3, scene 3, returned from Ireland

and deserted by his allies, Richard laments his plight standing on the walls of Flint Castle where he pledges to give his jewels for beads, his gorgeous palace for a hermitage, and his "gay apparel for an almsman's gown" (148). How did the poor dress—the soldiers and almsmen, craftsmen and oysterwenches Richard names in the course of Shakespeare's play? Recent work on dress and clothing in Elizabethan and Jacobean England has focused on sartorial extravagance, on the development of fashion, on conspicuous consumption among the elite, and on fashion trespassing by actors and the socially aspirant.[3] How the majority of the population, which experienced downward mobility and for whom fashion was inaccessible, dressed has been largely ignored.[4] What can be said about sartorial economy, even sartorial penury, in early modern English culture? In what follows, I wish to consider unfashionable clothing, the coarse shirts and smocks, loose coats and jerkins, rough bands and hose, of russet, kersey, buckram, homespun, buff and scotch cloth, frieze and indifferent knit that were the common dress of the large majority of the early modern English population occasionally represented on the English stage. How was such cloth and the clothing made from it registered in English writing of the late sixteenth and early seventeenth centuries? What can be said about the relation of cloth and clothing to style?

The importance of cloth to the English economy has been widely acknowledged. The early Tudor period saw the growth of the cloth trade, especially along the London-Antwerp axis, and the dominance of that trade by the Merchant Adventurers. In Elizabeth's time, the still powerful old cloth industry suffered from competition abroad whenever war, plague, or bad harvest disrupted fairs and markets, but the "new draperies," luxury cloth manufactured for export, flourished.[5] Not only cloth but clothing itself also played an important role in the English economy. In his *Burns Journal,* Gregory King estimates spending on clothing at 25 percent of national expenditure, as compared with 10 percent or less in the twentieth century, and he calculated that some seventy-nine million garments of apparel were added to the national stock annually. Recent work has refined King's figures; N. B. Harte estimates that the poorest spent some 18 percent of their annual incomes on clothing, about £3, while the better off and very richest spent 28 percent and 15 percent respectively.[6]

In Shakespeare's England, clothing was real property and a medium of exchange. Social historians have begun to document that importance by looking at household accounts that register the ordering and purchase of clothing, at wills and bequests in which clothing is passed down to kin and servants, at the widespread practice of "turning" and the trade in second-hand clothes; they have also studied the availability of clothing outside London and other English towns through the travels of chapmen; finally, they have examined the rag trade and the high incidence of cloth and clothing theft.[7] Though in the first chapter of Marx's *Capital* he famously argues that gold has become the universal equivalent, he nevertheless registers the continuing economic importance of cloth and clothing obliquely in the choice of commodities, the coat and twenty yards of linen, he uses to demonstrate value and the effacement of labor. The examples of coat and linen in *Capital,* like recent biographical work on Marx's serial pawning of his own coat, show that cloth and clothing persisted as real property well into the nineteenth century.[8]

That clothing betokens social relations in early modern England is virtually a cliché. As Polonius pompously reminds Laertes, "the apparel oft proclaims the man" (*Hamlet,* 1.3.72). Clothes make men, or as Spenser put it, "Apparell is comonlye made according to theire Condicions, and theire Condicions are often times gouerned by theire garments."[9] Sumptuary legislation, livery, ballads and pamphlets, diatribes and homilies against excess in apparel, and the vestiarian controversy all testify to the significance of clothes as markers of status, gender, work, and religious faith.[10] In Francis Thynn's didactic poem (ca. 1568) *The Debate between Pride and Lowliness,* later pirated by Robert Greene and published in 1592 as *Quip for an Upstart Courtier,* Thynn catalogs the clothing of men of varied social statuses and the various trades. They are enumerated in the name of seeking a jury to decide a debate between pride and lowliness personified respectively in the poem by velvet and cloth breeches.[11] Thynn details the honest clothes of bakers, vintners, merchants, tanners, bricklayers, shoemakers, weavers, and husbandmen but especially praises the knight, "plaine in his apparel," who "spends his living on the poorer sort," offering hospitality rather than wearing silk.[12] The wearing of silk by the elite, he suggests, leads to destitution exemplified in the poem by a woman and her two children. In the stanza quoted below, we learn initially that both the woman and her daughter are wearing russet, the coarse homespun woolen cloth of a reddish-brown, gray, or neutral color used for the dress of peasants and country folk (*OED*) already in the fourteenth century.[13] In the B text of *Piers Plowman,* for example, "Charite . . . is as gladde of a goune of a graye russet / As of a tunicle of tarse or of tyre scarlet" (15.167).[14] But in Thynn's poem, the russet the woman and her daughter wear is so worn that their naked bodies can be seen through the threadbare fabric:

> The woman and the wench were clad in russet
>> Both course and olde, and worne so very neere,
> That ye might see cleane through both sleeve and gusset
>> The naked skinne; whereas it dyd appeere.[15]

By specifying "gusset," originally a piece of flexible material that filled up a space under the arms at the joints between two adjacent pieces of mail, and subsequently a triangular piece of material let into a garment to strengthen or to enlarge the sleeve at the armpit to permit ease of movement (*OED*), Thynn glances ironically at the association of gusset with mail, since their garments emphatically do not provide protection; but more importantly, in using this technical term he suggests that their clothes are designed for utility since the gusset was designed to provide ease of movement for labor. In the next stanza, he extends the paradoxical irony of russet so worn it is transparent when he observes the material and craftsmanship of their shoes and hose, only to reveal that the leather he describes is none other than their weather-beaten skin:

> The hosen and their shooes were all of one,
>> I meane both for the woorkmanshyp and leather,
> To wye their skinnes, for other had they none,
>> And chapped were they sore with wind and weather.

The poorest in early modern England, then as now, were women and children, who apparently wore almost nothing at all. Thynn's poem is not only allegorical homily but sturdy social critique, for the poor woman and her children, we learn, had been "copie holders of tenant right." They have fallen on hard times after having been ousted by a rapacious "churle" to whom the lord/landowner has leased his land for cash.[16]

The relation of "condition" to apparel was also racialized in the early modern period with legislation to ensure distinctions between the English and Irish and in attacks on the Irish mantle.[17] In a contemporary song now titled "The Irish Hallaloo," the Irish are contrasted with their English betters in "Beavers and Castors so good": "When they are driven along the Passes / They've nothing but Tatters to hang on their Asses. / Instead of their Mantles lined with Plush: / They're forc'd to seek Rags off ever Bush."[18] The poor, it would seem, took their clothes wherever they could find them: from their masters as livery if they were fortunate enough to be employed, but if not, stolen as they dried on bushes and shrubbery or even stripped from the bodies of the dead:

> We beggars reck nought of the carcass of the dead body, but do defy it; we look for old cast coats, jackets, hose, caps, belts and shoes, by their deaths which in their lives the[y] would not depart from . . . god send me of them.[19]

Whereas the poor sought clothing for the sake of modesty or to protect themselves from weather, for the better off dress maintained status distinctions, enabled social mobility and social emulation, and provoked anxiety about sartorial trespass. Whether in city comedy, personal letters and diaries, sermons or other genres, contemporaries satirized persons who dressed above their station and bemoaned the decline of the landed elite through the sale of land for the purchase of high fashion.[20] In the anonymous play *Thomas of Woodstock,* which dramatizes Richard II's history from the perspective of his uncles and particularly, as its title indicates, that of Thomas of Woodstock, Duke of Gloucester, clothing both plain and extravagant is central to the play's rhetoric and presentation of character. Woodstock is explicitly characterized from the outset by his refusal of the "braverie" worn by others of his rank and most importantly by Richard's ambitious minions. He is introduced as Plain Thomas, so named, we learn,

> For his plain dealing, and his simple clothing?
> "Let others jet in silk and gold," says he,
> "A coat of English frieze, best pleaseth me."[21]

Here the rhyme paradoxically distinguishes Woodstock's plain speech from the unrhymed pentameter of his brothers and establishes the contrast between Richard and his gaudily dressed favorites and Thomas of Woodstock's "country habit" (1.1.197), "t'other hose" and "frieze coat" (1.3.100–101). "Frieze," like russet, is also a coarse woolen cloth, but with a nap. Woodstock rehearses the standard Elizabethan and Jacobean anxiety that land is being razed, sold and worn on the shoulders of the elite: "A hundred oaks upon these shoulders hang / To make me brave upon your wedding day, / And more than that, to make my horse more tire, / Ten acres of good land are stitched up here" (1.3.95–98). In the conventional trope, generic forests are razed to pay for fashionable attire, but here, the choice of *oaks*, long associated with England and its kings, and explicitly with Richard later in the play (2.1.21; 4.2.181), emphasizes the cost of fashion not just to an individual estate but to the nation: Woodstock's wedding bravery, his "golden metamorphosis / From homespun housewifery" (75–76) as Richard dubs it, may even fell its king. But Woodstock, like Thynn's knight, sees that cost not so much in terms of a struggle between Crown and peerage, or its symbolic cost to the nation, but in material, if paternalistic terms, to its people. When the king and his favorites mock his "t'other hose" and "frieze coat," he responds:

> Ay, ay, mock on. My t'other hose, say ye?
> There's honest plain dealing in my t'other hose.
> Should this fashion last I must raise new rents,
> Undo my poor tenants, turn away my servants
> And guard myself with lace; nay, sell more land
> And lordships too, by th' rood. Hear me King Richard:
> If thus I jet in pride, I still shall lose,
> But I'll build castles in my t'other hose.
>
> (1.3.104–8)

When the queen demurs that the king but jests, Woodstock's rejoinder is explicit: "T'other hose! Did some here wear that fashion / They would not tax and pill the commons so!" (111–12), and he repeats that accusation later at 2.2, when Richard chides him for shedding his "golden rich habilements" donned in honor of the king's wedding and the coronation of his queen: "I'm now in my t'other hose, / I'm now myself, Plain Thomas, and by th' rood / In these plain hose I'll do the realm more good / Than these that pill the poor, to jet in gold" (34–37). Richard's blank charters and exploitation of the commons are the cost of fashion and excess in apparel, an equation set up again later in act 2, scene 3 when the queen turns her jewels and plate into coin to help "seventeen thousand poor and indigent" and commands trunks "of needful clothing / To be distributed amongst the poor" (20, 59–60).

Not only material want but moral qualities and political behaviors are insistently characterized in terms of clothes and cloth: Woodstock's

"mind suits with his habit / Homely and plain" (1.1.106–7), his heart
is likened to "plain frieze," and his judgments are "homespun." Green
exhorts Tresilian to "fashion to the time / The habit of your laws"
(1.2.39–40), and Tresilian, the ex-lawyer, speaks in the language of that
much maligned Renaissance craftsman, the tailor: "I will screw and
wind the subtle law / To any fashion that shall like you best" (45–46),
both verbs used to describe decorative trimming and plaiting. Tresilian ends by pledging he will make law "what's most suitable to all your
pleasures" (48). Though "suitable" clearly means fitting and appropriate, in the context of the play's reiterated language of dress, it plays on
"suit" in all its myriad meanings in early English drama: suit of clothes,
suit at law, suing or pleading, even a lover's suit or courtship. The play
on "suit" is presented most emphatically at the end of act 2, scene 3,
where the king's council spends its time devising new, foreign fashions
rather than managing English affairs of state:

> They sit in council to devise strange fashions,
> And suit themselves in wild and antic habits
> Such as this kingdom never yet beheld:
> French hose, Italian cloaks, and Spanish hats,
> Polonian shoes with peaks a hand full long,
> Tied to their knees with chains of pearl and gold.
> Their plumed tops fly waving in the air
> A cubit high above their wanton heads.
>
> (88–95)[22]

A few lines later, Richard reiterates to the queen, "Thou seest
already we begin to alter / The vulgar fashions of our homespun kingdom," and "We held a council to devise these suits" (3.1.47–48, 51).
The king's favorites, whom he has earlier endowed with the staves of
public office, prompting Woodstock to declare, "What transformation do mine eyes behold / As if the world were topsy-turvey turned!"
(2.2.142–43), are fashion designers: Greene devised "this fashion shoe;
/ Bushy the peake; Bagot and Scroope set forth / This kind coherence
'twixt the toe and knee / To have them chained together lovingly"
(52–55). This riot of fashion leads Woodstock to ask, "You've heard
of the fantastic suits they wear? Never was English king so habited,"
to which Lancaster responds: "We could allow his clothing, brother
Woodstock, / But we have four kings more are equaled with him. /
Ther's Bagot, Bushy, wanton Greene, and Scroop / In state and fashion without difference" (3.2.37–42). York protests: "Indeed, they're

more than kings, for they rule him." In *Thomas of Woodstock,* apparel fails at distinguishing the nobility from the vulgar, a point the play makes again later in the action in the witty scene in which a messenger from the king arrives at Woodstock's country estate attired in his courtly gear and refuses to dismount until he is inside, for fear of soiling his shoes. Once admitted, he mistakes the duke, Plain Thomas in his homespun, for a groom and sets him to walk his horse. Instead of maintaining social distinctions, clothing breaks down the difference between anointed king and his plebeian favorites, between duke and groom.

Thomas of Woodstock is usually dated 1591–94 and has generally been thought to be a source for Shakespeare's play.[23] Recently commentators have claimed the play represents a "far more important source for *Richard II* than critics have acknowledged" and that it "speaks both through what remains of it in *Richard II,* and through what Shakespeare left out or modified."[24] At act 2, scene 1 of Shakespeare's play when Gaunt chastises the king, he dubs his brother Gloucester "plain" as he is so frequently termed in the anonymous *Woodstock. Richard II* opens famously with Bolingbroke's staged challenge to Mowbray and accusation that "he did plot the Duke of Gloucester's death." Though critics have long observed that Mowbray's response to that accusation is difficult to follow, and that the references to Richard's part in the murder of Woodstock have been said to be vague, inconclusive, and ambiguous,[25] recently commentators have argued for the importance of the murder and the anonymous play that dramatizes it to Shakespeare's play and its Elizabethan audience. Not only do they argue that knowledge of *Thomas of Woodstock* was assumed in Shakespeare's opening scenes but they also suggest the play influenced his portrayal of Richard at Gaunt's death when he confiscates the Lancastrian property.[26]

But unlike the anonymous *Thomas of Woodstock,* Shakespeare seems deliberately to avoid description of Richard's sartorial excess. Whereas *Woodstock* emphasizes the sartorial extravagance of Richard and his minions in contrast with Plain Thomas's frieze coat and t'other hose, the buckram of Nimble and of Tresilian in his lawyer days, Shakespeare makes reference instead to specific items of clothing and emblems of kingship to highlight their symbolic significance: Bolingbroke's bonnet, with which we began, the gloves or gages of

Mowbray and Bolingbroke at the play's ceremonial beginning and in act 5, scene 3, the royal scepter, and most famously, Richard's contested crown. Though Shakespeare makes mention of "gay apparel," with Woodstock murdered before the action of *Richard II* opens, he doesn't rely on or develop the contrast of Gloucester's plain style with that of the king and his favorites central to the anonymous *Thomas of Woodstock*. In *Richard II* "gay apparel" figures differently. Instead of opposing Plain Thomas to gaudy Richard, Shakespeare, as generations of critics have noted, presents two Richards, the King Richard of the first half of the play who, even on his initial return from Ireland, imagines his bright sun will pluck the "cloak of night" from off the back of "murders, treasons and detested sins." That Richard, who calls attention to his "gay apparel," which, as we have noted, he offers to trade for an "almsman's gown," is contrasted with the self-reflective Richard, the so-called poet king of the second half of the play who divests himself of the material emblems of kingship until he is finally alone in prison, an unaccommodated man, his only "suit" his words.[27] The phrase "gay apparel" appears in another context in the play as well, in the subplot involving Aumerle's treason. At act 5, scene 2, the Duchess of York attempts to hide her son's treason from his father by claiming the treasonous letter plotting Bolingbroke's assassination is no more than a contract for "gay apparel" for the new king's coronation: "'tis nothing but some bond that he is entered into / For gay apparel 'gainst the triumph day" (65–66). Here the duchess substitutes "gay apparel" for treason, just as in the anonymous *Woodstock* sartorial extravagance is similarly equated with treason. When York reads the supposed bond for gay apparel and discovers the plot, it prompts his own call for apparel: "Give me my boots" (77), he cries, "Bring me my boots" (85) he repeats, and then again, "Give me my boots, I say" (88), to almost comic effect.

In *Thomas of Woodstock*, when Woodstock is imprisoned and about to be murdered, he writes to his nephew admonishing him "to govern like a virtuous prince" (5.1.187). In this invocation of the genre of "advice to a prince," Plain Thomas's homeliness is no longer his dress but style: "I know not what to write, / What style to use; nor how I should begin. / My method is too plain to greet a king" (206–8). Not only English and continental Renaissance drama and poetry but countless classical, medieval, and early modern treatises concerned with rhetoric draw upon such comparisons of rhetoric and style to dress: the argument is the body, the figures of speech or rhetoric, its clothing or ornament. As Edmund Bolton puts it in his 1610 treatise *The Elements of Armories,* implying an analogy as well between rhetoric and armor, "Style," is "the apparel of matter." Perhaps the best known Shakespearean example is the insistently ironic and often quoted moment in *Love's Labor's Lost* when Berowne promises "by this white glove" to forsake "taffeta phrases, silken terms precise / Three-pil'd hyperboles" in favor of "russet yeas and honest kersey noes." To demonstrate his sincere adoption of russet and kersey, the cloth/ style of the poor, in the following two lines he dubs Rosaline "wench," and swears "so God help me law" but nevertheless ends his amorous avowal by betraying his newly embraced plain style: his love, he vows, is "sans crack." Rosaline is quick to counter, "Sans 'sans,' I pray you," objecting to his use of French. Berowne's promised russet and kersey is framed by two signs of his membership in a fashion-conscious, educated elite: the white glove and the French "sans," doubly ironic since Shakespeare's English-speaking lords waiting on the King of Navarre should presumably, of course, *be* speaking French. Berowne's spruce taffeta, silk, and velvet suit to Rosaline fails, and he is banished to try his dressy wit instead on sickly ears.

Clothing and ornament, as many commentators have observed, makes the body culturally visible.[28] Even the female nude in the history of Western art "has always assumed the form dictated by contemporary fashion."[29] In her work on fashion, femininity, and cinema, Kaja Silverman argues,

> Clothing exercises as profoundly determining an influence upon living, breathing bodies as it does upon their literary and cinematic counterparts, affecting contour, weight, muscle development, posture, movement and libidinal circulation. Dress is one of the most important cultural implements for articulating and territorializing human corporeality—for mapping its erotogenic zones, and affixing sexual identity.[30]

Though Silverman is concerned here primarily with gender and sexuality, as her last clause suggests, dress also maps, as many have discussed, what we now term class, or in the early modern period, status hierarchies and degree. In early modern England, as Jane Ashelford observes in *Dress in the Age of Elizabeth I,* elite fashion shaped and molded the body in order to display an "elongated, tapering waist, wide circular ruff and swollen hips and arms common to both sexes."[31] Doublets and hose were shaped and fitted to bodies, and padding of various kinds emphasized the contrast between parts of the body, legs, crotch and torso in the case of men, torso and hips in the case of women.[32] But Ashelford ignores the clothing of the poor, which by contrast was typically coarsely cut, shapeless, sometimes loosely belted or buttoned garments with an open knee-length shirt and loose-fitting pants for men and skirts for women, which produced an undifferentiated body, a body whose shape could barely be discerned. Instead of gloves that articulated the fingers of the hand, the poor wore mittens, and clogs rather than shoes or boots. As clothing began in the course of the seventeenth century to be available for purchase "ready to wear" rather than bespoke, sizing was a slowly introduced innovation.[33] Since clothing, including its color and cut, was often dictated to the servant, laborer, or apprentice contractually as part of livery, style was the province of the elite; the poor were denied what social historians have termed "consumer sovereignty."[34] The pursuit of fashion so often noted in the early modern period, whether in sumptuary laws and their transgression or in the pursuit of foreign fashions and the extravagant spending of the elite, records not only status or social aspiration but erotic longing for a body fashioned by fashion itself.

In their important, wide-ranging study of Renaissance clothing, Ann Rosalind Jones and Peter Stallybrass insist on the constitutive power of dress not only for the subject but for the body politic. The putting on of clothes or investiture was constitutive, "the means by which a person was given a form or shape, a social function, a 'depth.'"[35] In his third antitheatrical satire in book 1 of *Virgidemiarum* (1598), Joseph Hall highlights this relation between dress and social function in the context of theater: "A goodly hoch-poch," he observes, "when vile Russettings, / Are match' t with monarchs, & with mighty kings." Hall's attack on actors, referred to metonymically by their russet clothing, actors who play the more opulently dressed parts of their betters, may also allude to the perceived danger of representations on the English stage of kings as beggars. In *Thomas of Woodstock*, as we have seen, when Gloucester is imprisoned and about to be murdered, he would seem to be enjoying the privileges of elite prisoners in the period: he seems to be wearing the frieze coat and t'other hose he has worn virtually throughout the play; he has access to the implements for writing; and he seems to sit musing about how to "dress" his advice to the king at some sort of furniture on stage.

But at the end of Shakespeare's *Richard II* we find Richard not merely bereft of kingly crown and scepter but seemingly dressed in the rags of a beggar, bereft of that apparel which marks him/makes him, a king. At act 5, scene 5, Richard famously studies how to compare his prison to the world and finds he cannot do it. His thoughts and doubts plot

> how these vain weak nails
> May tear a passage through the flinty ribs
> Of this hard world, my ragged prison walls
> (18–21)

Though certainly the Norton Shakespeare is right to gloss "ragged" as "rugged," in keeping with "flinty" and "prison walls," and thus make sense of Richard's imagining "unlikely wonders" or escape from prison, "nails" and "ribs" also invoke another network of images. They suggest that Richard alludes as well to the little world of man, to his own body clothed in nothing but beggarly rags that he would rend to escape the self as "seely beggar," in the stocks bearing his "misfortunes on the back" (29) whom the audience witnesses on stage.

> Thus play I in one person many people,
> And none contented. Sometimes I am a king;
> Then treason makes me wish myself a beggar,
> And so I am. Then crushing penury
> Persuades me I was better when a king.
> Then am I kinged again, and by and by
> Think that I am unkinged by Bolingbroke,
> And straight am nothing. But whate'er I be,
> Nor I, nor any man that but man is,
> With nothing shall be pleased till he be eased
> With being nothing.
> (31–41)

Crushing penury, as we have seen, meant rags and nakedness. As potentially seditious as the deposition scene itself when the king relinquishes crown and scepter, the representation of Richard in rags, as a beggar alone, imprisoned in the little world of Pomfret Castle, without the boots and gloves and gay apparel of the elite, without the crown and scepter of a king, with only his suit of words, this last scene of *Richard II* may have offered as forceful an enactment of peril to the body politic as the deposition scene itself.

The putting on of clothes or investiture, I repeat, was constitutive. As Jones and Stallybrass argue, it is "the means by which a person was given a form or shape, a social function, a 'depth'" (2). They rightly debunk notions of clothing as mere surface, notions that they acknowledge rest on philosophically suspect oppositions between surface and depth, inside and outside. In recognizing the constitutive force of dress and in rehabilitating the study of material culture and of objects, they go on to claim that our "interest in objects (including clothes) is characterized by *disavowal*" (10) arising out of the continuing power of such suspect oppositions. While recognizing the force of Jones's and Stallybrass's claim, we need to think critically about the preoccupation with early modern conspicuous consumption and elite fashion, with the silks and velvets, plush and embroidery, lace and starch, that has characterized work on fashion and clothing in early modern England, including my own. That preoccupation also speaks to what Jean Baudrillard and others have analyzed as our compulsion to serve the market, to enjoy the "fun system" of consumption.[36] It bespeaks our own interpellation into a political economy that prompts not only a staggering consumer debt compounded through the exercise of desires that may not be our own but also a cultural studies that too often abandons critique to collaborate fully with commodity fetishism.

FRENCH SHAKESPEARE

Dryden, Vigny's *Othello,* and British Cultural Expansion

The historical fate of the British Empire challenges the idea that explaining oneself to literal and figurative foreigners is an unnecessary activity.

—Margaret Ferguson, *Trials of Desire*

Car c'est au bord du français, uniquement, ni en lui ni hors de lui, sur la ligne introuvable de sa côte que, depuis toujours, à demeure, je me demande si on peut aimer, jouir, prier, crever de douleur ou crever tout court dans une autre langue ou sans rien en dire à personne, sans parler même.

—Jacques Derrida, *Le monolinguisme de l'autre*

L E MONOLINGUISME DE L'AUTRE OU LA PROTHÈSE DE L'ORIGINE, Jacques Derrida's meditation on linguistic and cultural identity, considers the paradox "I have but one language—yet that language is not mine" or, in a different formulation, "One never speaks but one language / one never speaks only one language." As the Stanford University Press catalog blurb for the English translation observes, the book is first a theoretical inquiry into the relation between persons and their "own" language, a word the catalog copy puts in scare quotes, an inquiry that meditates on the "structural limits, desires, and interdictions inherent in such 'possession.'"[1] It also presents an account of Derrida's own relation to his acculturation into the French language, French schools, French citizenship, as an Algerian Jew, a "franco-maghrébin," and thus explores the "dynamics of cultural-political exclusion and inclusion." The essay reflects on what makes us imagine a particular language as good for some things but not for others, on our investment in certain notions of linguistic purity, and on the problematics of linguistic and cultural translation. These questions are particularly pressing and salient in approaching translations of Shakespeare, which have long been met with what can only be termed Anglocentric derision.

Long before Shakespeare became the British "national poet" whom Maurice Morgann celebrated "as the patron spirit of world empire on which the sun will never set" and whose destiny, Morgann opined, was the total extinction of the French; even before, in fact, Shakespeare's First Folio saw print, booksellers were peddling their intellectual property in Shakespeare internationally.[2] I quote from W. W. Greg's *The Shakespeare First Folio:*

> The principal centre of the European book-trade at the time was the fair held every spring and autumn at Frankfort-on-the-Main, in connexion with which there was published a half-yearly advertisement known as the *Mess-Katalog.* This did not include English books, though English booksellers frequented the market to buy stocks of foreign and classical works. There was, however, an English edition published by John Bill, the King's Printer, under the title *Catalogus uniuersalis pro nundinis Francofurtensibis,* which contained an appendix of English works. And to our surprise we find that "A Catalogue of such Bookes as haue beene published, and (by authoritie) printed in English, since the last Vernall Mart, which was in Aprill 1622. till this present October 1622." contains the entry "Playes, written by M. William Shakespeare, all in one volume, printed by Isaack Iaggard, in. fol."[3]

"Our surprise," as Greg terms it, would seem to be prompted by two things: first, that the entry appears in 1622, before the First Folio is printed in 1623; and second, that we find the entry in such an "unexpected source," as he terms it, in a supplemental listing of *English* books to a *Latin* catalog for a *German* book fair. Greg cites F. P. Wilson, whose "fortunate discovery," as Greg terms it, brought this early advertisement to light. Wilson himself notes that it is "perhaps the only contemporary advertisement of the First Folio now extant," but both he and Greg agree that it "does not add to our knowledge of the First Folio."[4] Greg and Wilson are concerned with dating, and not with the fact of the First Folio's first being offered for sale on a European market. For my purposes, the ad insists that even before there were modern nation-states, Shakespeare was always already multilingual and international, an incipient global cultural commodity.

The globalization of culture is often assumed to be a late twentieth-century phenomenon, the result of an expansion and acceleration in the movement and exchange of ideas, commodities, and capital over vast distances and porous boundaries[5] Narratives of cultural imperialism abound about "Americanization" or Western cultural hegemony in which "transnational regimes of the imagination" are said to threaten cultural autonomies.[6] Such discourses often focus on borders and the negotiations that take place as nations and cultures become unsettled and hybrid. In what follows, I want to rethink current claims about the globalization of culture by insisting on a longer historical frame for understanding cultural competition. By considering the long cultural rivalry between England and France, and two specific chapters in that history, Dryden's *Of Dramatic Poesy* and the French romantic poet Alfred de Vigny's translation of *Othello,* I hope to show that cultural globalization has a much longer history than has been generally allowed.

Recently Deanne Williams has traced "the cultural legacy of the Norman Conquest in England from Chaucer to Shakespeare."[7] She argues that our "professional and disciplinary investment in the greatness of the English tradition, combined with a certain nostalgia for British imperialism, has meant that the profound cultural effects of the Norman Conquest have been frequently downplayed."[8] Williams brilliantly demonstrates the impact of the Norman cultural conquest on Chaucer, in the Corpus Christi cycles, on Caxton and his press, on Skelton and Hawes, and, briefly, on Shakespeare. At the end of her study, she even gestures toward its continuing impact in the seventeenth century on radicals like the Levellers who represented the English aristocracy as foreign occupiers to justify their demands for the abolition of monarchy and degree. Williams is careful to point out that popular English stereotypes and attitudes toward the French do not always correspond to actual historical situations and circumstances; instead she insists on the Conquest's "imaginative impact on English culture, and especially its literature."[9]

Dryden "through a crowd of French people"

At the end of Dryden's *Of Dramatic Poesy*, Eugenius, Lisideius, Crites, and Neander disembark from the barge on which their literary conference has taken place at Somerset Stairs, a popular landing place west of Somerset House convenient to Covent Garden. Critics have noted the way in which Dryden imbues their leave-taking and return to London with nostalgia:

> The company were all sorry to separate so soon . . . and stood a while looking back upon the water, which the moon-beams played upon, and made it appear like quick-silver.[10]

But they have rarely read on: "At last they went up through a crowd of French people, who were merrily dancing in the open air, and nothing concerned for the noise of guns which had alarmed the town that afternoon."[11] The French, who throughout the essay are characterized by their strictures and bienséance, their confining alexandrines, their unities and rules, here embody insouciant merrymaking oblivious to the noise of battle raging nearby.

Dryden's presentation of the French/English cultural rivalry in the *Essay,* often "considered the pioneering instance of modern literary criticism," demonstrates the impact both of the lingering premodern legacy Williams traces and of the seventeenth-century European dominance of French culture and taste.[12] Some recent commentators, who read backward from the imperial successes of the later eighteenth century and forward through the literary and culturally triumphant lens of Shakespeare's ensuing reputation, have read *Of Dramatic Poesy* in triumphalist, even if ideologically critical, terms as an assertion of English cultural and imperial power.[13] But Dryden's essay needs also to be considered in the context of the contemporary state of British relations with France in the early years of the Restoration, in the aftermath of the interregnum following the exile of the English court and of a large cohort of the British intelligentsia to Paris.

Dryden's essay compares the classical and modern drama, alludes briefly to other genres, and considers contemporary aesthetic problems such as the imitation of "Nature" and the use of rhyme, but it is most particularly concerned with the relative merits of the French and English theater. But that *cultural* competition is famously subjected at the outset to a military and commercial rivalry in the well-known frame with which the essay begins, the Battle of Lowestoft on June 3, 1665, an early encounter in the Second Anglo-Dutch war:[14]

> It was that memorable day, in the first summer of the late war, when our navy engaged the Dutch: a day wherein the two most mighty and best

appointed fleets which any age had ever seen disputed the command of the greater half of the globe, the commerce of nations, and the riches of the universe. (18)

Dryden's aggrandizing rhetoric—what Roland Barthes dubbed in his fine essay on rhetoric's imperial reach a "véritable empire, plus vaste et plus tenace que n'importe quel empire politique"—portrays the British mercantile competition with the Netherlands as a global struggle: "the greater half of the globe," he claims, struggling over "the riches of the universe."[15] As Laura Brown has argued in "Dryden and the Imperial Imagination," "Dryden's preamble encourages us to connect this aesthetic debate with 'the commerce of Nations,' and the inception of the mode of discourse and the discipline that we now understand as literary criticism, with the imperial imagination" (60). Though the French, the object of cultural competition in the essay itself, are conspicuously absent from the commercial and martial contest with which the essay opens, as Michael Neill has shown, the "struggle for literary supremacy" is presented in military terms as a "heroic contest."[16] By insisting at the outset on England's military and mercantile preeminence over the Dutch, Dryden displaces French cultural dominance and prepares his reader for the intellectual battle still to come in which English victory is in fact never assured.

Though Brown argues that the "literary debate is represented as a means of passing time while awaiting the outcome of the battle" (59), in fact the company only begins that debate once it believes Britain to be the military victor. As we learn at the outset, hearing "the noise of the cannon from both navies" in the City, "all men being alarmed . . . every one went following the sound as his fancy led him." Eugenius, Crites, Lisideius, and Neander take a barge down the Thames, shooting London Bridge, in hopes of ascertaining the results of the Anglo-Dutch encounter. One of Lisideius's servants provides the barge, a detail that marks the outing as a pastime associated with aristocratic leisure. The company begins its literary conversation only when a lack of sound, "by little and little," becomes "that happy omen of our nation's victory" (19). Technically, the essay's central concern, the literary rivalry with France, is not in fact "the equivalent of the literal battle with the Dutch," as Brown claims, for that rivalry can only be articulated once Neander and his companions infer the Dutch defeat. What in fact is said to prompt the literary debate is an aesthetic defect of the English themselves, that is, the bad poetry the British victory will produce, dread of which Crites articulates in commercial terms: "He could scarce have wished the victory at the price he knew he must pay for it, in being subject to the reading and hearing of so many ill verses" (19–20).

Now we have grown accustomed, given the current domination of literary studies by materialist and ideological analysis, to assume that the aesthetic is merely a displacement of the socioeconomic. In such a reading, Dryden's essay and its frame reveal Britain's struggle to supersede the Netherlands in dominating, as Brown argues, "the lucrative trade with East India, West Africa and the new world" (60). But I want to pause over that cultural competition by asking what Dryden is up to in framing his essay concerned so insistently with literary rivalry with France, with the Dutch military defeat? Critics and commentators of *Of Dramatic Poesy* generally declare that Neander, Dryden's persona and the defender of English drama, wins with the essay's last word.[17] Furthermore, the subsequent success of Shakespeare and English drama, at least from an Anglocentric point of view, has overshadowed the rivalries the essay dramatizes. But defeat of the French cultural model is less definitive than is generally claimed.[18]

First, of course, there is the evidence of Dryden's own dramatic practice, which notoriously accepts French aesthetic standards and employs them in his own drama. As endless studies of Shakespearean revision and adaptation from the Restoration until well into the nineteenth century have shown, he and many of his contemporaries rewrote Shakespeare's plays to make them conform to the unities of time, place, and action and to neoclassical decorum as defined by the French. Though Dryden and his contemporaries often claimed Shakespeare's failure to observe the unities and other neoclassical tenets was a minor flaw that his genius overcame, in practice Shakespeare as we know him rarely mounted the boards; instead, the plays were silently corrected, revised, reworked, cut, and rewritten. Though Dryden represents himself the heir of Fletcher, Jonson, and Shakespeare, from whom in fact he borrows little, as David Bruce Kramer has noted, he "suppresses . . . his substantial debt to the still-living writers in the French tradition."[19] Neander claims that "we have borrowed nothing from them; our plots are weaved in English looms" (65), a metaphor that relies on nostalgia for the old-time English mercantile cloth trade. In fact, many Restoration plays, including a number of Dryden's, weave their plots on French and also Spanish looms.[20]

Second, Dryden's *Essay,* usually considered, as we have noted, "the pioneering instance of modern literary criticism" (59), itself relies heavily on Corneille's literary criticism, which it frequently lifts verbatim or paraphrases from his prefaces, "Discours," and "Examens."[21] Dryden even uses Corneille's own arguments against certain neoclassical strictures to reveal their limitations and defend English dramatic practice. And as at least one commentator on Dryden has noted, the essay is "a kind of French play" that employs the typical French method of the long revelatory speech or discourse, as Neander himself dubs such speeches, also the very term Dryden uses to refer to the *Essay* itself.[22]

Third, Dryden employs French words and expressions, several for the first time in English, and not only technical terms from the drama and its criticism, such as "des Trois Unités," "la liaison des scenes," "la catastrophe," and "le dénouement" but also newly imported expressions including "ballette," "à propos" and "mal à propos," and Frenchisms such as "embarrass," "propatic," "examen," and "in vogue."[23] In appropriating a point in French from Corneille in the 1667 edition of the "Essay," Dryden repeats a grammatical or typographical error from Corneille's own text, which he then corrects in the 1684 and 1693 editions. Though Dryden occasionally names Corneille, he more often speaks of "the French poet" or poets; and whereas Racine had supplanted Corneille by the time Dryden wrote *Of Dramatic Poesy,* Racine is never named in the *Essay* at all.

Throughout the long eighteenth century, French theatrical taste and practice continued to have a profound impact on contemporary English drama and on revivals and productions of earlier plays, particularly those of Shakespeare. Similarly, on the other side of the Channel, French theatrical taste and practice influenced the reception and translation of Shakespeare in France. Early translators rewrote Shakespeare to make the plays conform to neoclassical canons and taste: blank verse became prose or alexandrines, the unities were observed, clowns were cut, and Shakespeare's language rendered to conform to the conventions of Racine's diction. Voltaire notoriously condemned Shakespeare as a savage with imagination whose work could only please audiences in London and Canada, a colonialist prejudice that also tells us what he thought about London audiences.[24] But in the aftermath of the French Revolution and the defeat of Napoleon by Wellington at Waterloo, the balance of cultural power begins to change. Whereas Dryden had proclaimed English superiority while in fact conforming to French taste, by the nineteenth century the French inability to appreciate, understand, and properly translate Shakespeare becomes notorious. Even today in his recent popularizing study, *Shakespeare Goes to Paris: How the Bard Conquered France,* John Pemble condescends and patronizes, mocks and condemns, using the metaphor of battle from his title throughout. He betrays a breathtaking nationalist prejudice that would seem to support the view of a recent French critic who argues that the continuing cult of Shakespeare represents solace for British postimperial abjection.[25] In describing early nineteenth-century efforts to improve on earlier translations, for example, Pemble opines that "the drive for authenticity seems only to expose the inadequacy of the French language."[26] He disparages what he terms "the puppets of conventional classical drama" (100) and the "old fusty repertoire" (120), by which he seems to refer to the work of Corneille, Molière, and Racine. Of Alfred de Vigny's translation of *Othello,* Pemble declares of both French poet and audience, "Neither was yet ready for the real thing" (106). Yet "the real thing" had a celebrated success in Vigny's Paris and seems in fact to have been what prompted him to translate *Othello.*[27]

Vigny's *Le more de Venise* and Shakespeare's *Othello*

When Shakespeare was initially performed in France in the aftermath of Napoleon's defeat at Waterloo, *Othello* was apparently booed from the stage with shouts dubbing the playwright "Wellington's lieutenant" and with calls for the actors to "Parle[r] français."[28] But by 1827, a troupe of English Shakespearean actors led by a contingent mostly from Covent Garden under the theater manager/actor Charles Kemble and perhaps emulating the recent success of the French actress and former mistress of Napoleon Mademoiselle George's highly touted visit to London, stormed Paris with a run of some ten months, performing in English at the Odéon Theater, from the fall of 1827 until midsummer 1828. Though the French Romantics' well-known romance with Shakespeare has conventionally been explained as a reaction against neoclassical canons and taste, a definitive battle in the ongoing debate between ancients and moderns, it needs also to be understood as an early skirmish in an ongoing struggle over the globalization of culture. Napoleon, who extended the French empire to Africa and attempted to conquer Russia, is said to have objected to the substitution of Shakespeare for Homer, as he put it, thus displacing his rivalry with the English onto the aesthetic debate between ancients and moderns.[29] Contemporaries recognized the potential of cultural expansion: in the extravagantly illustrated program produced to commemorate the English troupe's visit to France, *Souvenirs du theatre anglais,* the author, M. Moreau, observes, "C'est par ces conquêtes pacifiques que deux nations, également fières et généreuses, cimenteront une union formée sous les auspices des arts" (It is through such peaceful conquests that two equally proud and generous nations will cement a union formed under the auspices of the arts). Following Napoleon's defeat, the British empire expanded its reach and influence across Europe and the globe largely unhampered by competing western powers.

Famously, the success of the English troupe in Paris prompted a flurry of romantic cultural production. Shakespeare's mongrel mix of genres, his disregard for the unities of time, place, and action, and the diction of his plays inspired dramas by Hugo and Dumas, Delacroix's series of lithographs and canvases on *Hamlet,* Théophile Gautier's libretto for *Giselle,* and some half-dozen works by Berlioz among many others. Though commentators have generally claimed that this interest was prompted by aesthetic ideals, it is worth considering the evidence from the vantage of cultural competition and expansion.[30]

The visit of the English troupe and expansion across the channel in 1827 seems in fact to have been motivated by the search for new markets on both sides of the channel.[31] The first decades of the nineteenth century were a dismal moment for the so-called patent theaters in London, Covent Garden and Drury Lane.[32] Granted patents by Charles II in the seventeenth century that were subsequently confirmed by the Licensing Act of 1734, Covent Garden and Drury Lane were the only theaters officially permitted to perform the serious drama, particularly Shakespeare, in London. By the first decade of the nineteenth century, they had fallen on hard times. Not only was there the war with France but within six months time both theaters were completely destroyed by fire, Covent Garden in September 1808 and Drury Lane in February 1809. Once rebuilt, both theaters raised the price of admission, a move that provoked the so-called Old Price Riots that continued for over two months and eventually ended in a rollback. The smaller London theaters provided plenty of competition, either through new theatrical forms such as the burletta, attributed to the French, or through performances of Shakespeare and other examples of the serious drama that got around the patent rules by, for example, playing the piano throughout performances or changing play titles—*Othello* became, for example, *Is He Jealous?*

Kemble's retirement as manager and the arrival of the well-known English actor Edmund Kean brought new theatrical, but not financial, successes to the London theater scene. When in the fall of 1827 a group of English actors that included Kemble and members of his Covent Garden troupe, Harriett Smithson from Drury Lane, and actors from a number of other, smaller theaters made its way to Paris in the wake of the 1826 bank failures and ensuing financial crisis, they were seeking new venues in which to perform. The severe financial difficulties of the patent theaters were such throughout the teens and twenties that Parliament finally established a "Select Committee Appointed to Inquire into the Laws Affecting Dramatic Literature," which interviewed the most famous actors and theatrical managers of the day. Among the questions posed to those who had spent time in Paris was whether the support of the arts by the French government, as opposed to the so-called free market stance of the English, had an impact on the current sorry state of English theatrical affairs. As Macready put it in response to the question "Is there not a great demand for Genius upon the stage in France?"— "It would be paid amply no doubt in France, much more highly than here."[33] When Kemble and the others left London for Paris in 1827, they were seeking, we have seen, new markets—in short, a financial bailout, and saw the French capital as a good bet. Following their success, at least five other English troupes visited Paris over the next decade, with varying success, all in search of financial remuneration.[34]

The English troupe played *Romeo and Juliet, Othello,* and *Hamlet* to packed houses that included all the major artists and writers of the day. Alfred de Vigny's letters show that these productions prompted him to translate first *Romeo and Juliet* with a partner, and then *Othello* on his own.[35] Vigny claimed to have learned English from his wife, Lydia Bunbury, an Englishwoman born in French Guiana, and from Shakespeare himself, whose name he spelled Schakespeare. He began work on his translation soon after the English troupe's run — the first date in the manuscript is October 1828; his *Le More de Venise* was produced by the Comédie française in 1829 and had a brief but only partially successful run. Famously, it was the first time the French word for handkerchief, *mouchoir,* had ever been spoken on the serious French stage, much to the vexation of the great French actress Mlle Mars, who played Desdemona. In a prefatory letter to his translation, Vigny ironically observes that it had taken a century of translation before the word *mouchoir* could make its entry onto the French stage.[36] Generations of Anglo-American critics have belittled and mocked the French unwillingness to translate Shakespeare's English word.[37] Their reluctance is seen as effete, a refusal of "low" words, the words of everyday life, and their translations or substitutions as euphemistic — according to a recent review in the *Economist,* as "lexical political correctness."[38] "Handkerchief" was variously translated in the eighteenth and early nineteenth century as a "billet" or letter, or more fancifully, as a bandeau of diamonds, and later, as a "tissu" or cloth. But that reluctance deserves further attention and analysis.

Mouchoir in French is quite a different word from *handkerchief* in English, even though it is certainly the best literal, if not cultural, translation. If you look up "handkerchief" in a French/English dictionary, *mouchoir* is its lexical equivalent, but as Walter Benjamin famously observed, even lexical equivalents do not mean the same thing.[39] *Mouchoir* is from the common French word *moucher,* which means to blow one's nose and comes from the Latin word *muccere,* meaning to empty the nose of mucus. In terms of cultural translation, *mouchoir* in fact does not convey the English sense of handkerchief, a euphemism if ever there was one. *Handkerchief* is a compound word made up of the Old English word *hand* and the French derived word, *kerchief,* from Middle English but derived from the Old French word *couvre-chef,* or head covering, thus the euphemism, covering for the hand. At the very moment we chastise the French for their euphemistic refusal to translate *handkerchief* with the word *mouchoir,* with its etymological link to snot and thus its quite different affect, Shakespeare uses the aristocratically marked, euphemistic word that etymologically means hand covering. Othello initially terms the handkerchief a *napkin,* as does Iago in the same scene, again from the French *nappe* or tablecloth, and the diminutive suffix from Middle Dutch *kin,* as in Perkin or Chaucer's Jankin. The etymological history of *handkerchief* and *mouchoir,* and the cultural disputes over its translation, insist that "no semantic form is timeless. When using a word we wake into resonance . . . its entire previous history."[40] That previous history returns us to my epigraph and Derrida's insistence—"I have but one language—yet that language is not mine." Shakespeare's English is not "pure"; he never speaks only one language; he, and for that matter the French Vigny, speak only one language. Translation has long been a contested term and practice. At least from the time of the early Church fathers, translators and commentators of the Bible and other texts have recognized the distinction between literal translation and the translation of sense, or as Jerome put it in his letter "Ad Pammachius": "non verbum e verbo sed sensum exprimere de sensu" (not word for word, but sense for sense).[41] In his well-known lecture "On the Different Methods of Translation" (1813), Schleiermacher distinguishes between word-for-word translation, in which the reader or audience is untroubled, merely a textual consumer, and cultural translation, in which language becomes strange to itself and thus "present" through the transposition of thought into another universe of thought, an entirely other milieu or culture.[42] Translation is never a simple transfer, of course, but an inscription in another interpretation of the world. Heidegger reflected on translation's role in constituting meaning in which difference and identity are two sides of a gulf that translation, also a *trahison,* the French for treason or betrayal, brings together.[43] As Walter Benjamin reflects in his work on translation, "Fidelity and freedom in translation have traditionally been regarded as conflicting tendencies," but he goes on to profess that "a translation touches the original lightly and only at the infinitely small point of the sense, thereupon pursuing its own course according to the laws of fidelity in the freedom of linguistic flux." Translation entails license and betrayal, yet as Benjamin poignantly understood, it is translation that permits for the afterlife of a text by allowing it to continue to live in different cultural moments and far-flung cultural geographies.[44]Instead of focusing only on national literary histories in studying Dryden's literary criticism or Shakespeare and his translators, we need to think and read comparatively. We must recognize that efforts at cultural globalization were already underway in the seventeenth-century imperial ambitions of France, and subsequently in the eighteenth- and nineteenth-century imperial ambitions of Britain. As the recent spate of world literature anthologies, job announcements, and calls for counting, graphing, and mapping eagerly proclaim, the era of "world literature" may be upon us, but we need to understand that its twenty-first-century manifestation has a history.[45] The nineteenth-century popularity and interest in *Othello* in France must be seen, for example, as a part of the post-Enlightenment dialogue on race prompted by the abolition of slavery in the aftermath of the French Revolution, its subsequent reinstitution by Napoleon in 1802, and then by the growing abolitionist movement that led to the abolition of slavery in England in 1833 and in France in 1848. The highly successful Alexandre Dumas, grandson of a French aristocrat and an Afro-Caribbean slave, wrote the introduction to the first complete edition of Shakespeare's works in French published in 1839. Already in the first decades of the nineteenth century, literary magazines such as the *Magasin encyclopédique* reported on the latest English novels and on plays performed at Covent Garden and Drury Lane.[46] The aptly named liberal, anticlerical French journal *Le Globe*, which had subscribers and was sold all over Europe, followed world literary developments by reviewing newly published writing not only from Europe and North America—that is, western literature—but from Brazil and South America, Mexico, India, Egypt, and throughout the Middle East.

If we return to the *Mess-Katalog* with its English supplement advertising for sale the not-yet-printed First Folio in Germany, we are reminded that cultural globalization and what we are calling world literature began long before Goethe's often quoted pronouncement of 1827, exactly contemporaneous with the visit of the English actors to Paris: "National literature is now a rather meaningless term. The epoch of world literature is at hand."[47] We need to think seriously about what it means that Hector Berlioz was said to have been driven to a profound melancholy ("mélancolie profonde") by seeing Shakespeare's plays performed at the Odéon in 1827, though he didn't know a word of English and followed the plays using the abbreviated eighteenth-century prose translations of Pierre Le Tourneur.[48] That experience led to the composition of some of Berlioz's best-known works. We need to ask as well what it means that the most lauded productions of Shakespeare in 2006, not only hot tickets in the United States and Britain but globally, were the wildly successful Russian *Twelfth Night* directed by Declan Donnellan and the so-called Indian *A Midsummer Night's Dream* in which a multilingual cast from across India and Sri Lanka performed the play in multiple languages including English, Hindi, Bengali, Tamil, Sinhalese, Malayalam, Marathi, and Sanskrit. Of that production, the BBC News opined that it showed "how globalization has affected even the most time-honoured literary works."[49] Of the Chekhov International Theatre Festival's production of *Twelfth Night,* Ben Brantley of the *New York Times* observed, "You find yourself thinking you have rarely heard the sense of Shakespeare rendered with such enlightening exactness and musicality, when the words you're listening to are not remotely like English, Elizabethan or otherwise."[50] In fact, of course, they weren't "like" English at all; they were Russian. Shakespeare's language is, in Derrida's resonant paradox, both ours and not ours.

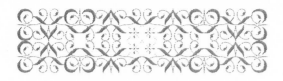

NOTES

Introduction

1. See, for example, Stephen Guy-Bray's 2006 MLA talk, "Against Reproduction," Carla Freccero, *Queer/Early/Modern* (Durham, N.C.: Duke University Press, 2006), and Valerie Traub, *The Renaissance of Lesbianism in Early Modern England* (Cambridge: Cambridge University Press, 2002), all of which are psychoanalytically inflected in their approach to material embodiment, gender, sexuality, and desire.

2. Carolyn Heilbrun, review of *The Woman's Part, Shakespeare's Division of Experience,* and *Man's Estate," Signs* 8 (1982): 182–86. I am grateful to Margaret Ferguson for her incisive comments on my discussion of the mimetic model and Heilbrun's review.

3. Karen Newman, "Comment on Heilbrun's Review of *The Woman's Part, Shakespeare's Division of Experience,* and *Man's Estate," Signs* 10 (1985): 601–3.

4. As Peter Erickson observes in his essay "The Moment of Race in Renaissance Studies," *Shakespeare Studies* 26 (1998): 27–36, the study of race in Shakespeare is not new, but since the late 1980s there has been a "concerted, collective level of activity with a more powerful cumulative force." For earlier work on race in Shakespeare, see G. K. Hunter, "*Othello* and Colour Prejudice," *Proceedings of the British Academy* 53 (1968): 139–63, and his "Elizabethans and Foreigners," *Shakespeare Survey* 17, *Shakespeare in His Image,* ed. Allardyce Nicoll (Cambridge: Cambridge University Press, 1964); Eldred Jones, *Othello's Countrymen: The African in English Renaissance Drama* (Oxford: Oxford University Press, 1965); Elliot Tokson, *The Popular Image of the Black Man in English Drama, 1550–1688* (Boston: G. K. Hall, 1982).

5. Jyotsna Singh, "Othello's Identity, Postcolonial Theory, and Contemporary African Rewritings of *Othello,*" in *Women, "Race," and Writing in the Early Modern Period,* ed. Margo Hendricks and Patricia Parker (London: Routledge, 1994), 290. See also Dympna Callaghan, "Re-reading Elizabeth Cary's *The Tragedie of Mariam,*

Faire Queene of Jewry," on feminist criticism's "habitual tendency to take gender as the diacritical difference of culture," in the same volume (163).

6. On this expansion, see in particular Margaret W. Ferguson's important essay "Juggling the Categories of Race, Class, and Gender," which appeared in the same collection as Singh's essay cited above, 209–24.

7. See Stephen Heath's prescient *The Sexual Fix* (New York: Schocken Books, 1984).

8. Nigel Wood and Barbara Rasmussen, eds., *Theory and Practice, The Merchant of Venice* (London and Toronto: Open University and Toronto University Press, 1996), 102–23.

9. See, for example, my "Directing Traffic: Subjects, Objects, and the Politics of Exchange," *differences: A Journal of Feminist Cultural Studies* (Summer 1990): 41–54.

10. Peter Baker, Sarah Webster Goodwin, and Gary Handwerk, eds., *The Scope of Words* (New York: Peter Lang, 1991), 167–78. An earlier, highly abbreviated version of the essay appeared in the *Shakespeare on Film Newsletter* in 1982 based on an early conference paper.

11. Juliet Fleming, "*The French Garden*: An Introduction to Women's French," *ELH* 56 (1989): 19–51.

12. Viviana Comensoli and Paul Stevens, eds., *Discontinuities: New Essays on Renaissance Literature and Criticism* (Toronto: University of Toronto Press, 1998), 96–113.

13. Harold Bloom, Shakespeare: *The Invention of the Human* (New York: Riverhead Books, 1998), 3.

14. See most recently Ann Rosalind Jones and Peter Stallybrass, *Renaissance Clothing and the Materials of Memory* (Cambridge: Cambridge University Press, 2001), and my chapter "Dressing Up: Sartorial Extravagance in Early Modern London" in *Fashioning Femininity and English Renaissance Drama* (Chicago: University of Chicago Press, 1991).

15. See, for example, John Tomlinson, *Cultural Imperialism: A Critical Introduction* (Baltimore: Johns Hopkins University Press, 1991), and Bruce Robbins, *Feeling Global: Internationalism in Distress* (New York: New York University Press, 1999). On the dangers of a "homogenization of global culture," see Lisa Lowe and David Lloyd, *The Politics of Culture in the Shadow of Capital* (Durham, N.C.: Duke University Press, 1997), 1.

1. Myrrha's Revenge

An earlier, shorter version of this essay was presented at a Brown University conference on Ovid and the Ovidian influence in March 1979. I wish to thank Charles Segal, William Carroll, and S. Clark Hulse for reading this paper and making many welcome suggestions and comments.

1. Don Cameron Allen, "On *Venus and Adonis*," in *Elizabethan and Jacobean Studies Presented to Frank Perry Wilson*, ed. Herbert Davis and Helen Gardner

(Oxford: Oxford University Press, 1959), 100; on Adonis's unwillingness, see also T. W. Baldwin, *On the Literary Genetics of Shakespeare's Poems and Sonnets* (Urbana: University of Illinois Press, 1950); Geoffrey Bullough, *Narrative and Dramatic Sources of Shakespeare* (New York: Routledge and Kegan Paul,1957), vol. 1, 7; William Keach, *Elizabethan Erotic Narratives* (New Brunswick, N. J.: Rutgers University Press, 1977), and S. Clark Hulse, "Shakespeare's Myth of *Venus and Adonis*," *Proceedings of the Modem Language Association* 93 (1978). The one exception is A. Robin Bowers, "'Hard Armours' and 'delicate Amours' in Shakespeare's *Venus and Adonis*," *Shakespeare Survey* 12 (1979), who argues that Adonis does acquiesce by kissing Venus and is, therefore, destroyed by the boar, a symbol of lust. Bowers's allegorical reading fails to explain why, if Venus herself represents lust, she so vehemently opposes Adonis's hunting of the boar; he also ignores Venus's jealousy and confessed frustration in lines 597–98; 607–10; J. D. Jahn presents a more convincing argument that Adonis, though reluctant, nevertheless tempts Venus, in "The Lamb of Lust: The Role of Adonis in Shakespeare's *Venus and Adonis*," *Shakespeare Survey* 6 (1972). The willing Adonis of earlier myth can be found in *Orphic Hymns,* No. 56; Theocritus, *Idylls,* 1, 3, 15; Bion, "Epitaphium Adonidis"; Hyginus, *Fabulae,* 164, 271; and Fulgentius, *Mythologia,* III. For a summary of earlier criticism and major issues raised by *Venus and Adonis,* particularly the debate as to its "seriousness," see J. W. Lever, "The Poems," *Shakespeare Survey* 16 (1962): 19–22, and more recently, Keach, *Elizabethan Erotic Narratives.*

2. In book 10 of the *Metamorphoses* we learn only that Venus, grazed by an arrow of Cupid's, has fallen in love with Adonis and forgotten her usual haunts and occupations. Transformed by love, she goes about dressed like Diana and hunts animals, warning Adonis against the lion and wild boar. When he asks why, Venus stops to rest and tells him a story. Before beginning her warning tale of Atalanta, Venus places her head and neck in the lap of the reclining youth and interrupts her own words with a kiss ("inque sinu iuvenis posita cervice reclinis / sic ait ac mediis interserit oscula verbis" *Metamorphoses* 10. 558–59). All quotations are cited from W. S. Anderson's Teubner edition, *P. Ovidii Nasonis Metamorphoses* (Leipzig, 1977). In Renaissance pictorial representations Adonis is always depicted with his head in Venus's lap, a change from Ovid that reflects the aggressive Venus of earlier as well as later versions of the myth.

3. G. P. V. Akrigg, *Shakespeare and the Earl of Southampton* (Cambridge, Mass.: Harvard University Press, 1968), 196.

4. Leslie A. Fiedler, *The Stranger in Shakespeare* (New York: Stein and Day, 1972), 23ff. See also William Empson's introduction to the Signet edition of the *Narrative Poems,* ed. William Burto (New York: New American Library, 1968), xx, and Stephen's discourse in the library in the Scylla and Charybdis chapter of Joyce's *Ulysses.*

5. *Problems in Titian, Mostly Iconographic* (New York: New York University Press, 1969); Panofsky notes that "the painting ordered by Philip II remained in England for several years and was widely accessible in sixteenth-century prints by Giulio Santo (dated 1559) and Martino Rota (died 1583)" (153); Keach, *Elizabethan Erotic Narratives,* 56; see also David Rosand, "Titian and the 'Bed of Polyclitus,'"

Burlington Magazine 1, no. 17 (1975): 242–45; and John Doebler's article in *Shakespeare Quarterly* 33 (1982): 480–90, "The Reluctant Adonis: Titian and Shakespeare."

6. "Mother Venus: Temptation in Shakespeare's *Venus and Adonis*," *Shakespeare Studies* 11 (1978): 13.

7. "Self and Eros in *Venus and Adonis*," *Centennial Review* 10 (1976): 351–71.

8. Bullough, *Narrative and Dramatic Sources of Shakespeare*, notes the relationship between the Hermaphroditus and Narcissus myths and Shakespeare's portrayal of Adonis, 1.162–63; see also Allen, "On *Venus and Adonis*," who suggests another possible source in the story of Hippolytus, the chaste hunter. He points out that "ancient poets and mythographers sometimes said that a jealous Mars or an avenger Apollo sent the boar that killed Adonis, but Passerat, a French contemporary of Shakespeare's, invented a new, and perhaps more congenial legend. Diana sent the boar to revenge the killing of Hippolytus." In addition, there is a supporting hint in the interpolated tale of Atalanta and Hippomenes found in Ovid's version of the myth. "Hippomenes (ἵππο-μένος, passion or strength of a horse) has a connection with Hippolytus and with Adonis's stallion that [a poet] with 'small Greek' would notice," 107; Donald G. Watson, "The Contrarieties of *Venus and Adonis*," *Studies in Philology* 75 (1978): 32–63, explains Adonis's reluctance as a witty reversal of Petrarchan roles.

9. Baldwin, *On the Literary Genetics*, 84.

10. See, for example, Brooks Otis, *Ovid as an Epic Poet* (Cambridge: Cambridge University Press, 1970).

11. Ibid., 225ff.

12. See W. S. Anderson's commentary in his edition of books 6–10, *Ovid's Metamorphoses* (Norman: University of Oklahoma Press, 1972), 519.

13. *Ovide moralisé*, ed. C. De Boer (Wiesbaden: Martin Sandig, 1966, rpt. from 1936 ed.). All references are to this edition; *Ovid's Metamorphoses*, trans. Arthur Golding, 1567, ed. John Frederick Nims (New York: Simon and Schuster, 1965), 265.

14. See W. Atallah, *Adonis dans la littérature et l'art grecs* (Paris : Klincksieck, 1966), and Marcel Detienne, *Gardens of Adonis: Spices in Greek Mythology*, trans. Janet Lloyd (New York: Humanities Press, 1977), both of whom review the ancient sources of the myth. Medieval and Renaissance commentaries also recognize Venus's part in Myrrha's love for her father (see Raphael Regius, *P. Ovidii Metamorphosis* [1526], sig. M6ᵛ).

15. Keach admits that "there is a submerged suggestion of incest, a suggestion which glances at the story of Adonis's mother Myrrha," but he ignores the significance of his own glancing remark (*Elizabethan Erotic Narratives*, 77); see also Rebhorn, "Mother Venus," who notes the incestuous implications of Venus's role as mother (3).

16. Baldwin, *On the Literary Genetics*, 4.

17. Regius, *P. Ovidii Metamorphosis*, sig. M6ᵛ. Baldwin quotes a similar *argumentum* derived from Regius's commentary, 87.

18. Jacques Lacan, "Le séminaire sur 'La Lettre volée,'" *Ecrits I* (Paris, 1966), 19–78.

19. See, for example, the work of Pierre Macherey, *Pour une théorie de la production littéraire* (Paris: Maspero, 1966); Terry Eagleton, *Criticism and Ideology* (Atlantic Highlands, N. J.: New Left Books, 1976); and Shoshana Felman's introduction to "Literature and Psychoanalysis," special issue, *Yale French Studies* 55–56 (1977).

20. Spenser's portrayal of Venus's relation to Adonis as maternal in book 3 of the *Faerie Queene* (1590) must inevitably have influenced Shakespeare's characterization of Venus and Adonis. In the Garden of Adonis Spenser describes the goddess as "great Mother Venus" who "takes her fill" of a "wanton boy," an epithet which conflates Adonis and Cupid. For a discussion of Spenser and Shakespeare's different uses of Ovid, see Ellen Aprill Harwood, "*Venus and Adonis:* Shakespeare's Critique of Spenser," *Journal of the Rutgers University Library* 39 (1977): 44–60; Rebhorn assembles the evidence for Shakespeare's maternal Venus, "Mother Venus," 1–3; for an earlier classical account in which Venus's relation to Adonis is portrayed as maternal, see Charles Segal, "Adonis and Aphrodite, Theocritus, *Idyll* III, 48," *L'antiquité classique* 38 (1969): 82–88.

21. Allen, "On *Venus and Adonis,*" 109; see also A. C. Hamilton, "Venus and Adonis," *Studies in English Literature* 1 (1961): 14; Richard Lanham, *The Motives of Eloquence* (New Haven, Conn.: Yale University Press, 1976), 86; and Keach, *Elizabethan Erotic Narratives,* for whom the incestuous maternal-filial imagery suggests "not a scandalous unnaturalness, but a connection between the erotic and the maternal aspects of the feminine psyche," 77.

22. Kahn claims that the comparison of the boy Adonis to a flower is unconventional and therefore emphasizes his youth and peculiar role with relation to Venus ("Self and Eros in *Venus and Adonis,*" 357). On the contrary, the comparison of young men, particularly young men who die prematurely, to flowers dates from Homer and would have been well known to Shakespeare from many sources including the story of Nisus and Euryalus in the *Aeneid.*

23. Quoted by Rufus Putney, "*Venus and Adonis:* Amour with Humor," *Philological Quarterly* 20 (1941): 536.

24. Erich Neumann, *The Origin and History of Consciousness,* trans. R. F. C. Hull (New York: Harper, 1954), 78. See also Hereward T. Price, "The Function of Imagery in *Venus and Adonis,*" *Papers of the Michigan Academy of Sciences, Arts and Letters* 31 (1945): 295–96, who calls the boar "Venus in her most terrible aspect."

25. Ibid., 47; in his discussion of the Adonis myth, Atallah points out that Adonis's effeminacy and the phallic character of the boar probably date from the Alexandrian period, not from any so-called primitive past (*Adonis dans la littérature et l'art grecs,* 48-49, 63–74).

26. Hunting the boar is traditionally associated with the hero's initiation. For a review of the medieval and Renaissance pedigree of the boar as a symbol of male virility, see A. T. Hatto, "*Venus and Adonis* — and the Boar," *Modern Language Notes* 41 (1946): 353–61. Hatto also points to Shakespeare's own use of the boar as a sexual-phallic symbol in *Cymbeline* 2.5.

27. Hatto notes the boar's role as a usurper both in *Venus and Adonis* and *Richard III*, 3.2 and 5.2. With amusing understatement, he calls the Venus-Adonis-boar relation an "unusual triangular situation," 361.

28. It has long been remarked that the sexual roles of Venus and Adonis are reversed to enable Shakespeare to describe a homosexual rather than heterosexual relation—obliquely enough, however, for the poem to have won the approval of the Archbishop of Canterbury, who licensed it in 1593. For late classical and Italian examples of the boar justifying his "kiss," see Hatto, "*Venus and Adonis*—and the Boar," and Hulse, "Shakespeare's Myth of *Venus and Adonis*," 94, who cites the pseudo-Theocritean "Death of Adonis," accepted as Theocritus, No. 30, in the Renaissance. Hulse notes that the poem was translated anonymously into English as *Sixe Idillia* (1588; rpt. London 1922); cited by Gregorio Giraldi, *De Deis Gentium*, and imitated by Ronsard and Minturno, "De Adoni ab Apro Interempto" in *Epigrammata et Elegia*, 7a-8b, bound with *Poemata* (Venice, 1564).

29. *Violence et le sacré* (Paris: Grasset, 1972); see *Diacritics* (March 1978), devoted to Girard's work, and more recently Larry E. Shiner, "The Darker Side of Hellas: Sexuality and Violence in Ancient Greece," *Psychohistory Review* 9 (1980): 111–35.

30. Lévi-Strauss argues that the function of primary myth is to bridge the gap between conflicting values through a "series of mediating devices each of which generates the next one by a process of opposition and correlation. . . . The kind of logic in mythical thought is as rigorous as that of modern science. . . . (The difference lies, not in the quality of the intellectual process, but in the nature of the things to which it is applied)"; *Structural Anthropology,* trans. Claire Jacobson and Brooke G. Schoepf (New York: Basic Books, 1963), 226, 230.

31. "Shakespeare's Myth of Venus and Adonis," 95.

32. In his *Gardens of Adonis,* Detienne argues that the legend is not a fertility myth at all, but a myth about seduction: "The two episodes (Myrrha and Adonis) involve a double seduction, that of the mother as well as that of the son. . . . As in the story of Myrrha, seduction makes it possible to bring together two terms that are usually held apart," 64.

33. See Hugh Parry, "Ovid's *Metamorphoses:* Violence in a Pastoral Landscape," *Transactions and Proceedings of the American Philological Association* 95 (1964): 268–82, for a discussion of Ovid's exploitation of the erotic connotations of the hunt.

34. Both Detienne, *Gardens of Adonis,* and Parry, "Ovid's *Metamorphoses,*" 277, point out the powerful and dangerous qualities of the sun and its associations with sexuality.

2. Hayman's Missing *Hamlet*

1. In his essay "Francis Hayman's Illustrations of Shakespeare," *Shakespeare Quarterly* 9 (1958): 145, W. Moelwyn Merchant notes that Hayman's drawing "is doubly theatrical in that the 'murder of Gonzago' is played below a musi-

cians' gallery, while the two principal groups in the audience are strongly placed downstage."

2. Ibid., 145.

3. W. Moelwyn Merchant, *Shakespeare and the Artist* (London: Oxford University Press, 1959), 46.

4. Marcia Allentuck, "Sir Thomas Hanmer Instructs Francis Hayman: An Editor's notes to his Illustrator (1744)," *Shakespeare Quarterly* 27 (1976): 288–315.

5. Merchant, *Shakespeare and the Artist,* 46.

6. Ibid., 47.

7. *The Riverside Shakespeare,* gen. ed. G. Blakemore Evans (Boston: Houghton Mifflin, 1974).

8. Merchant notes, rightly I think, that "the Queen and Polonius direct attention to Claudius's agitation by looks of innocent concern, but with no tension of pose or gesture" (*Shakespeare and the Artist,* 46).

9. Whether this figure is Ophelia or simply one of the Queen's attendants is impossible to say. The figure is also found in the small study of the play scene by Hayman at the Folger Shakespeare Library. Ophelia is present, sitting as she is in the illustration, as is the figure behind the Queen, but in the study that figure lacks detail. The care with which her expression is rendered in the Vauxhall Gardens painting and the absence of any spectators other than the major characters suggest that the figure may be Ophelia. I am grateful to Charles Babcock at Ohio State University for suggesting that if this figure is indeed Ophelia, her gaze seems to be directed outside the painting and therefore perhaps at Hamlet himself (personal communication).

10. We have no indication of how the paintings were hung in relation to the Prince of Wales in his Pavilion at the gardens. See L. Gowing, "Hogarth, Hayman, and the Vauxhall Decorations," *Burlington Magazine* 95 (1953): 4ff., and J. G. Southworth, *Vauxhall Gardens* (New York: Columbia University Press, 1941).

11. For an interesting discussion of the reliance of the spectator on prior information, here knowledge of the play *Hamlet,* see E. H. Gombrich, "Standards of Truth: The Arrested Image and the Moving Eye," *Critical Inquiry* 7 (1980): 237–73.

12. We might compare the effect of the missing Hamlet in Hayman's painting with that of the missing sovereigns in Velázquez's *Las Meninas.* Though absent, King Philip IV and Maria, his wife, nevertheless order the entire representation. See Michel Foucault, *The Order of Things (Les mots et les choses)* (New York: Pantheon, 1971; Vintage rpt. 1973).

13. Merchant, "Francis Hayman's Illustrations of Shakespeare," 145. I am grateful to Jean Miller at the Folger, who permitted me, even though the library was closed to readers, to see both this painting and the 1744 Hanmer edition in which Hayman's drawings are interleaved with the engravings by Gravelot.

14. The most interesting attempt to deal with the independence of the literary illustrator, and indeed with the verbal-visual problem, is W. J. T. Mitchell's *Blake's Composite Art* (Princeton: Princeton University Press, 1978), particularly his first chapter.

15. M. C. Salaman, ed., *Shakespeare in Pictorial Art* (*Studio*, Special Number, 1916), 16; T. S. R. Boase, "Illustration of Shakespeare's Plays in the Seventeenth and Eighteenth Centuries," *Journal of the Warburg and Courtauld Institutes* 10 (1947): 90; Merchant, "Francis Hayman's Illustrations," 45, and *Shakespeare and the Artist*, 45.

3. Renaissance Family Politics
and Shakespeare's *The Taming of the Shrew*

1. This would seem to be Rosyer's neighbor's duty. The OED cites Lupton's *Sivgila*, p. 50 (1580), as an early use of *cowlstaff*: "If a woman beat hir husbande, the man that dwelleth next unto hir sha ride on a cowlstaffe."

2. PRO STAC 8,249/19. I am grateful to Susan Amussen for sharing her transcription of this case, and to David Underdown for the original reference. We do not know the result of Rosyer's complaint since only the testimony, not the judgment, is preserved.

3. Louis Montrose, "'Shaping Fantasies': Gender and Power in Elizabethan Culture," *Representations* 1 (1983): 61–94.

4. See Natalie Z. Davis, "Women on Top," in *Society and Culture in Early Modern France* (Stanford, Calif.: Stanford University Press, 1975); H. P. Thompson, "Rough Music: 'Le Charivari Anglais,'" *Annales ESC* 27 (1972): 285–312.

5. In *The Taming of a Shrew*, the frame tale closes the action; Sly must return home after his "bravest dreame" to a wife who "will course you for dreaming here tonight," but he claims: "Ile to my / Wife presently and tame her too." See Geoffrey Bullough, *Narrative and Dramatic Sources of Shakespeare* (London: Routledge and Kegan Paul, 1957), 1:108.

6. See Montrose's discussion of the Amazonian myth, "'Shaping Fantasies,'" 66–67.

7. *Réponse à John Lewis* (Paris, 1973), 91–98.

8. Fredric Jameson, *The Political Unconscious* (Ithaca, N.Y.: Cornell University Press, 1981), 35.

9. Montrose, "'Shaping Fantasies,'" 62, after Gayle Rubin.

10. (1.1.57–58); all references are to the New Arden edition, ed. Brian Morris (London: Methuen, 1981).

11. See, for example, Robert Greene's *Penelope's Web* (1587), which presents the Renaissance ideal of womanhood—chastity, obedience and silence—through a series of exemplary tales; see also Ruth Kelso, *Doctrine for the Lady of the Renaissance* (Urbana: University of Illinois Press, 1956); Linda T. Fitz, "'What says the Married Woman?': Marriage Theory and Feminism in the English Renaissance," *Mosaic* 13 (1980): 1–22; the books Suzanne Hull examines in her *Chaste, Silent, and Obedient: English Books for Women, 1475–1640* (San Marino, Calif.: Huntington Library, 1982); and most recently Lisa Jardine, *Still Harping on Daughters* (Sussex, Eng.: Harvester Press, 1983), 103–40.

12. See, among others, Lawrence Stone's *The Crisis of the Aristocracy, 1558–1641*

(Oxford: Clarendon Press, 1965), and Keith Wrightson's *English Society, 1580–1680* (New Brunswick, N.J.: Rutgers University Press, 1982), esp. chaps. 5 and 6. I am grateful to David Underdown for referring me to Wrightson.

13. Stone cites Swetnam, *Family,* 137; for references to *Hic Mulier,* see David Underdown, "The Taming of the Scold: The Enforcement of Patriarchal Authority in Early Modern England," in *Order and Disorder in Early Modern England,* ed. Anthony Fletcher and John Stevenson (Cambridge: Cambridge University Press, 1985), 116–36.

14. Underdown, "The Taming of the Scold," 119.

15. Ibid., 121.

16. Ibid., citing E. P. Thompson.

17. Montrose, "'Shaping Fantasies,'" 64–65.

18. Ibid. See also Davis, "Women on Top," and Thompson, "Rough Music," cited above.

19. See, for example, 1.1.65, 105, 121, 123; 2.1, 26, 151; for the social context of witchcraft in England, see Alan Macfarlane, *Witchcraft in Tudor and Stuart England* (New York: Harper and Row, 1970), and Keith Thomas, *Religion and the Decline of Magic* (London: Routledge and Kegan Paul, 1971).

20. On the importance of the gaze in managing human behavior, see Michel Foucault, *Surveiller et punir* (Paris: Gallimard, 1975); see also Laura Mulvey's discussion of scopophilia in "Visual Pleasure and Narrative Cinema, " *Screen* 16 (1975): 6–18, and Luce Irigaray's more philosophical *Speculum de l'autre femme* (Paris: Minuit, 1974).

21. Kate's speech at 3.2.8, 18–20 makes clear this function of his lateness and his "mad-brain rudesby." She recognizes that this shame falls not on her family but on her alone: "No shame but mine . . . Now must the world point at poor Katherine / Lo, there is mad Petruchio's wife, if it would please him come and marry her." Although Katherine to herself, she recognizes that to others she will be "Petruchio's wife."

22. See Marianne Novy's discussion of the importance of the father and paternity in her essay "Patriarchy and Play in *The Taming of the Shrew,*" *English Literary Renaissance* 9 (1979): 273–74.

23. Underdown, "The Taming of the Scold," 120.

24. See Novy's detailed discussion of Kate's puns, animal imagery, and sexual innuendoes in this scene, "Patriarchy and Play," 264, and Martha Andreson-Thom's "Shrew-Taming and Other Rituals of Aggression: Baiting and Bonding on the Stage and in the Wild," *Women's Studies* 9 (1982): 121–43.

25. *Collected Papers,* trans. Joan Riviere (London: Hogarth Press, 1948), 2:51–59.

26. Ibid., 51.

27. For a discussion of female fantasy, see Nancy K. Miller, "Emphasis Added: Plots and Plausibilities in Women's Fiction," *PMLA* 97 (1981): 36–48.

28. *Collected Papers,* 2:57.

29. Ibid., 58.

30. See Joan Riviere's essay on female masquerade in *Psychoanalysis and Female*

Sexuality, ed. H. Ruitenbeek (New Haven, Conn.: College and University Press, 1966); also of interest is Sir Thomas Elyot's *Defense of Good Women* in which Zenobia is allowed autonomy in relation to her husband but exhorted to dissemble disobedience. See Constance Jordan, "Feminism and the Humanists: The Case of Thomas Elyot's *Defense of Good Women,*" *Renaissance Quarterly* 36 (1983): 195.

31. Freud describes a similar strategy of evasion, *Collected Papers,* 2:58.

32. "Comic Structure and the Humanizing of Kate in *The Taming of the Shrew,*" in *The Woman's Part,* ed. Carolyn Ruth Swift Lenz, Gayle Greene, and Carol Thomas Neely (Urbana: University of Illinois Press, 1980). Bean quotes the "antirevisionist" Robert Heilbrun, "The *Taming* Untamed, or, the Return of the *Shrew,*" *Modern Language Quarterly* 27 (1966): 147–61. For the revisionist view, see Coppélia Kahn's "*Taming of the Shrew:* Shakespeare's Mirror of Marriage," *Modern Language Studies* 5 (1975): 88–102.

33. Bean, "Comic Structure and the Humanizing of Kate in *The Taming of the Shrew,*" 66.

34. Ibid., 67–70.

35. See Nancy K. Miller's discussion of the mystification of defloration and marriage in "Writing (from) the Feminine: George Sand and the Novel of Female Pastoral," in *The Representation of Women: Selected Papers from the English Institute* (Baltimore: Johns Hopkins University Press, 1983), 124–52.

36. *Ce sexe qui n'en est pas un* (Paris : Minuit, 1977), 134ff.

37. *Speculum de l'autre femme,* particularly 282–98. Contemporary handbooks often seem an uncanny description of woman as Other: the popular preacher Henry Smith, whose *Preparative to Marriage* was published in 1591, suggests that marriage is an equal partnership, but goes on to declare that "the ornament of women is silence; and therefore the Law was given to the man rather than to the woman, to shewe that he shoulde be the teacher, and she the hearer" (quoted in Novy, "Patriarchy and Play," 278).

38. Irigaray, *Speculum de l'autre femme,* 74, quoted and translated by Miller, "Emphasis Added," 38.

39. Miller, "Emphasis Added," 38.

40. Joel Fineman, "The Turn of the *Shrew,*" in *Shakespeare and the Question of Theory,* ed. Patricia Parker and Geoffrey Hartman (London: Methuen, 1985), 141–44.

41. See D. A. Miller's discussion of the "narratable" in *Narrative and Its Discontents* (Princeton, N.J.: Princeton University Press, 1981), especially the chapter on Austen.

42. Jameson, *The Political Unconscious,* 79, 56.

4. "And wash the Ethiop white"

1. Whitney chose the woodcuts from a collection of Christopher Plantyn, the well-known printer whose shop published *A Choice of Emblemes.* See Charles H. Lyons, *To Wash an Aethiop White: British Ideas about African Educability, 1530–1960* (New York: Columbia Teachers' College Press, 1975), iv–v.

2. For references to this proverb in Elizabethan and Jacobean drama, see Robert R. Cawley, *The Voyages and Elizabethan Drama* (Boston: D.C. Heath, 1938), 85ff.

3. E. V. Lucas, *Highways and Byways in Sussex* (London: Macmillan, 1904), 311. I am grateful to Peter Stallybrass for this reference.

4. M. R. Ridley, ed., *Othello* by William Shakespeare, Arden edition (London: Methuen, 1958, rpt. 1977), li. All references are to this edition.

5. Martin Orkin notes the telling preference in South Africa for Ridley's edition. Though aware of the political dimensions of *Othello* criticism, Orkin recuperates Shakespeare's play by claiming its universality in expressing the limitations of "human" judgments (184). His article, "*Othello* and the Plain Face of Racism," appeared in *Shakespeare Quarterly* 38 (1987): 166–88, after this essay was in press.

6. For a useful general discussion of black and white and their cultural associations, see the opening chapter of Harry Levin's *The Power of Blackness* (New York: Alfred A. Knopf, 1958).

7. Winthrop Jordan, *White over Black* (Chapel Hill: University of North Carolina Press, 1968), 7.

8. Stephen Orgel, *The Jonsonian Masque* (Cambridge, Mass.: Harvard University Press, 1967, rpt. New York: Columbia University Press, 1981), 120.

9. For a general account of the classical materials, see Frank M. Snowden Jr. *Before Color Prejudice* (Cambridge, Mass.: Harvard University Press, 1983).

10. All the passages quoted appear in the 1600 edition of R. Hakluyt, *The Principal Navigations, Voyages, Traffiques & Discoveries of the English Nation,* ed. Walter Raleigh (Glasgow: J. MacLehose, 1904), 7:262, in which Best's *Discourse* was reprinted in a substantially cut version. The story of the origins of blackness in Noah's son Chus is also found in Leo Africanus's popular *Historie of Africa* (1526).

11. Jordan observes that "English experience was markedly different from that of the Spanish and Portuguese who for centuries had been in close contact with North Africa and had actually been invaded and subjected by people both darker and more highly civilized than themselves. . . . One of the fairest-skinned nations suddenly came face to face with one of the darkest peoples on earth" (*White over Black,* 6).

12. Hakluyt's book is said to have been a prime motivator of English colonial expansion and to have increased the profits of the East India Company by some £20,000; see Walter Raleigh's essay in Hakluyt 1:92.

13. Best, in Hakluyt, 7:263–64. Talmudic and midrashic commentaries, which inspired interest in the humanist sixteenth century, seem to have been the source for the link between blackness and the curse on Cham; see Jordan, *White over Black,* 17–20, 35–39.

14. Jacques Derrida, "Racism's Last Word," trans. Peggy Kamuf, *Critical Inquiry* 12 (1985): 292.

15. See Frank Whigham's entry "Courtesy as a social code" in the *Spenser Encyclopedia,* ed. A. C. Hamilton, David A. Richardson, and Donald Cheney (Toronto: University of Toronto Press, 1997), 195, and his *Ambition and Privilege* (Berkeley: University of California Press, 1984).

16. July 11 and 18, 1596, in John Roche Dasent, ed., *Acts of the Privy Council*

(London: Mackie, 1902), 26, 16, 20. These proclamations must be read in light of the similar dislike and resentment, based on economic distinctions, between the English and the Fleming and Huguenot clothworkers who fled religious persecution and emigrated to England. The clothworkers, however, not only brought needed skills; they were also European, more like the English than an African could ever be, and though they generated hostility, there is no evidence of similar legislation to oust them from England. See C. W. Chitty, "Aliens in England in the Sixteenth Century," *Race* 8 (1966): 129–45, and Anthony Barker, *The African Link* (London: Frank Cass, 1978), 30.

17. See Paul L. Hughes and James F. Larkin, eds., *Tudor Royal Proclamations* (New Haven, Conn.: Yale University Press, 1969), 3:221.

18. Rudolf Wittkower, "Marvels of the East: A Study in the History of Monsters," *Journal of the Warburg and Courtauld Institutes* 5 (1942): 159–97, provides a thorough review, particularly of the visual material. Mary Louise Pratt's analysis of two modes of travel writing, the scientific-informational and the subject-centered, experiential, is suggestive not only for reading her nineteenth-century texts but also for earlier examples, which already manifest signs of the distinctions she draws; "Scratches on the Face of the Country; or, What Mr. Barrow Saw in the Land of the Bushmen," *Critical Inquiry* 12 (1985): 119–43.

19. These accounts are strikingly similar to discourses about the New World, but comparison of the two would require another study.

20. See, among others, John Lok's *Second Voyage to Guinea* (1554), in Hakluyt, 6:154–77; William Towerson's voyage (1556–57), in Hakluyt, 6:177–212; George Fenner's voyage (1556), in Hakluyt, 6:266–84; and finally Richard Jobson, *The Golden Trade* (1623), ed. Walter Rodney (London: Dawsons, 1968), 65–67. Lok's long and interesting account also appeared in the 1589 edition of Hakluyt as Robert Gainsh's voyage.

21. This passage did not appear in the French but in the Latin *De Republica* (Bodin, 1601, LI, 8^V); the English translation is that of Richard Knolles (London, 1606), available in a facsimile edition: J. Bodin, *The Six Bookes of a Commonweale,* ed. Kenneth Douglas McRae (Cambridge, Mass.: Harvard University Press, 1962), 3: viii. Knolles is quoted in David B. Davis, *The Problem of Slavery in Western Culture* (Ithaca, N.Y.: Cornell University Press, 1966), 112.

22. For a review of Portuguese and Spanish sources, see Katherine George, "The Civilized West Looks at Primitive Africa: 1400–1800," *Isis* 49 (1958): 62–72. For a general view of Elizabethans and foreigners, see G. K. Hunter, "Elizabethans and Foreigners," *Shakespeare Survey* 17 (1964): 37–52. On the representation of blacks on the English stage, see Eldred Jones, *Othello's Countrymen: The African in English Renaissance Drama* (Oxford: Oxford University Press, 1965); G. K. Hunter, "*Othello* and Colour Prejudice," *Proceedings of the British Academy* 53 (1967): 139–63; and more recently, Elliot H. Tokson, *The Popular Image of the Black Man in English Drama, 1550–1688* (Boston: G.K. Hall, 1982).

23. Indians and other New World peoples are similarly represented, as in *The Tempest,* in which Caliban is called a devil.

24. Keith Thomas, *Religion and the Decline of Magic: Studies in Popular Beliefs in Sixteenth- and Seventeenth-Century England* (London: Weidenfeld and Nicolson, 1971), 475.

25. Quoted from R. Burton, *Admirable Curiosities* (1703), in Hyder Rollins, "An analytical Index of the Ballad Entries in the Registers of the Stationers of London," *Studies in Philology* 21 (1924): 53. Teratological treatises often attributed monstrous births to the maternal imagination and desire, linking femininity to the production of monsters. As Marie Helène Huet, in "Living Images: Monstrosity and Representation," *Representations* 4 (1983), observes, the "monster publicly signals all aberrant desire, reproves all excessive passion and all illegitimate fantasy" (74). A contemporary English source specifically for the link between the maternal imagination and blackness is Sir Thomas Browne's *Pseudodoxia Epidemica* (1646). Ernest Martin, *Histoires des monstres* (Paris, 1880) traces the theory of monstrosity and the maternal imagination, 266–94.

26. See Kenneth Burke, *A Grammar of Motives* (Berkeley: University of California Press, 1969), quoted in Stephen Greenblatt, *Renaissance Self-Fashioning from More to Shakespeare* (Chicago: University of Chicago Press, 1980), 306. Recently Eve Sedgwick, in *Between Men: English Literature and Homosocial Desire* (New York: Columbia University Press, 1985), has deconstructed such versions of "consubstantiality" by showing how the female body, at once desired object and subject of discourse, becomes the territory across which male bonds, which she terms homosocial, are forged.

27. The Folio reading "Travellours historie," with, as Greenblatt notes, its generic implications, seems to me more convincing than "travel's history," since the tale Othello tells is drawn from accounts such as Mandeville's and repeated by the early Elizabethan travelers recorded in Hakluyt.

28. Linda Williams's essay "When the Woman Looks," in *Revision: Essays in Feminist Film Criticism,* ed. Mary Ann Doane, Patricia Mellencamp, and L. Williams (Frederick, Md.: American Film Institute, 1984), motivates part of the following discussion of *Othello.*

29. Homi Bhabha's notion of hybridity, which he defines as "the revaluation of the assumption of colonial identity through the repetition of discriminatory identity effects" in "Signs Taken for Wonders: Questions of Ambivalence and Authority under a Tree outside Delhi, May 1817," *Critical Inquiry* 12 (1985): 154, is suggestive for my reading of *Othello.*

30. Bernard Spivak, *The Allegory of Evil* (New York: Columbia University Press, 1958), 415ff.

31. Casual assumptions about the Shakespearean audience are problematic, and the "we" of my own critical discourse is equally so. Shakespeare's audience was not a classless, genderless monolith. The female spectators at a Globe performance, both the whores in the pit and the good English wives Stephen Gosson chastises for their attendance at the theater in *The Schoole of Abuse,* view the play from different perspectives from those of the white male audience of whatever social and economic station. As women, if we are implicated in Iago's perspective and

Othello's tragedy, we are unsexed, positioned as men; however, if we identify with Desdemona, we are punished. See the interesting work on female spectatorship in film theory by Laura Mulvey, "Visual Pleasure and the Narrative Cinema," *Screen* 16 (1975): 6–18, and Mary Ann Doane, "Film and the Masquerade: Theorizing the Female Spectator," *Screen* 23 (1983): 74–87.

32. In Leo Africanus's *Historie of Africa,* the "Portugals" are most often singled out as the destroyers of Africa and her peoples. From this perspective, the Iberian origins of Iago's name suggest that his destruction of Othello/Africa can be read as an allegory of colonialism. For detailed if occasionally dubious parallels between Leo's *Historie* and *Othello,* see Rosalind Johnson, "African Presence in Shakespearean Drama: *Othello* and Leo Africanus' *Historie of Africa,*" "African Presence in Early Europe," a special issue of *Journal of African Civilizations* 7 (1985): 261–87.

33. Compare Thomas Becon's lively description of a whore in his *Catechisme,* 20.2.5, in his *Workes* (London, 1564), typical of such representations in the period: "The whore is never satisfied, but is like as one that goeth by the way and is thirsty; even so does she open her mouth and drink of everye next water, that she may get. By every hedge she sits down, & opes her quiver against every arow." Becon makes explicit what is only implied in *Othello:* the link between female orifices — ear, mouth, genitals — and the perceived voraciousness of females.

34. This alternative sexual economy suggests another trajectory of desire in *Othello,* which cannot be explored further here. Iago's seduction is also cast in terms of the aural/oral, as for example when he claims to pour "pestilence into his [Othello's] ear" (2.3.347). For an interesting discussion of *Othello* and the "pathological male animus toward sexuality," particularly Desdemona's, see Edward A. Snow, "Sexual Anxiety and the Male Order of Things in *Othello,*" *English Literary Renaissance* 10 (1980): 388.

35. I am grateful to Rey Chow and the other members of the Brown University seminar "Cultural Constructions of Gender" (1987) at the Pembroke Center for Teaching and Research on Women for valuable discussion of the play's sexual economies.

36. Rymer in *Critical Essays of the Seventeenth Century,* ed. Joel Elias Spingarn (Bloomington: Indiana University Press, 1957), 221. For the status of blacks and moors in Renaissance Venice, see Giorgio Fedalto, "Stranieri a Venezia e a Padova," in *Storia della cultura veneta dal primo quattrocento al concilio di Trento,* ed. Girolamo Arnaldi and M. P. Stocchi (Vicenza: N. Pozza, 1976), 3:499–535.

37. For an excellent discussion of gender and class in *Othello,* see Peter Stallybrass, "Patriarchal Territories: The Body Enclosed," in *Rewriting the Renaissance: The Discourses of Sexual Difference in Early Modern Europe,* ed. Margaret Ferguson, Maureen Quilligan, and Nancy Vickers (Chicago: University of Chicago Press, 1986), 123–44.

38. For a psychoanalytic reading of Othello's relation to "the voice of the father," see Snow, "Sexual Anxiety and the Male Order of Things in *Othello,*" 409–10.

39. Quoted in Jordan, *White over Black,* 28.

40. See James Walvin, *The Black Presence* (New York: Schocken Books, 1972),

13, and Folarin Shyllon, *Black People in Britain, 1555–1833* (Oxford: Oxford University Press, 1977). It is worth noting that slavery between Europe and Africa was reciprocal. W. E. B. Du Bois, *The World and Africa* (New York: Viking, 1947), points out that during the sixteenth century "the [black] Mohammedan rulers of Egypt were buying white slaves by the tens of thousands in Europe and Asia" (52). Blond women were apparently in special demand: quoted in Wayne B. Chandler, "The Moor: Light of Europe's Dark Age," in "African Presence in Early Europe," special issue, *Journal of African Civilizations* 7 (1985): 144–75. He points out that "moors" were black and that historians' efforts to claim their tawniness represent racial prejudice.

41. Postlewayt writes in order to justify the Royal African Company's attempts to regain its monopoly; his pamphlet is exemplary, but many others could also be cited. Quoted in Walvin, *The Black Presence,* 51–52.

42. Rymer's attack on Shakespeare in the age of growing Shakespeare idolatry prompted other critics to a different tack—to dispute Othello's blackness altogether rather than reprehend it.

43. This same slippage from blackness to femininity is implicit in the commonly believed notion that apes and Negroes copulated, and especially that "apes were inclined wantonly to attack Negro women." For contemporary references, see Jordan, *White over Black,* 31.

44. Rymer's characterization of Emilia as "the meanest woman in the Play" (Spingarn, *Critical Essays,* 254) requires comment. The moralism of his "Short View" might lead most readers to award Bianca that superlative, but predictably Rymer cannot forgive Emilia her spunky cynicism toward men and her defense of women.

45. Norbert Elias, *The Civilizing Process: The History of Manners,* trans. Edmund Jephcott (New York: Urizen, 1978), 14–52.

46. Guido Ruggiero, *The Boundaries of Eros: Sex Crimes in Renaissance Venice* (New York: Oxford University Press, 1985), 61–62. I am grateful to Jonathan Goldberg for this reference.

47. My argument about the handkerchief has much in common with Stallybrass's in "Patriarchal Territories."

48. Lawrence Ross, "The Meaning of Strawberries in Shakespeare," *Studies in the Renaissance* 7 (1960): 225–40.

49. Lynda Boose in her "Othello's Handkerchief: The Recognizance and Pledge of Love," *English Literary Renaissance* 5 (1975): 360–74, argues that the handkerchief represents the lovers' consummated marriage and wedding sheets stained with blood, a sign of Desdemona's sexual innocence. She links the handkerchief to the folk custom of displaying the spotted wedding sheets as a proof of the bride's virginity

50. Sigmund Freud, "Fetishism," in *Sexuality and the Psychology of Love* (1927), ed. Phillip Rieff (New York: Collier, 1963, rpt. 1978), 215, 216.

51. See, for example, 1.3.402; 3.3.433.

52. Snow, "Sexual Anxiety and the Male Order of Things in *Othello,*" associates

the spotted "napkin" not only with Desdemona's stained wedding sheets but also with menstrual blood. He argues that the handkerchief is therefore "a nexus for three aspects of woman—chaste bride, sexual object, and maternal threat" (392).

53. For a discussion of critical attitudes toward Desdemona, and particularly this line, see S. N. Garner, "Shakespeare's Desdemona," *Shakespeare Studies* 9 (1976): 232–52.

54. *Renaissance Self-Fashioning from More to Shakespeare*, 244.

55. Tony Bennett, "Text and History," in *Re-Rereading English*, ed. Peter Widdowson (London: Methuen, 1982), 229.

56. For a discussion of the problem of representation and colonialist discourse, see Edward Said, *Orientalism* (New York: Pantheon, 1978).

5. Portia's Ring

1. This essay is based in part on two previously published articles, "Portia's Ring: Unruly Women and Structures of Exchange in *The Merchant of Venice*," *Shakespeare Quarterly* 38 (1987): 19–33, and "Directing Traffic: Subjects, Objects, and the Politics of Exchange," *differences: A Journal of Feminist Cultural Studies* (Summer 1990): 41–54.

2. Claude Lévi-Strauss, *The Elementary Structures of Kinship*, ed. Rodney Needham (Boston: Beacon Press, 1969), 115.

3. Gayle Rubin, "The Traffic in Women: Notes on the 'Political Economy' of Sex," in *Toward an Anthropology of Women*, ed. Rayna Reiter (New York: Monthly Review, 1975), 157–210.

4. There are numerous exceptions to the claim that "feminists . . . have reproduced the paradigm of exchange," but I am describing a dominant approach employed particularly within white Anglo-American feminist critical practice, based in anthropology and history, and which often recuperates radical appropriations of Lévi-Strauss's paradigm to its own empiricist ethos.

5. *Essai sur le don,* trans. Ian Cunnison (rpt. New York: Norton, 1967), 11–12.

6. Simone de Beauvoir, *The Second Sex,* trans. H. M. Parshley (Harmondsworth: Penguin, 1976), 17.

7. Pierre Bourdieu, *Outline of a Theory of Practice,* trans. Richard Nice, *Studies in Social Anthropology* 16 (Cambridge: Cambridge University Press, 1977), 58.

8. Rubin, "The Traffic in Women," 177.

9. *Ce sexe qui n'en est pas un* (Paris: Minuit, 1977), 189, my translation. Also available in English translation, *This Sex Which Is Not One,* trans. Catherine Porter with Carolyn Burke (Ithaca, N.Y.: Cornell University Press, 1985).

10. "Sexualism and the Citizen of the World: Wycherley, Sterne, and Male Homosocial Desire," *Critical Inquiry* 11 (1984): 227. For a more extended discussion, including a fine chapter on Shakespeare's sonnets, see her *Between Men: English Literature and Male Homosocial Desire* (New York: Columbia University Press, 1985). See also Lars Engle, "'Thrift is Blessing': Exchange and Explanation in *The Merchant of Venice*," *Shakespeare Quarterly* 37 (1986): 20–37, for a discussion of Sedgwick's work in relation to *Merchant*.

11. Lawrence Stone, *The Family, Sex, and Marriage in England, 1500–1800* (New York: Harper, 1977), 128.

12. See the work of the Cambridge demographers on age at marriage in the early modern period, especially Peter Laslett, *The World We Have Lost* (New York: Scribner's, 1984), 81–90.

13. Appropriately unmarked since in Tudor and Jacobean England, marriages were arranged for men as well as women, and they were arranged by both male and female "more prudent and mature heads," not just by fathers as Stone implies. See Keith Wrightson, *English Society, 1580–1680* (New Brunswick, N.J.: Rutgers University Press, 1982), 71–79, and Muriel St. Clare Byrne, ed., *The Lisle Letters, an Abridgement* (Chicago: University of Chicago Press, 1981), 198–99.

14. E. P. Thompson, "Happy Families," *New Society* 8 (1977): 499–501, and Wrightson, *English Society*.

15. See among others work by Irene Dash, *Wooing, Wedding, and Power: Women in Shakespeare's Plays* (New York: Columbia University Press, 1981); Peter Erickson and Coppélia Kahn, eds., *Shakespeare's Rough Magic: Renaissance Essays in Honor of C. L. Barber* (Newark: University of Delaware Press, 1985); Coppélia Kahn, *Man's Estate: Masculine Identity in Shakespeare* (Berkeley: University of California Press, 1981); Carol Thomas Neely, "Constructing the Subject: Feminist Practice and the New Renaissance Discourses," *English Literary Renaissance* 18 (1988): 5–18; Marianne Novy, *Love's Argument: Gender Relations in Shakespeare* (Chapel Hill: University of North Carolina Press, 1984); and Marilyn Williamson, *The Patriarchy of Shakespeare's Comedies* (Detroit: Wayne State University Press, 1986).

16. On the seeming centrality of the woman as desired object, see Julia Kristeva, *Texte du roman* (The Hague: Mouton, 1970), 160, 60.

17. See Lisa Jardine, *Still Harping on Daughters: Women and Drama in the Age of Shakespeare* (Brighton: Harvester Press; Totowa, N.J.: Barnes and Noble, 1983), 68–102.

18. See E. T., *The Lawes Resolution of Womens Rights* (1632), also known as *The Woman's Lawyer*, which gathers together in one volume contemporary laws about women, property, and marriage. In book 2, xxxii, there is an extended discussion of the gifts given at marriage. In "'Thrift is Blessing,'" Lars Engle claims that Portia's name suggests the marriage portion, a common means of relieving debt in early modern England. Though it is conceivable that an audience might hear "Portia" as an aural pun on "portion," the name is not etymologically related to the Latin *portio, -onis*, a share, part, proportion, but the Latin *porcus*, pig, and the Roman clan, the Porcii, breeders of pigs.

19. John Wing, *The Crowne Conjugall or the Spouse Royal* (London, 1632), sig. K2ʳ.

20. See particularly Wallace T. MacCaffrey, "Place and Patronage in Elizabethan Politics," in *Elizabethan Government and Society*, ed. S. T. Bindoff, J. Hurstfield, and C. H. Williams (London: University of London, Athlone Press, 1961), 97–125. For a discussion of prestation and literary fictions in Elizabethan culture, see Louis Adrian Montrose, "Gifts and Reasons: The Contexts of Peele's *Araygnement of Paris*," *ELH* 47 (1980): 433–61. For a more detailed account of Jacobean gift

giving, see Coppélia Kahn's "'Magic of bounty': *Timon of Athens,* Jacobean Patronage, and Maternal Power," *Shakespeare Quarterly* 38 (1987), especially 41ff.

21. See William Vaughn, *The Golden Grove* (London, 1600), sig. M8ʳ.

22. Stone, *The Family, Sex, and Marriage in England,* 216, 229–31.

23. See R. H. Tawney, *Religion and the Rise of Capitalism* (New York: New American Library, 1947); Lawrence Stone, *The Crisis of the Aristocracy, 1558–1641* (Oxford: Clarendon Press, 1965); Christopher Hill, *The Century of Revolution: 1603–1714* (New York: Norton, 1982); and Wrightson, *English Society.*

24. *The Merchant of Venice,* ed. John Russell, The Arden Shakespeare (1955; rpt. London: Methuen, 1977), 3.2.149–71. All future references are to this edition.

25. Kenneth Burke calls this figure the "'noblest synecdoche,' the perfect paradigm or prototype for all lesser usages, [which] is found in metaphysical doctrines proclaiming the identity of 'microcosm' and 'macrocosm.' In such doctrines, where the individual is treated as a replica of the universe and vice versa, we have the ideal synecdoche." *A Grammar of Motives and a Rhetoric of Motives* (Cleveland: Meridian, 1962), 508.

26. For a contemporary discussion of the giving of rings, see Henry Swinburne, *Treatise of Spousals or Matrimonial Contracts* (London, 1686), but written and published much earlier; see also Anne Parten, "Re-establishing Sexual Order: The Ring Episode in *The Merchant of Venice,*" *Selected Papers of the West Virginia Shakespeare and Renaissance Association* 6 (1976): 27–34. Parten also remarks this link between Portia's ring and her submission. Engle, "'Thrift Is Blessing,'" claims that Portia's actions in the final acts represent "her triumphant manipulation of homosocial exchange" and her "absolute mastery" (37).

27. Daniel Tuvill, *St. Pauls Threefold Cord* (London, 1635), sigs. B4ᵛ–B5ᵛ.

28. *The Aeneid of Virgil: A Verse Translation,* trans. Alan Mandelbaum (Berkeley: University of California Press, 1971), 161. Virgil knew the simile from the end of Hesiod's prologue to the *Theogony,* but Shakespeare would only have known it, of course, through Virgil.

29. George Puttenham, *The Arte of English Poesie* (1589), in *English Literary Criticism: The Renaissance,* ed. O. B. Hardison Jr. (London: Peter Owen, 1967), 177.

30. Thomas Wilson, *The Arte of Rhetorique* (1560), in Hardison, ed., *English Literary Criticism,* 42.

31. Ibid., 45.

32. Natalie Zemon Davis, *Society and Culture in Early Modern France* (1965; rpt. Stanford, Calif.: Stanford University Press, 1975), 130. Davis refers to the work of several anthropologists including Gluckman, Turner, Bateson, Fliigel, Delcourt, and Meslin.

33. See, for example, Clara Claiborne Park, "As We Like It: How a Girl Can Be Smart and Still Popular," in *The Woman's Part: Feminist Criticism of Shakespeare,* ed. Carolyn Ruth Swift Lenz, Gayle Greene, and Carol Thomas Neely (Urbana: University of Illinois Press, 1980), 100–116; Irene Dash, *Wooing, Wedding, and Power,* and more recently, Peter Erickson's *Patriarchal Structures in Shakespeare's Drama* (Berkeley: University of California Press, 1985).

34. See Parten, "Re-establishing Sexual Order," 32.

35. John Knox, *The First Blast of the Trumpet Against the Monstrvovs Regiment of Women* (London, 1558), sigs. 16ʳ–17ʳ.

36. *De Studiis et litteris,* trans. William H. Woodward, in *Vittorino de Feltre and Other Humanist Educators* (Cambridge, 1897), 124, 126, quoted in Constance Jordan, "Feminism and the Humanists: The Case of Sir Thomas Elyot's *Defence of Good Women,*" *Renaissance Quarterly* 36 (1983): 192. See also Vives's discussion of women and eloquence in Foster Watson, ed., *Vives and the Renascence Education of Women* (New York: Longmans, Green, and Co., 1912), 48–56, and More's letters, quoted in Watson, esp. 179ff. Similar exhortations can be found in Protestant tracts. On the position of the learned lady in the Renaissance, see Lisa Jardine, "'O decus Italiae virgo,' or The Myth of the Learned Lady in the Renaissance," *Historical Journal* 28 (1985): 799–819, and the opening pages of "Cultural Confusion and Shakespeare's Learned Heroines: 'these are old paradoxes,'" *Shakespeare Quarterly* 38 (1987): 1–18.

37. See Walter Cohen, "*The Merchant of Venice* and the Possibilities of Historical Criticism," *English Literary History* 49 (1983): 779–81, which appears in part in his recent book, *Drama of a Nation: Public Theater in Renaissance England and Spain* (Ithaca, N.Y.: Cornell University Press, 1985), and Robert Weimann's discussion of inversion and wordplay in *Shakespeare and the Popular Tradition in the Theatre,* ed. Robert Schwartz (Baltimore: Johns Hopkins University Press, 1978), esp. 39–48, 120–50.

38. Cohen, "*The Merchant of Venice* and the Possibilities of Historical Criticism," 776–83.

39. Norman Holland presents a number of psychoanalytic accounts of the link between rings and female sexuality in *Psychoanalysis and Shakespeare* (New York: McGraw-Hill, 1966), 238–331; for folktale sources, see, for example, the Tudor jest book *Tales and Quick Answers* (1530) cited in Parten, "Re-establishing Sexual Order," 27.

40. See in particular Engle, "'Thrift is Blessing,'" who argues for Portia's "absolute mastery" in act 5, (37), and Richard Horwich, who claims that the ring trick is "a device by which she may exercise her free will," in "Riddle and Dilemma in *The Merchant of Venice,*" *Studies in English Literature* 18 (1977): 199.

41. C. L. Barber claims, "No other comedy . . . ends with so full an expression of harmony. . . . And no other final scene is so completely without irony about the joys it celebrates," *Shakespeare's Festive Comedy* (1957; rpt. Princeton, N.J.: Princeton University Press, 1972), 187.

42. Davis, "Women on Top," 150.

43. See Jacques Derrida, *Of Grammatology,* trans. Gayatri C. Spivak (Baltimore: Johns Hopkins University Press, 1977), and *Writing and Difference,* trans. Alan Bass (Chicago: University of Chicago Press, 1978).

44. Judith Butler, *Gender Trouble: Feminism and the Subversion of Identity* (New York: Routledge, 1990), 141.

45. Margaret Ferguson, "Juggling the Categories of Race, Class, and Gender: Aphra Behn's *Ooronoko,*" *Women's Studies* 19 (1991): 163.

46. Commentators have often remarked on Shakespeare's introduction of the

theme of friendship in the relation between Antonio and Bassanio, a shift from the paternal/filial relationship of *Il Pecorone* usually recognized as *The Merchant of Venice*'s primary source. Recent critics who explain Antonio's melancholy as a loss of friendship include Leonard Tennenhouse, "The Counterfeit Order of *The Merchant of Venice*," in *Representing Shakespeare: New Psychoanalytic Essays,* ed. Murray M. Schwartz and Coppélia Kahn (Baltimore: Johns Hopkins University Press, 1980), 57–66, and Keith Geary, "The Nature of Portia's Victory: Turning to Men in *The Merchant of Venice*," *Shakespeare Survey* 37 (1984): 55–68. Graham Midgley, "*The Merchant of Venice:* A Reconsideration," *Essays in Criticism* 10 (1960): 119–33; W. H. Auden, "Brothers and Others," *The Dyer's Hand and Other Essays* (New York: Random House, 1962); Lawrence W. Hyman, "The Rival Lovers in *The Merchant of Venice*," *Shakespeare Quarterly* 21 (1970): 109–16; and W. Thomas MacCary, *Friends and Lovers: The Phenomenology of Desire in Shakespearean Comedy* (New York: Columbia University Press, 1985), claim a homoerotic impulse in Antonio's attachment.

6. Ghostwriting

1. *Hamlet* (Baltimore, Md.: Penguin, 1957); all references are to this edition.

2. See J. Magny, "Claude Chabrol: L'écorce et le noyeau," *Téléciné,* June, 1976, for a reading of Chabrol's work as ideological analysis.

3. For an interesting discussion of the problems involved in comparing film with a literary text, see Barbara Herrnstein Smith's response to Seymour Chatman in "Narrative Versions, Narrative Theories," *Critical Inquiry* 7 (1980): 213–36.

4. Chabrol called *Ophélia* a thriller and claimed that all his films share features with the genre, *Image et Son,* December 1961. For a useful introduction and filmography, see Angelo Moscariello, *Chabrol* (Firenze: La Nuova Italia, 1977).

5. See Gilles Deleuze and Carmelo Bene, "Un manifeste de moins," *Superpositions* (Paris: Minuit, 1979), 87–131, for a discussion of intertextuality as subtraction.

6. See, for example, André Green, "L'écran de face, un oeil derrière la tête," *Psychanalyse et cinéma* (1971): 15–22; Christian Metz, "The Imaginary Signifier," *Screen* 16 (1975): 49–54; and more recently, Mary Ann Doane's "Misrecognition and Identity," *Ciné-tracts* (1980): 25–32.

7. Metz, "The Imaginary Signifier," 51ff.

8. Sigmund Freud, *The Ego and the Id, Standard Edition* (London and New York: Hogarth Press, 1953–74), vol. 19, claims that the ego, in psychoanalytic theory the *locus* of identity, is always linked to the body; see also Jacques Lacan, "Le stade du miroir," *Ecrits I* (Paris: Seuil, 1968), who analyzes the process of identification whereby a child recognizes his *imago* in a mirror, and the subsequent consequences of this recognition for the development of the ego.

9. Freud, "The 'Uncanny,'" *On Creativity and the Unconscious: Papers on the Psychology of Art, Literature, Love, and Religion,* trans. Alix Strachey, ed. Benjamin Nelson (New York: Harper and Row, 1958), 122–61.

10. On Chabrol's preoccupation with "la bêtise," see Jean Louis Comolli, *L'avant scène* 92 (May 1967).

11. Freud, "The 'Uncanny,'" 159.

12. Jeffrey Mehlman, "Poe Pourri: Lacan's Purloined Letter," *Semiotext(e)* 1 (1975): 51–68.

13. Traditional criticism has remarked the baroque quality and emphatic theatricality of Chabrol's production (Moscariello, *Chabrol* 27). In his brief consideration of *Ophélia,* Moscariello also notes that Yvan's transformation of reality into spectacle not only criticizes the notion of realism but confutes the principles of Aristotelean logic as well, 30. See also G. Frezza, "Negazione e finzione nell'ultimo Chabrol," *Filmcritica,* August 1973.

14. Sarah Kofman, "Le double e(s)t le diable," *Quatre romans analytiques* (Paris, 1973), 137–81, emphasizes the importance of writing to Nathanael, the protagonist of Hoffmann's story "The Sandman" that Freud analyses: "La fiction a sur lui plus d'effet que la vie, le substitue progressivement à elle: simple représentant de la vie, elle finit par prendre sa place, apportant avec elle folie et mort. La littérature comme mimésis qui se substitue à la vie est une perversion de la créature qui rivalise avec Dieu: mimésis diabolique."

15. Hamlet himself is not unmindful of the power of tales and stories. Through metaphor Hamlet makes of the ghost's account the matter of books: "thy commandment all alone shall live within the book and volume of my brain"; in 5.2, when Hamlet is dying, he calls on Horatio "to tell my story."

16. In an interview with Chabrol, Jean André Fieschi points out the importance of figures like Lucy/Ophélia in Chabrol's films whose "normalcy" serve to emphasize the strangeness of his other characters (*Cahiers du cinéma,* May 1963).

17. Ibid., 58; Fieschi in fact calls the film "un gag tragique," a joke that backfires. Critics have often noted Chabrol's attack on realism characteristically carried out by emphasizing the artifice of his texts with the joke or "beffa."

18. Freud, *An Outline of Psycho-analysis, Standard Edition* (London and New York: Harper and Row, 1953–74), vol. 23, 192.

7. Englishing the Other

1. R. Hakluyt, *The Principal Navigations, Voyages Traffiques & Discoveries of the English Nation* (1600), ed. Walter Raleigh (Glasgow, 1903–5), 7:306–7.

2. Steven Mullaney, "Strange Things, Gross Terms, Curious Customs: The Rehearsal of Cultures in the Late Renaissance," *Representations* 3 (1983): 40–67. We know from other records that these two "Eskimos" eventually did "use as man & wife" because a child was born to the couple in England.

3. See Mullaney's *The Place of the Stage* (Chicago: University of Chicago Press, 1988), 82.

4. In Bakhtin's formulation, *heteroglossia* is only possible in the novel and certain other genres from which it developed because of the dialogic organization of novelistic discourse, the presence of an authorial or narrative voice in dialogic relation to the many-voicedness of characters and genres. In drama, Bakhtin complains, "There is no all-encompassing language that addresses itself dialogically to separate languages, there is no second plotless (nondramatic) dialogue outside that

of the (dramatic) plot." Though the dramatic immediacy of theatrical representation obscures the fact that the audience watches a constructed world, theatrical representation on the Elizabethan and Jacobean stage, so different from the
naturalistic "fourth wall" bourgeois theater that Bakhtin seems to have in mind,
provides a formal equivalent to an authorial voice, to a narrator, and particularly in
Henry V with its choral preludes that remind the audience of the conventions of
theater. The conventions of the Elizabethan theater, including acting styles, transvestism, prominent use of rhetoric and of microgeneric intrusions—from the no-
vella to letter writing—establish a dialogic relation with the characters' voices and
prevent what Bakhtin calls the domination of "unitary language." M. M. Bakhtin,
The Dialogic Imagination, trans. Michael Holquist and Caryl Emerson (Austin:
University of Texas Press, 1981), 266.

5. Ibid., 272.

6. M. A. K. Halliday, *Language as Social Semiotic* (London: Edward Arnold,
1978), 35.

7. J. H. Walter, ed., *Henry V* (London: Methuen; 1954, rpt. 1984), 4.1.250–55.
All references are to this edition, which relies primarily on the Folio text.

8. See, for example, Norman Rabkin, *Shakespeare and the Problem of Meaning*
(Chicago: University of Chicago Press, 1981), 33–62. But as Stephen Greenblatt
observes, "The very doubts that Shakespeare raises serve not to rob the king of his
charisma but to heighten it, precisely as they heighten the theatrical interest of the
play. . . . prodded by constant reminders of a gap between real and ideal, facts and
values, the spectators are induced to make up the difference, to invest in the illusion of magnificence, to be dazzled by their own imaginary identification with the
conqueror"; "Invisible Bullets: Renaissance Authority and its Subversions, *Henry
IV* and *Henry V,*" in *Political Shakespeare,* ed. Jonathan Dollimore and Alan Sinfield
(London: Methuen, 1985), 43. Greenblatt assumes too easily this imaginary "identification with the conqueror," thereby ruling out contestatory voices and producing a monolithic audience, marked here by the definite article—ungendered, un-
classed. The female spectator is faced either with a kind of specular masquerade in
which she dons a masculine subject position and identifies with the conqueror, or
alternatively, masochistic identification with the doubly subject Katherine, woman
and synechdochic representative of a conquered France.

9. Cited in Jonathan Dollimore and Alan Sinfield, "History and Ideology: The
Instance of *Henry V,*" in *Alternative Shakespeares,* ed. John Drakakis (London:
Methuen, 1985), 224.

10. Dollimore and Sinfield, "History and Ideology," 226.

11. Rowe emended the Folio's "desire" to "defile," which Walter accepts in the
Arden edition. Though "defile" is, of course, consistent with "dash'd" and "spitted,"
the Folio's "desire" stresses the sexual violence against women I am emphasizing
here.

12. Mullaney, "Strange Things," 87.

13. Nancy Vickers, "Diana Described: Scattered Woman and Scattered Rhyme,"
Critical Inquiry 8 (1981): 265–80.

14. Laura Mulvey, "Visual Pleasure and Narrative Cinema," *Screen* 16 (1975): 6–18; Paul Willemen, "Voyeurism, the Look, and Dwoskin," *Afterimage* 6 (1976): esp. 44–45.

15. Gayle Rubin, "The Traffic in Women: Notes on the 'Political Economy' of Sex," in *Toward an Anthropology of Women,* ed. Rayna Reiter (New York: Monthly Review Press, 1975).

16. On female destinies and the erotic plot, see Nancy Miller, *The Heroine's Text* (New York: Columbia University Press, 1980).

17. Kathleen McLuskie observes of Shakespeare's plays generally that "sex and sexual relations" are "sources of comedy" and "narrative resolution" rather than part of the conflict or the serious business of war and politics. See "The Patriarchal Bard: Feminist Criticism and Shakespeare: *King Lear* and *Measure for Measure*" in *Political Shakespeare,* ed. Jonathan Dollimore and Alan Sinfield (Ithaca, N.Y.: Cornell University Press, 1985), 92.

18. Lévi-Strauss, *The Elementary Structures of Kinship,* trans. James Harle Bell, John Richard von Sturmer, and Rodney Needham (Boston: Beacon Press, 1969), 115. For a fuller discussion of exchange and feminist theory, see my "Directing Traffic: Subjects, Objects, and the Politics of Exchange," *differences* 2 (1990): 41–54.

19. Julia Kristeva, *Texte du roman* (The Hague: Mouton, 1970), 160.

20. Luce Irigaray, *Ce sexe qui n'en est pas un* (Paris: Les Editions de Minuit, 1977), 189, my translation. (See also chaps. 3 and 5.)

21. Eve Kosofsky Sedgwick, "Sexualism and the Citizen of the World: Wycherley, Sterne, and Male Homosocial Desire," *Critical Inquiry* 11 (1984): 227. See also her *Between Men: English Literature and Male Homosocial Desire* (New York: Columbia University Press, 1985).

22. Michel Serres, "Platonic Dialogue," in *Hermes, Literature, Science, Philosophy,* ed. Josue V. Harari and David Bell (Baltimore: Johns Hopkins University Press, 1982), 67.

23. Michel Serres, *Le parasite* (Paris: Grasset, 1980).

24. Serres's notion of dialogue and the *tiers exclu* in particular helps to make sense of that final moment in *The Elementary Structures of Kinship* when Lévi-Strauss admits women "could never become just a sign and nothing more, since even in a man's world she is still a person, and since in so far as she is defined as a sign she must be recognized as a generator of signs . . . in contrast to words, which have wholly become signs, woman has remained at once a sign and a value," *Le parasite,* 496.

25. J. H. Walter, xxviii; Herschel Baker, *The Riverside Shakespeare* (Boston: Houghton Mifflin, 1974), 931.

26. Walter, xxviii.

27. Mullaney, *The Place of the Stage,* 87.

28. The "source" of this attribution of influence is M. L. Radoff, "The Influence of French Farce in *Henry V* and *The Merry Wives of Windsor,*" *MLN* 48 (1933): 427–35. The cornerstone of his argument is the pun on "con," which turns up in contemporary French farces and "would seem a highly improbable . . . mere

coincidence," 435. He neither cites the farces nor gives evidence they were available in England. More importantly, puns on "con" are ubiquitous. James Bellot's French phrase book, published during the Huguenot immigrations to England, offers several clear correspondences with the phonetic renderings of Katherine's accented English, "dat" for "that," "de" for "the," "den" for "then," "wat" for "what," and "fout" for "foot." *Familiar Dialogues* (London, 1586), unique copy at the Folger Shakespeare Library.

29. An exception is Walter Cohen, in *Drama of a Nation* (Ithaca, N.Y.: Cornell University Press, 1985), who is interested in precisely the problem of the incompleteness of the generic kinds, "romantic comedy" and "national historic drama." He notes that "the basic fallacy of the history play is to assume that politics is everything and consequently to minimize the impact on national affairs of social relations between the aristocracy and other classes," 220.

30. Dollimore and Sinfield, "History and Ideology," 214.

31. For Bakhtin's formulation of carnival, see *Rabelais and His World,* trans. Helene Iswolsky (Bloomington: Indiana University Press, 1984); see also *Critical Inquiry* 10 (1983), a forum on Bakhtin. See also Wayne Booth's discussion of Bakhtin's work on Rabelais, "Freedom of Interpretation: Bakhtin and the Challenge of Feminist Criticism," *Critical Inquiry* 9 (1982): 45–76.

32. Jacques Derrida, *Positions,* trans. Alan Bass (Chicago: University of Chicago Press, 1972), 41–42.

8. Cultural Capital's Gold Standard

1. For one such recent critique, see James Holstun, "Ranting at the New Historicism," *English Literary Renaissance* 19, no. 2 (1989): 189–225.

2. Marc Shell, *Money, Language, and Thought* (Berkeley: University of California Press, 1982), 6. On the gold standard, see also Walter Benn Michaels, *The Gold Standard and the Logic of Naturalism* (Berkeley: University of California Press, 1987) and especially Jean-Joseph Goux, *Symbolic Economies: After Marx and Freud,* trans. Jennifer Curtiss Gage (Ithaca, N.Y.: Cornell University Press, 1990). All references are to this edition.

3. Insofar as the production of any early author continues to constitute cultural capital, Shakespeare is that author; the plays epitomize the canon as the continuing proliferation of new editions and texts demonstrates, even as the standard plays of Jonson, Marlowe, and others go out of print. The availability of Middleton in Gary Taylor's mammoth new edition will inevitably shift pedagogic interest even further away from Marlowe and Jonson, though it is unlikely even to jostle the Shakespeare industry.

4. John Guillory, *Cultural Capital: The Problem of Literary Canon Formation* (Chicago: University of Chicago Press, 1993). All references appear in parentheses in the text.

5. See, for example, Peder J. Zane's "When Scholars Dig Not Only Tassels but Sequins" in the *New York Times,* 6 August 1995, reporting on the upcoming First

Annual International Conference on Elvis Presley, at the University of Mississippi, at which well-known Elvis impersonators, "The Mexican Elvis," and other "media personalities" were to take part. According to university sources interviewed by the *Times,* academic conferences are boring and in need of juicing up (2).

6. Although Maurice Charney claimed in his 1973 bibliographic essay on *Timon* that "older studies of divided or non-Shakespearian authorship are now more or less obsolete," ("*Coriolanus* and *Timon of Athens,*" in *Shakespeare: Select Bibliographical Guides,* ed. Stanley Wells [London: Oxford University Press, 1973], 225), *Timon of Athens* will be included in Gary Taylor's projected edition of Middleton's works. Also on authorship, see M. W. A. Smith, "The Authorship of *Timon of Athens,*" *Transactions of the Society for Textual Scholarship* 5 (1991): 195–240. Titles of recent essays include "An Embryonic *Lear,*" "Notes toward a More Finished *Timon,*" and "Word Links between *Timon of Athens* and *King Lear.*" The locus classicus for the play as unfinished is Una Ellis-Fermor, "*Timon of Athens:* An Unfinished Play," *Review of English Studies* 18 (1942): 270–83; see also Ninian Mellamphy, "Wormwood in the Wood outside Athens: *Timon* and the Problem for the Audience," in *"Bad" Shakespeare: Revaluations of the Shakespeare Canon,* ed. Maurice Charney (Rutherford, N.J.: Farleigh Dickinson University Press; London and Toronto: Associated University Presses, 1988), 170.

7. Frank Kermode, introduction to *Timon of Athens, The Riverside Shakespeare,* ed. G. Blakemore Evans (Boston: Houghton Mifflin, 1974), 1441.

8. Maurice Charney, "*Timon of Athens* on Stage and Screen," in *The Tragedy of Titus Andronicus,* ed. Charney, bound with *The Life of Timon of Athens,* ed. Sylvan Barnet, originally published in 1963 (New York: New American Library; Markham, Ontario: Penguin, 1989), 249.

9. A. C. Bradley, *Shakespearean Tragedy* (1905) (London: Macmillan; New York: St Martin's, 1966), 200. In his review of *Timon* criticism and bibliography, Charney notes that Coleridge established the comparison with *Lear,* which "pairing is one of the commonplaces of *Timon* criticism, although there is no external evidence at all, or even a specific-allusion, by which to date the play" ("*Coriolanus* and *Timon,*" 226).

10. See especially the important essay by Coppélia Kahn, "'Magic of Bounty': *Timon of Athens,* Jacobean Patronage, and Maternal Power," *Shakespeare Quarterly* 38, no. 1 (1987): 34–57; see also Michael Chorost, "Biological Finance in Shakespeare's *Timon of Athens,*" *English Literary Renaissance* 21, no. 3 (1991): 349–70. *Timon* has been wildly successful onstage, for example, in Michael Langham's stunning production at Stratford, Ontario, in 1991.

11. Barbara Correll, unpublished essay "Easy Come, Easy Go: Capitalism and Castration in *Timon of Athens* and *Old Fortunatus.*" For a recent essay still concerned with Jacobean patronage and gift giving but in terms of what she calls its sodomitical economy, see Jody Greene, "'You Must Eat Men': The Sodomitic Economy of Renaissance Patronage," *GLQ: A Journal of Lesbian and Gay Studies* 1, no. 2 (1994): 163–97. Her essay came to my attention after I had written my own; although our approaches to *Timon* differ, we share an interest in the play's

adumbration of sodomy. Whereas Greene's attention is focused on "the impossibility of writing a play about the limits of male friendship in the Renaissance without recourse to the vocabulary of sodomy" (165), I am concerned with the ways in which commentators have turned away from *Timon's* sodomitical economy.

12. See John Dixon Hunt, "Shakespeare and the Paragone: A Reading of *Timon of Athens,*" in *Images of Shakespeare,* ed. Werner Habicht, D. J. Palmer, Roger Pringle, and Philip J. Brockbank (Newark: University of Delaware Press, 1988), 47–63.

13. William Shakespeare, *Timon of Athens,* ed. H. J. Oliver, The Arden Shakespeare (London: Methuen, 1929, rpt. 1959). All references are to this edition.

14. Barbara Johnson, "Apostrophe, Animation, and Abortion." *diacritics* 16, no. 1 (1986): 29–30.

15. Jonathan Culler, *The Pursuit of Signs* (Ithaca, N.Y.: Cornell University Press, 1981), 135–55; on apostrophe as performative, see especially Johnson, "Apostrophe, Animation, and Abortion."

16. If, as Culler argues, apostrophe substitutes the "temporality of discourse" for "referential temporality," the lyric *now* for narrative, or in this case, dramatic, extension (149, 154), then apostrophe also helps to make sense of other of the play's so-called unusual imperfections, particularly its episodic structure.

17. T. J. B. Spencer, "Shakespeare Learns the Value of Money: The Dramatist at Work on *Timon of Athens,*" *Shakespeare Survey* 6 (1953): 75–78.

18. Stephen Greenblatt, *Shakespearean Negotiations: The Circulation of Social Energy in Renaissance England* (Berkeley: University of California Press, 1988), 1.

19. An exception is H. J. Oliver, who states that "North's *Plutarch*" was "Shakespeare's main source for the story of Timon" (*Timon,* xxxii). But Oliver claims of the Life of Alcibiades that Shakespeare merely "glanced through it at this or a later stage of his career" (xxxiii) and ignores the Life's insistence on Alcibiades' homoerotic attachments.

20. Kenneth Muir, *The Sources of Shakespeare's Plays* (New Haven, Conn.: Yale University Press, 1978), 218.

21. T. J. B. Spencer, ed., *Shakespeare's Plutarch: The Lives of Julius Caesar, Brutus, Marcus Antonius, and Coriolanus in the Translation of Sir Thomas North* (Harmondsworth, Middlesex: Penguin, 1964).

22. David C. Green, *Plutarch Revisited: A Study of Shakespeare's Last Roman Tragedies and Their Source* (Salzburg: Universitat Salzburg, 1979), 1.

23. Geoffrey Bullough, *Narrative and Dramatic Sources of Shakespeare* (London: Routledge, 1964), 6:249.

24. Alexander Dyce, ed., *Timon, a Play Now First Printed* (for the Shakespeare Society; London, 1842).

25. Plutarch. *The Lives of the Noble Grecians & Romans Compared Together by that Grave Learned Philosopher and Historiographer Plutarke of Chaeronea,* trans. into French by James Amyot and from French into English by Thomas North, 1579; 1603 (London: Nonesuch, 1929), 5 vols. All references are to this edition.

26. See Greene, "'You Must Eat Men'"; Alan Bray, "Homosexuality and the Signs of Male Friendship in Elizabethan England," in *Queering the Renaissance,*

ed. Jonathan Goldberg (Durham, N.C.: Duke University Press, 1994), 40–61; and Goldberg's *Sodometries: Renaissance Texts, Modern Sexualities* (Stanford, Calif.: Stanford University Press, 1992).

27. Terence [T. J. B.] Spencer's essay "'Greeks' and 'Merrygreeks': A Background to *Timon of Athens* and *Troilus and Cressida*" is particularly interesting in its avoidance of drawing the conclusion required by its own evidence. Spencer details the Greeks' general reputation for depravity by looking in turn at drunkenness, deceit, dishonesty, and the libidinous habits of Greek women, with only a brief reference to the "'Greek vice'" via a quotation from *Troilus* (231); in *Essays on Shakespeare and Elizabethan Drama in Honor of Hardin Craig,* ed. Richard Hosley (Columbia: University of Missouri Press, 1962), 223–33.

28. Edmund Spenser, *Spenser: Poetical Works,* ed. J. C. Smith and E. De Selincourt (London: Oxford University Press, 1970) 422, 423.

29. Christopher Marlowe, *Edward the Second,* ed. W. Moelwyn Merchant. The New Mermaids edition (London: Benn, 1967).

30. Goux, *Symbolic Economies,* 23, quoting from Jacques Lacan, *Ecrits* (Paris: Seuil, 1966).

9. Charactery

1. L. C. Knights, *How Many Children Had Lady Macbeth? An Essay in the Theory and Practice of Shakespeare Criticism* (Cambridge: Gordon Fraser, 1933); see also John Britton's "A. C. Bradley and those Children of Lady Macbeth," *Shakespeare Quarterly* 12 (1961): 349–51. Britton quotes from a letter from Knights attributing the phrase to F. R. Leavis. For a recent approach to character in Shakespeare, see Marjorie Garber, "Fatal Cleopatra," in her *Quotation Marks* (New York: Routledge, 2003). On writing about characters as if they were people, see David A. Brewer, *The Afterlife of Character, 1726–1825* (Philadelphia: University of Pennsylvania Press, 2005), who also quotes this well-known passage from Berger (see note 2).

2. Harry Berger Jr., "What Did the King Know and When Did He Know It? Shakespearean Discourses and Psychoanalysis," *South Atlantic Quarterly,* 88 (1989): 811–62.

3. Harold Bloom, *Shakespeare: The Invention of the Human* (New York: Riverhead Books, 1998), 17.

4. "Soul of the Age," *New York Times Book Review,* November 1, 1998.

5. Theophrastus's *Characters,* which became known in England in the 1590s following the publication of Causaubon's edition (1592–99), consists in sketches of vicious types said to have been influenced by Aristotle's classification of virtuous types in the *Ethics.*

6. Sir Thomas Overbury, *The Overburian Characters,* ed. W. J. Paylor (Oxford: Blackwell, 1936).

7. Quoted from *The Shakespeare Allusion-Book: A Collection of Allusions to Shakespeare from 1591 to 1700* (Freeport, N.Y.: Books for Libraries Press, 1909, rpt. 1970), 2:246.

8. E. A. Horsman, "Dryden's French Borrowings," *Review of English Studies* 1, no. 4 (1950): 346–51.

9. Jonathan Goldberg, *Voice Terminal Echo: Postmodernism and English Renaissance Texts* (New York: Methuen, 1986), 68–100.

10. Harry Berger Jr., "What Did the King Know."

11. Margreta de Grazia and Peter Stallybrass, "The Materiality of the Shakespearean Text," *Shakespeare Quarterly* (1993): 267.

12. On Pope and Shakespearean character, see Random Cloud, "'the very names of the Persons': Editing and the Invention of Dramatic Character," in *Staging the Renaissance,* ed. David Scott Kastan and Peter Stallybrass (New York: Routledge, 1991), 88–96.

13. *Die Traumdeutung* (1899), first published in English in 1913.

14. Brewer, *The Afterlife of Character,* 83.

15. *The Shakespeare Allusion-Book,* 1:330–31

16. *Twelfth Night,* ed. J. M. Lothian and T. W. Craik (London: Routledge, 1975, rpt. 1988). All references are to this edition. The Arden, Norton, Pelican/Penguin, and Riverside editions all gloss *character* in this line as "appearance." The line is precisely about whether the captain's outward appearance or character corresponds with his mind, his interiority.

17. We need to distinguish between work that uses such categories anachronistically by judging actions, behaviors, and plots ahistorically, and work that eschews anachronism and instead uses such categories to analyze theoretical problems historically.

18. On the production of inwardness in Shakespeare, see, inter alia, Karen Newman, *Shakespeare's Rhetoric of Comic Character* (London: Methuen, 1985); Harry Berger Jr., "What Did the King Know"; Katharine Eisman Maus, *Inwardness and Theatre in the English Renaissance* (Chicago: University of Chicago Press, 1995), and on the sonnets, Anne Ferry, *The "Inward" Language: Sonnets of Wyatt, Sidney, Shakespeare, Donne* (Chicago: University of Chicago Press, 1983).

19. *Coriolanus,* ed. Philip Brockbank, The Arden Shakespeare (London: Routledge, 1976). All references are to this edition.

20. Morris W. Croll, "'Attic' and Baroque Prose Style," in *Style, Rhetoric and Rhythm: Essays by Morris W. Croll,* ed. J. Max Patrick and Robert O. Evans, with John W. Wallace (Princeton, N.J.: Princeton University Press, 1969), 216. See also Lynne Magnusson's brief note on this passage in "'I paint him in the character': Prose Portraits in *Coriolanus,*" *English Language Notes* 25 (1987): 33–36.

21. Joseph Hall, *Heaven upon Earth and Characters of Vertues and Vices,* ed. Rudolf Kirk (New Brunswick, N.J.: Rutgers University Press, 1948). For the best account of the genre in early modern England, see J. W. Smeed, *The Theophrastan "Character"* (Oxford: Clarendon, 1985), 1–46.

22. Hall is generally credited with being the first practitioner of the genre in English and is recognized for his inclusion, different from Theophrastus, of both virtues and vices among his characters.

23. Smeed, *The Theophrastan "Character,"* 2.

24. D. A. Traversi, "Coriolanus," *Scrutiny* 6 (1937); L. C. Knights, *Further*

Explorations (London : Chatto and Windus, 1965); Paul A. Cantor, *Shakespeare's Rome: Republic and Empire* (Ithaca, N.Y.: Cornell University Press, 1976); Janet Adelman, "'Anger's My Meat' : Feeding, Dependence, and Aggression in *Coriolanus,*" in *Representing Shakespeare: New Psychoanalytic Essays,* ed. Murray M. Schwartz and Coppélia Kahn (Baltimore: Johns Hopkins University Press, 1980); Coppélia Kahn, *Roman Shakespeare: Warriors, Wounds, and Women* (London: Routledge, 1997); and James Kuzner, "Unbuilding the City: *Coriolanus* and the Birth of Republican Rome," *Shakespeare Quarterly* 58 (2007): 174–99.

25. Words from *Ant* to *batten* of what was then called the *New English Dictionary* appeared in 1885; Shaw's coinage *bardolatry* appeared in the preface of his *Plays for Puritans* (1901) and subsequently in the dedicatory epistle to *Man and Superman.* In the coinage *bardolatry,* the suffix *ery* has the contracted form *ry,* which appears with increasing frequency.

26. Sir Thomas Overbury, *The Overburian Characters,* ed. W. J. Paylor (Oxford: Blackwell, 1936), 92.

27. "How Many Children Had Lady Macbeth?" was originally announced in *Scrutiny* and appeared in 1933; it was subsequently reprinted in Knights's *Explorations: Essays in Criticism* (London: Chatto and Windus, 1946, rpt. New York University Press, 1964); Arthur Sewell, *Character and Society in Shakespeare* (Oxford: Clarendon, 1951); Wolfgang Clemen, *Shakespeare's Soliloquies* (Cambridge: Cambridge University Press, 1964).

28. Reprinted in *Approaches to Shakespeare,* ed. Norman Rabkin (New York: McGraw-Hill, 1964), 52.

10. Sartorial Economics and Suitable Style

1. *The Tragedy of King Richard II,* ed. Stephen Greenblatt, The Norton Shakespeare (New York: Norton, 1997), 1.4.30, 35. All references are to this edition.

2. On the clothing of common soldiers, see Henry J. Webb, "Falstaff's Clothes," *MLN* 59 (1944): 162–64.

3. See among many studies Lawrence Stone, *The Crisis of the Aristocracy, 1558–1641* (Oxford: Clarendon, 1965); the several studies of Tudor and Jacobean costume by Janet Arnold; Jane Ashelford, *Dress in the Age of Elizabeth I* (New York: Holmes and Meier, 1988); Karen Newman, *Fashioning Femininity and English Renaissance Drama* (Chicago: University of Chicago Press, 1991), chap. 7; Ann Rosalind Jones and Peter Stallybrass, *Renaissance Clothing and the Materials of Memory* (Cambridge: Cambridge University Press, 2000); and Linda Levy Peck, *Consuming Splendor: Society and Culture in Seventeenth-Century England* (Cambridge: Cambridge University Press, 2005). At the 2008 meeting of the Renaissance Society of America, no fewer than fifteen sessions, each with three speakers, were devoted to the rubric "Dress and Identity." Though an occasional paper considered the dress of the Irish, or a sartorial marker imposed on an ethnic group, virtually every paper addressed the clothing of the elite, or alternatively, persons of a lower social status dressing in clothing above their degree. An important new source on clothing in the early modern period in England will be the database being prepared as

part of a new research project, "Clothing, Culture, and Identity in Early Modern England," described in a note with that title that appeared in *Textile History* 34 (2003): 229–34, by Mark Merry, Catherine Richardson, and Graeme Murdock. On sartorial extravagance, see also Kaja Silverman, "Fragments of a Fashionable Discourse," in *Studies in Entertainment: Critical Approaches to Mass Culture,* ed. Tania Modleski (Bloomington: Indiana University Press, 1986).

4. Keith Wrightson ends his discussion of early modern English population and resources by noting that Gregory King estimated that in 1688 at least half the English population could barely "provide an adequate maintenance for their families. The poor had emerged as a massive and permanent element in English society" *(English Society, 1580–1680* [New Brunswick, N.J.: Rutgers University Press, 1982], 148). On downward mobility, see Wrightson, 140–48. See also Wrightson's essay with John Walter, "Dearth and the Social Order in early modern England," *Past & Present* 71 (1976), 22–42, and J. D. Chambers, *Population, Economy, and Society in Pre-Industrial England* (Oxford: Oxford University Press, 1972).

5. On cloth and the English economy, see Joan Thirsk, *Economic Policy and Projects* (Oxford: Clarendon, 1978); Margaret Spufford, *The Great Reclothing of Rural England* (London: Hambledon Press, 1984); and Eric Kerridge, *Textile Manufacture in Early Modern England* (Manchester: Manchester University Press, 1985); on the "new draperies," see D. C. Coleman, "Innovation and its Diffusion: The 'New Draperies,'" *Economic History Review* 22 (1969): 417–29.

6. N. B. Harte, "The Economies of Clothing in the Late Seventeenth Century," *Textile History* 22 (1991): 286. Harte's figures are for the late seventeenth century, when the stabilization of population growth, agricultural innovation, and improved distribution that resulted in slowly improving real wages apparently enabled a somewhat higher rate of consumption. See also John Hatcher, "Labour, Leisure, and Economic Thought before the Nineteenth Century," *Past & Present* 160 (1998): 94–95. On the distribution of clothing, or money to redeem clothing in pawn, to the poor, see Linda Hayner, "The Responsibilities of the Parishes of England for the Poor, 1640–1660," *Proceedings of the South Carolina Historical Association* (1983): 76–84. On the size of the cloth and clothing companies in comparison with other major companies, see Steve Rappaport, *World within Worlds: Structures of Life in Sixteenth-Century London* (Cambridge: Cambridge University Press, 1989), 394–99, and Jones and Stallybrass, *Renaissance Clothing and the Materials of Memory,* 17, 178, and passim.

7. See Carole Shammas, *The Pre-Industrial Consumer in England and America* (Oxford: Clarendon, 1990); Harte, "The Economies of Clothing in the Late Seventeenth Century"; and Lorna Weatherill, "Consumer Behavior, Textiles, and Dress in the Late Seventeenth and Early Eighteenth Centuries," *Textile History* 22 (1991): 277–96 and 297–310, and her *Consumer Behaviour and Material Culture in England, 1660–1760* (New York: Routledge, 1988); D. C. Coleman, *The British Paper Industry, 1495–1860* (Oxford: Clarendon, 1958); Donald Woodward, "Swords into Ploughshares: Recycling in Pre-industrial England," *Economic History Review* 38 (1985), 175–91; and F. G. Emmison, *Elizabethan Life: Disorder* (Chelmsford: Essex

Co. Council, 1970), who notes the "scores of indictments for stealing clothes" and whose appendixes document the high incidence of cloth theft. On second-hand clothing, see Beverly Lemire, "Consumerism in Preindustrial and Early Industrial England: The Trade in Secondhand Clothes," *Journal of British Studies* 27 (1988): 1–24; John Styles, "Clothing the North: The Supply of Non-Elite Clothing in the Eighteenth-Century North of England," *Textile History* 25 (1994): 139–66; and Jones and Stallybrass, *Renaissance Clothing and the Materials of Memory,* chap. 1. For contemporary representations of the textile guilds, see *The Works of Thomas Deloney,* ed. F. O. Mann (Oxford: Clarendon, 1912), particularly *Iacke of Newberie* and *Thomas of Reading.*

8. On Marx's own relation to the market in clothes, see Peter Stallybrass, "Marx's Coat," in *Border Fetishisms: Material Objects in Unstable Spaces,* ed. Patricia Spyer (New York and London: Routledge, 1998), 183–207.

9. Edmund Spenser, *A Vewe of the Present State of Irelande, The Complete Works of Edmund Spenser,* ed. Edwin Greenlaw (Baltimore: Johns Hopkins University Press, 1949), 10.121. In the case of the theater, clothes not only registered class distinctions but made the boy a woman and, on early seventeenth-century London streets, sometimes apparently made a woman a man. See most recently Stephen Orgel, *Impersonations: The Performance of Gender in Early Modern England* (Cambridge: Cambridge University Press, 1996).

10. On sumptuary legislation, see Frances E. Baldwin, "Sumptuary Legislation and Personal Regulation in England," *Johns Hopkins University Studies in Historical and Political Science* 44 (1926) and N. B. Harte, "State Control of Dress and Social Change in Pre-Industrial England," in *Trade, Government, and Economy in Pre-Industrial England: Essays Presented to F. J. Fisher,* ed. D. C. Coleman and A. H. Johns (London: Weidenfeld and Nicholson, 1976), 132–65; on livery, see Shammas, *The Pre-Industrial Consumer in England and America*; *Satrical Songs and Poems on Costume in Early English Poetry, Ballads, and Popular Literature* (London: Percy Society, 1849), vol. 27. The best single example of the Puritan attack on fashion is the frequently quoted Philip Stubbes, *The Anatomie of Abuses in Ailgna of Philip Stubbes,* ed. F. J. Furnivall (London, 1877–82); on state-supported attacks on sartorial excess, see the frequently quoted "Homily against Excess of Apparel." On the vestiarian controversy, see M. M. Knappen, *Tudor Puritanism: A Chapter in the History of Idealism* (Chicago: University of Chicago Press, 1939); Patrick Collinson, *Godly People: Essays on English Protestantism and Puritanism* (London: Hambledon Press, 1983), and his *The Elizabethan Puritan Movement* (Oxford: Clarendon, 1990). On fashion, status, and gender more generally, see René König, *The Restless Image,* trans. F. Bradley (London: George Allen and Unwin Limited, 1973), and J. C. Flugel, *The Psychology of Clothes* (London: Hogarth Press, 1930).

11. See also *A Pleasaunt Dialogue or Disputation between the Cap and the Head* (London: Henry Denham, 1565).

12. On complaints about excess of dress and the decline of hospitality, see Joan R. Kent, "Attitudes of Members of the House of Commons to the Regulation of 'Personal Conduct' in late Elizabethan and Early Stuart England," *Bulletin of the*

Institute of Historical Research 46 (1973): 41–71. See also Felicity Heal, "The Idea of Hospitality in Early Modern England," *Past & Present* 102 (1984): 66–93.

13. On russet, see also Jones and Stallybrass, *Renaissance Clothing and the Materials of Memory,* 229–44.

14. The *OED* defines *tarse* as a rich and costly oriental material often used in the West in the fourteenth and fifteenth centuries and *trye* as "choice" or "excellent," both in contrast to russet. Thanks to Martha Rust for the *Piers Plowman* reference.

15. Francis Thynn, *The Debate between Pride and Lowliness,* ed. J. Payne Collier (London: Shakespeare Society, 1841); in her research for *The Great Reclothing of Rural England,* Spufford was unable to find examples of ordinary clothing except for those excavated from a Shetlands bog. In other words, clothing in the period was worn to rags and then either exported for paper making abroad or, later, sold for paper making at home. See Coleman, "Innovation and its Diffusion," and the many examples in Shakespeare of "patches" as a substantive for the poorer sort.

16. For another contemporary critique of the effects of conspicuous consumption on the ploughman, see Middleton's *Father Hubbard's Tales, or The Ant and the Nightingale* (1604).

17. The Irish mantle was worn across social classes and was most troublesome to many when it became fashionable among the English themselves. See Margaret Rose Jaster, "'Fashioninge the Minde and Condicions': The Uses and Abuses of Apparel in Early Modern England" (Ph.D. diss., University of Maryland, 1994), and Jones and Stallybrass, *Renaissance Clothing and the Materials of Memory.*

18. D'Urfey's *Songs Compleat Pleasant and Divertive: Set to Musicke* (London: W. Pearson for J. Tonson, 1719), 4:199–200.

19. Quoted from W. Bullein, *A Dialogue against the Pestilence* (1593) by Woodward, "Swords into Ploughshares," 79.

20. On clothing and the elite, see Stone, *The Crisis of the Aristocracy;* for a concise consideration of dress, status, and social mobility, see Lisa Jardine, *Still Harping on Daughters* (Sussex: Harvester, 1983), 141–68; but for a cautionary word about the preoccupation with "emulation" in work on consumer behavior and dress later in the period, see Lorna Weatherill, "Consumer Behavior, Textiles, and Dress in the Late Seventeenth and Early Eighteenth Centuries." See also my *Fashioning Femininity and English Renaissance Drama* and Jones and Stallybrass, *Renaissance Clothing and the Materials of Memory.*

21. *Thomas of Woodstock, or Richard the Second, Part One,* ed. Peter Corbin and Douglas Sedge (Manchester: Manchester University Press, 2002),1.1.99–102. All references are to this edition.

22. On this Polish shoe, the "crackowe," see Thomas Wright, *The Romance of the Shoe, Being the History of Shoemaking* (London: C. J. Farncombe, 1922), 78–79.

23. Rossiter lays out the parallels in the introduction to his edition, *Woodstock: A Moral History,* ed. A. P. Rossiter (London: Chatto and Windus, 1946).

24. Paula Blank, "Speaking Freely about *Richard II*," *JEGP* 96 (1997): 327–48. For a countervailing view, see MacD. P. Jackson, "Shakespeare's *Richard II* and the

Anonymous *Thomas of Woodstock,*" *Medieval and Renaissance Drama in England* 14 (2001): 17–65. Drawing on various empirical studies of the British Library manuscript in which *Woodstock* is preserved, he argues that *Woodstock* is an early seventeenth-century play based on Shakespeare rather than one of his sources. It remains to be seen whether Jackson's exhaustive argument concerning the date of the anonymous *Woodstock* will be widely accepted, but my argument does not depend on which play predates the other.

25. Larry Champion, "The Functions of Mowbray: Shakespeare's Maturing Art in *Richard II,*" *Shakespeare Quarterly* 26 (1975): 3–7; *Richard II,* ed. J. Dover Wilson (Cambridge: Cambridge University Press, 1939), lxviii; E. M. W. Tillyard, *Shakespeare's History Plays* (New York: Macmillan, 1946); and A. P. Rossiter, introduction to *Woodstock.*

26. A. L. French, "*Richard II* and the Woodstock Murder," *Shakespeare Quarterly* 22 (1971): 337–44.

27. For a concise review of Richard as "bad king, good poet," see Madhavi Menon, "*Richard II* and the Taint of Metonomy," *ELH* 70 (2003): 653–75.

28. Silverman, "Fragments of a Fashionable Discourse," 145, drawing on the work of Eugénie Lemoine-Luccioni, *La robe: Essai psychanalytique sur le vêtement* (Paris: Editions du Seuil, 1983).

29. See Ann Hollander, *Seeing through Clothes* (New York: Viking, 1975): "The placement, size, and shape of the breasts, the set of the neck and shoulders, the relative girth and length of the rib cage, the exact disposition of its fleshly upholstery, front and back—all these, along with styles of posture both seated and upright, are continually shifting according to the way clothes have been variously designed in history" (91), quoted in Silverman, "Fragments of a Fashionable Discourse," 145–46.

30. Silverman, "Fragments of a Fashionable Discourse," 146.

31. Ashelford, *Dress in the Age of Elizabeth,* 43. See also John Twyining, *London Dispossessed: Literature and Social Space in the Early Modern City* (New York: St. Martin's, 1998), who observes that ruffs and other elite fashions that inhibited bodily movement "emphasized and displayed the fact that the wearer was a person of leisure," 101.

32. On the codpiece, for example, see Marjorie Garber, "Fetish Envy," *October* 54 (1990): 45–56.

33. See John Styles, "Product Innovation in Early Modern London," *Past & Present* 168 (2000): 124–69; on sizing see his "Clothing the North," 161ff.

34. Shammas, *The Pre-Industrial Consumer in England and America.*

35. Jones and Stallybrass, *Renaissance Clothing and the Materials of Memory,* 2.

36. In claiming that our relation to objects is characterized by "disavowal," Jones and Stallybrass write against the critique of objects mounted by Jean Baudrillard's series of books on objects and consumption, *Le système des objets* (Paris: Gallimard, 1968); *La société de consommation, ses mythes, ses structures* (Paris: SGPP, 1970); *Simulacres et simulations* (Paris: Galilée, 1981); and *Les stratégies fatales* (Paris: Grasset, 1983).

11. French Shakespeare

Second epigraph: "For it is on the edge of French, neither solely from within it nor from outside of it, on its always and forever vanishing shore, that I wonder if one can love, experience pleasure, pray, die of sorrow, or even just die in another language, or without saying anything of it to anyone, without speaking itself" (translation mine). Jacques Derrida, *Le monolinguisme de l'autre ou la prothèse d'origine* (Paris: Galilée, 1996), 14. Translated by Patrick Mensah as *Monolingualism of the Other, or The Prosthesis of Origin* (Stanford, Calif.: Stanford University Press, 1998).

1. See the Stanford online catalog at http://www.sup.org/book.cgi?book_id.

2. Quoted in Michael Dobson, *The Making of the National Poet: Shakespeare, Adaptation, and Authorship, 1660–1769* (Oxford: Clarendon, 1992), 228.

3. W. W. Greg, *The Shakespeare First Folio* (Oxford: Clarendon, 1955). On the Frankfort book fair, see particularly James W. Thompson's edition of *The Frankfort Book Fair; the Francofordiense Emporium of Henri Estienne* (Chicago: Caxton Club, 1911).

4. F. P. Wilson, "The Jaggards and the First Folio of Shakespeare," *TLS,* November 5, 1925, 737.

5. See, for example, John Tomlinson, *Cultural Imperialism: A Critical Introduction* (Baltimore: Johns Hopkins University Press, 1991), and Bruce Robbins, *Feeling Global: Internationalism in Distress* (New York: New York University Press, 1999).

6. Imre Szeman, "Culture and Globalization, or The Humanities in Ruins," *CR: The New Centennial Review* 3 (2003): 92. On unequal translation patterns and the ways in which they produce significant cultural "trade imbalances," see Lawrence Venuti, *The Scandals of Translation: Towards an Ethics of Difference,* (New York: Routledge, 1998). Venuti goes on to argue, however, that translation's effects cannot be "anticipated or controlled," 171). See A. Appadurai, *Modernity at Large: Cultural Dimensions of Globalization* (Minneapolis: University of Minnesota Press, 1996), on the ways in which metropolitan and dominant cultures are absorbed or indigenized (32, 42).

7. Deanne Williams. *The French Fetish from Chaucer to Shakespeare* (Cambridge: Cambridge University Press, 2004), 2.

8. Ibid., 3.

9. Ibid., 12.

10. John Dryden, *Of Dramatic Poesy and other Critical Essays,* ed. George Watson (New York: J. M. Dent, 1962), 1, 92. All references are to this edition and will be cited by page number in the text.

11. An exception is Michael Neill's essay "'An artificiall following of nature': Dryden, Etherege and the Perfection of Art," in *Style: Essays on Renaissance and Restoration Literature and Culture in Memory of Harriett Hawkins,* ed. Allen Michie and Eric Buckley (Newark: University of Delaware Press, 2005). On the association between the French and dancing, see Jean Howard's "Ballrooms and Academies: Producing the Cosmopolitan Body in West End London, " *Theater of a City:*

The Places of Londong Comedy, 1598–1642 (Philadelphia: University of Pennsylvania Press, 2007), 162–208.

12. Laura Brown, "Dryden and the Imperial Imagination," in the *Cambridge Companion to John Dryden,* ed. Steven Zwicker (Cambridge: Cambridge University Press, 2004), 59–74; all references will be noted in the text. See George Williamson, "The Occasion of *An Essay of Dramatic Poesy,*" *Modern Philology* 44 (1946): 1–9, on the debate between Thomas Sprat and Samuel Sorbière as a provocation for Dryden's essay.

13. See, for example, Brown, "Dryden and the Imperial Imagination," 59.

14. See Mary Thale, "The Framework of *An Essay of Dramatic Poesy,*" *Papers on Language and Literature* 8 (1972): 362–69, and Daniel Ennis, "Tactical Victory: Dryden's *Essay of Dramatic Poesy* and the Battle of Lowestoft," *Restoration and Eighteenth Century Theatre Research* 14 (1999): 38–54.

15. Roland Barthes, "L'ancienne rhétorique : Aide-mémoire," *Communications* 16 (1970) : 172–229.

16. Neill, "'An artificiall following of nature,'" 185.

17. See, for example, Howard Weinbrot, *Britannia's Issue: The Rise of British Literature from Dryden to Ossian* (Cambridge: Cambridge University Press, 1993). But see Neill, "'An artificiall following of nature,'" who insists on the unresolved ending of Dryden's debate (183).

18. On French cultural influence, see the early studies of L. Charlanne, *L'influence française en Angleterre au XVIIe siècle* (Paris, 1906), and Georges Ascoli, *La Grande-Bretagne devant l'opinion française* (Geneva: Slatkine, 1971, rpt. from Paris: Gamber, 1927–30), 2 vols. See also the more recent collection, *France et Grande-Bretagne de la chute de Charles Ier à celle de Jacques II (1649–1688),* ed. Christopher Smith and Elfrieda Dubois (Norwich, England: University of East Anglia, 1990).

19. David Bruce Kramer, *The Imperial Dryden: The Poetics of Appropriation in Seventeenth-Century England* (Athens: University of Georgia Press, 1994), 26.

20. On translations and performances of French plays in seventeenth-century England, see André Blanc, "Les traductions anglaises de Corneille," in Smith and Dubois, eds., *France et Grande-Bretagne de la chute de Charles Ier à celle de Jacques II,* 177–96.

21. Brown, "Dryden and the Imperial Imagination," 59. On Dryden's debt to Corneille, see J. Aden, "Dryden, Corneille, and the *Essay on Dramatic Poesy,*" *Review of English Studies* 6 (1955): 147–56.

22. Michael Gelber, *The Just and the Lively: The Literary Criticism of John Dryden* (Manchester: Manchester University Press, 1999), 58.

23. On French/English linguistic exchange, see Isabelle Landy-Houillon, "Le langage et son double ou les échanges linguistiques entre la France et l'Angleterre : L'example de Claude Mauger (1653)," in Smith and Dubois, eds., *France et Grande-Bretagne de la chute de Charles Ier à celle de Jacques II,* 129–41.

24. *Dissertation sur la tragedie ancienne et moderne* (1749) and Voltaire to Bernard Joseph Saurin, December 4, 1765, Letter D13025 of *The Complete Works of Voltaire,*

ed. Theodore Besterman, vol. 113 (Banbury Oxfordshire: Cheney and Sons, 1973), 436–37.

25. Michèle Willems, *La genèse du mythe shakespearien, 1660–1780* (Paris: PUF, 1979).

26. John Pemble, *Shakespeare Goes to Paris: How the Bard Conquered France* (London: Hambledon and London, 2005), 89.

27. See J. L. Borgerhoff, *Le theater anglais à Paris sous le Restauration* (Paris, 1912); Victor Leathers, *British Entertainers in France* (Toronto: University of Toronto Press, 1959); and *Souvenirs du théâtre anglais* (Paris: Henri Gaugain, 1827).

28. Stirling Haig, "Vigny and *Othello*," *Yale French Studies* 33 (1964): 53–64.

29. Eric Partridge, *The French Romantics' Knowledge of English Literature (1820–1848)* (1924, rpt. Geneva: Slatkine, 1974), 21. See also Jonathan Bate, "The Politics of Romantic Shakespearean Criticism: Germany, England, France," *European Romantic Review* 1 (1990): 1–26. Bate shows how Shakespeare "served as a weapon against the hegemonic tendencies of French neo-classical culture" (3).

30. As Richard Foulkes observes in his recent *Performing Shakespeare in the Age of Empire* (Cambridge: Cambridge University Press, 2002), British actors had long ventured overseas; colonial expansion and improvements in transport simply accelerated that expansion (3).

31. An excellent overview of the 1827 visit to Paris that also details the efforts of French theater managers in organizing the visit can be found in Peter Raby's *Fair Ophelia: A Life of Harriet Smithson Berlioz* (Cambridge: Cambridge University Press, 2003).

32. On the plight of the London theater in the early nineteenth century, see Joseph Donohue, *The Cambridge History of British Theatre, 1660 to 1895* (Cambridge: Cambridge University Press, 2004), vol. 2; Foulkes, *Performing Shakespeare in the Age of Empire;* and Raby, *Fair Ophelia,* passim.

33. "Report from the Select Committee Appointed to Inquire into the Laws Affecting Dramatic Literature," *British Parliamentary Papers, Stage and Theatre,* ed. Marilyn L. Norstedt (Shannon: Irish University Press Series, 1968), 135.

34. See Partridge, *The French Romantics' Knowledge of English Literature,* 195ff.

35. *Correspondance d'Alfred de Vigny 1816-juillet 1830,* ed. Madeleine Ambrière (Paris: Presses Universitaires de France, 1989). On the multiple texts and revisions of Vigny's *Le more de Venise,* see José Lambert, "Shakespeare and French Nineteenth-Century Theatre: A Methodological Discussion," in *Geschichte, System, Literarische Übersetzung: Histories, Systems, Literary Translations,* ed. Harald Kittel (Berlin: Erich Schmidt, 1992), 66–90.

36. Alfred de Vigny, *Oeuvres complètes: Théâtre I* (Paris: Gallimard, 1986), 408.

37. See, for example, Pemble, *Shakespeare Goes to Paris;* Haig, "Vigny and *Othello,*" and the entry "Shakespeare on the Continent," *The Drama to 1642* in *The Cambridge History of English and American Literature* (Cambridge: Cambridge University Press, 1907–21). For a review of eighteenth- and nineteenth-century French translations of *Othello,* see Margaret Gilman, *Othello in French* (Paris: Champion, 1925). See also, from a French perspective, Jean-Michel Deprats, "The

'Shakespearian Gap' in French," *Shakesepare Survey: Shakespeare and Language,* ed. Stanley Wells (1997). Ironically, as Peter Raby argues in his study of Harriett Smithson, "French commentators were generally more concerned than their English counterparts about the integrity of the Shakespearean texts used in the theatre" (46). Stendhal famously complained about the adulterated Shakespearean texts he saw performed in London (*Examiner,* November 26, 1821), cited in Raby, *Fair Ophelia.*

38. "French Hissing," *Economist,* April 2, 2005.

39. See Benjamin's well-known discussion of *brot* and *pain* in "The Task of the Translator," and Carol Jacobs, "The Monstrosity of Translation," *MLN* 90 (1975), in which she translates Benjamin as follows: "literality thoroughly overthrows all reproduction of meaning . . . and threatens directly to lead to incomprehensibility" (761).

40. George Steiner, *After Babel: Aspects of Language and Translation* (Oxford: Oxford University Press, 1975, rpt. 1998), 24. See also the introduction to Sandra Bermann and Michael Wood, eds., *Nation, Language, and the Ethics of Translation* (Princeton, N.J.: Princeton University Press, 2005): "Language remains radically impure, haunted by endless semantic contexts" (4).

41. Saint Jerome, *Lettres,* ed. J. Labout (Paris: Les Belles Lettres, 1953), vol. 3, 57.

42. For an interesting discussion of Schleiermacher on translation and his nationalist aims, see Lawrence Venuti, *The Translator's Invisibility: A History of Translation* (New York: Routledge, 1995).

43. See particularly his work on the pre-Socratics and Anaximander's fragment translated in *Early Greek Thinking,* ed. D. F. Krell and F. A. Capuzzi (New York: Harper and Row, 1975). On translation as betrayal, as "traducing," see also Barbara Johnson, *Mother Tongues: Sexuality, Trials, Motherhood, Translation* (Cambridge, Mass.: Harvard University Press, 2003), 15–17.

44. Walter Benjamin, "The Task of the Translator," *Illuminations,* ed. Hannah Arendt, trans. Harry Zohn (New York: Schocken Books, 1969), 79, 80, 71. But see Carol Jacobs's fine essay "The Monstrosity of Translation," in which she offers a critique of the organic metaphor implied in "afterlife," and Johnson, *Mother Tongues,* who observes, "The inevitability of betrayal is the only evidence we actually have that there is something to betray," 17.

45. See Franco Moretti, *Graphs, Maps, Trees* (New York: Verso, 2005), based on essays that originally appeared in the *New Left Review* in 2003.

46. On the impact of English publishing practices on the distribution and popularity of English authors during this period in France, particularly Scott, Byron, and the Galignani offshore editions, see William St. Clair's important study *The Reading Nation in the Romantic Period* (Cambridge: Cambridge University Press, 2004).

47. Recorded in Goethe's conversations with Johann Peter Eckermann, January 1827, *Conversations with Eckermann, 1823–1832,* trans. John Oxenford (New York: Farrar, Straus and Giroux, 1982).

48. See the account of Berlioz's melancholy, which led him to spend nights

sleeping outdoors, to sit for hours in a trance in cafés, etc., in "Miss Smithson et Hector Berlioz," *Revue Britannique* (1879): 299–315. Berlioz ultimately married Harriett Smithson; see Raby, *Fair Ophelia.*

49. Vincent Dowd, "India Shakespeare play tours UK" at http://news.bbc. co.uk/2/hi/south_asia/6453489.stm.

50. *New York Times,* November 9, 2006. This production offered English subtitles that elicited odd comments from reviewers. Natalie Anglesey reviewing for *The Stage* in Edinburgh, May 30, 2006, observed that "such is the clarity of Declan Donnellan's reading of the text, combined with first rate performers, that the English subtitles were almost unnecessary," while Lyn Gardner of the *Guardian* enthused "just forget them," they are a "useless distraction."

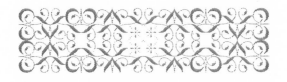

PUBLICATION HISTORY

Chapter 1 was previously published as "Myrrha's Revenge: Ovid and Shakespeare's Reluctant Adonis," *Illinois Classical Studies* 9 (1985): 251–66.

Chapter 2 was previously published as "Hayman's Missing *Hamlet*," *Shakespeare Quarterly* 34, no. 1 (1983): 73–79. Copyright Folger Shakespeare Library. Reprinted with permission of the Johns Hopkins University Press.

Chapter 3 was previously published as "Renaissance Family Politics and Shakespeare's *The Taming of the Shrew*," *English Literary Renaissance* 16 (1986): 86–101.

Chapter 4 was previously published as "'And wash the Ethiop white': Femininity and the Monstrous in *Othello*," in *Shakespeare Reproduced*, ed. Jean Howard and Marion O'Connor (London: Methuen, 1987), 141–62.

Material in chapter 5 was previously published as "Portia's Ring: Unruly Women and Structures of Exchange in *The Merchant of Venice*," *Shakespeare Quarterly* 38, no. 1 (1987): 19–33. Copyright Folger Shakespeare Library. Reprinted with permission of the Johns Hopkins University Press.

Material in chapter 5 was previously published as "Reprise: Gender, Sexuality, and Theories of Exchange in *The Merchant of Venice,*" in *Theory and Practice, "The Merchant of Venice,"* ed. Nigel Wood and Barbara Rasmussen (London and Toronto: Open University and Toronto University Press, 1996), 102–23.

Chapter 6 was previously published as "Ghostwriting: *Hamlet* and Claude Chabrol's *Ophélia,*" in *The Scope of Words,* ed. Peter Baker, Sarah Webster Goodwin, and Gary Handwerk (New York: Peter Lang Publishing, 1991), 167–78.

Chapter 7 was previously published as "Englishing the Other: 'Le tiers exclu' and Shakespeare's *Henry V,*" in Karen Newman, *Fashioning Femininity and English Renaissance Drama* (Chicago: University of Chicago Press, 1991). Copyright 1991 by the University of Chicago. All rights reserved.

Material in chapter 8 was previously published as "Rereading Shakespeare's *Timon of Athens* at the fin de siècle," in *Shakespeare and the Twentieth Century: The Selected Proceedings of the International Shakespeare Association World Congress,* ed. Jonathan Bate, Jill L. Levenson, and Dieter Mehl (Newark: University of Delaware Press, 1998), 378–89.

Material in chapter 8 was previously published as "Cultural Capital's Gold Standard: Shakespeare and the Critical Apostrophe in Renaissance Studies," in *Discontinuities in Contemporary Renaissance Criticism,* ed. Viviana Comensoli and Paul Stevens (Toronto: University of Toronto Press, 1998), 96–113.

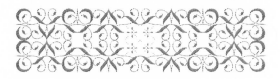

INDEX

culture: cultural identity, 136–37; cultural poetics, 96; French, 139; globalization of, 138, 144, 148; and power, 143

Cupid (mythological character), 4

Davis, Natalie Zemon, 70, 75

Death Goddess, 8

degree, 45, 88, 139. *See also* class; status

Derrida, Jacques, 45, 48, 136, 147, 149

Desdemona (character): desire of, 51–52, 58; fairness, 41, 42; marriage to Othello, 41–42, 48–49; murder by Othello, 42; purity of, 41

desire: and marriage, 63; mimetic, 9; monstrous, 48–53; and myth, 10–12; sexual, 10; of women, 51–52, 58

Detienne, Marcel, 11

devil, 45, 47

difference: and Desdemona, 51–53, 56–57; and ethnography, 87; and gender, 88; and identity, 147; and Katharine, 90; in modern period, 40; and sex/race code, 51; sexual, 9, 10, 50, 57, 87, 92, 93–94. *See also* other

domestic violence, 23, 27, 29, 30–31

Donnellan, Declan, 149

Drury Lane theater, 13, 144, 148

Dryden, John, 114–15; *Of Dramatic Poesy,* 138–43, 147–48

Dumas, Alexandre, 148

Earle, John, 114

Earl of Southampton (Henry Wriothesley), 1, 7

economics, 59, 98

E. K., 109

Elizabeth I, Queen of England, 24, 46, 85–86, 124; and female rule, 29

Emilia (character), 42

Engle, Lars, 167n18

Eskimos, 85–87

Eugenius (character), 138–39, 140

Eurydice. *See* Orpheus and Eurydice story

exchange: clothing as, 124–25; in film, 78, 82–84; of gifts, 59–60, 65, 101, 103–4, 105, 110; sexual, 90–91, 93–94; theory, 59–60, 62, 64, 75–76, 92–93; of women, 59–64, 75, 76, 90–92

Falstaff (character): and character, 115–17, 121–22; and personality, 112; and popular culture, 95; punishment, 120

family politics, 25–27

femininity: and blackness, 57; cultural, 51; and monstrous, 56; on sexual inversion, 71. *See also* women

feminist literary criticism: on objectification of women, 62; on traffic in women, 59, 61, 75, 92; on woman as other, 60–61

Ferguson, Margaret, 136

film and spectator, 79–80

Fineman, Joel, 35

Forman, Simon, 24

Frazer, James, 11

Freud, Sigmund: and Chabrol's *Ophélia,* 78; on compulsion to repeat, 80–81; on familial model, 9; on father as symbolic, 35; on *Hamlet,* 79, 83, 116; on hysterical symptoms, 33–34, 36; on myth, 11; and narcissim, 105; on *Oedipus Rex,* 84; *Outline of Psycho-analysis,* 84; on repression, 82, 84; on uncanny, 81–82

Frobisher, Martin, 85–86

Gauguin, Paul, 96

Gaunt, John of, Duke of Lancaster (character), 123, 129–30

Geertz, Clifford, 113

gender: and clothing, 132; and

incest, 3–5, 7–8, 9, 60
intertextuality, 69, 78
Irigaray, Luce, 35–36, 62, 92; and
    mimeticism, 35–37

James, Richard, 117
Jameson, Fredric, 26–27
jealousy, 9
Johnson, Barbara, 102, 104
Johnson, Samuel, 94–95
Jones, Ann Rosalind, 133, 135
Jones, Robert Edmond, 15–16
Jordan, Winthrop, 42
Jung, Carl Gustav, 11

Kahn, Coppélia, 2
Kate (character): abuse by, 30–31; and
    animal analogies, 31; final speech,
    34, 36–37; and linguistic power, 28,
    30, 32–33, 35–36; and Petruchio,
    26, 31–33, 35; puns, 32, 33, 34,
    36; taming of, 26, 30, 34, 37; on
    women's submission, 34
Katharine, Princess of France
    (character), 89–92, 94, 95
Kean, Edmund, 145
Kemble, Charles, 143, 145
Kenrick, William: *Falstaff's Wedding*,
    116–17
Kermode, Frank, 101
King, Gregory: *Burns Journal*, 124
kinship system, 59, 61–62, 65
Knight, L. C., 122
Knox, John: *First Blast of the Trumpet
    against the Monstrous Regiment of
    Women*, 72
Kramer, David Bruce, 141
Kristeva, Julia, 92

La Bruyère, Jean de, 114
Lacan, Jacques, 5, 110
Laertes (character), 125
Lancaster, Duke of (character). *See*
    Gaunt, John of, Duke of Lancaster
language: character as, 116; as

constitutive, 104; and cultural
    capital, 98; and cultural identity,
    136–37; French, 142; and identity,
    28, 32; and translation, 145–49; and
    women, 28, 32, 72, 89
Launcelot Gobbo (character), 73
Leo Africanus: *Historie of Africa*, 47
Lesurf, Yvan (character), 79–84
Le Tourneur, Pierre, 148
Lévi-Strauss, Claude : on exchange
    of women, 59–60, 64–65, 92;
    on incest, 60; on language,
    62; phallocentrism of, 61; as
    structuralist, 11
Lisideius (character), 138–39, 140
literacy, 100
literary criticism, 112–14, 139, 142, 147
literary production, 112, 141
love: frustrated, 3; and gender, 10;
    perverse, 3; reluctant, 1–2
Lucy/Ophélia (character), 82, 83–84

Maclise, Daniel, 14–15
Maenads, 8
Mandeville, John, 46
Marcus Antonius, 107–8
Maria, wife of Roberto Bono, 55
Marlowe, Christopher, 109–10
marriage: arranged, 63; as commercial
    transaction, 65; and desire, 63; and
    difference, 86–87; as exchange of
    women, 92; as partnership, 34; and
    sex, 32; and subjection of women,
    68
Marx, Karl: post-Marxism, 98, and
    general equivalent, 105, and
    clothing, 125
Mary Tudor, 72
Mauss, Marcel: *Essai sur le don,* 59–60
McLuskie, Kathleen, 173n17
mediation, 11
Mehlman, Jeffrey, 82
men: beloved of gods, 3; and masculine
    identity, 26; and power, 53;
    reluctant, 2; sexuality, 9. *See*

Ovid: Adonis's character, 1, 2; and
   Bianca and Lucentio, 32; and
   Shakespeare's *Venus and Adonis,* 3–7
Ovide moralisé, 4

parody, 78
pathological communication, 93–94
patriarchy: and community ritual,
   23–25; and familial bonds, 10;
   homosocial aspect, 62, 64, 75, 76,
   92–93, 109; as master narrative, 10
Pear's Soap (advertisement), 38–39
Pemble, John: *Shakespeare Goes to Paris,*
   143
personality, 112, 113, 122
Petruchio (character): animal imagery
   and Kate, 31–35; taming of Kate,
   26, 30, 34, 37
Phaeton myth, 43
phallocentrism, 61
pharmakos, 9
Plutarch, 107–8, 110
Poe, Edgar Allen: "The Purloined
   Letter," 5
Polonius (character), 18, 125
Portia (character): exchange of, 64–65;
   linguistic labor, 72–73, 74–75; love
   for Bassanio, 66–67; name, 167n18;
   as prince, 69; ring of, 67–68,
   69–70, 71, 73–74; as unruly woman,
   72, 74, 76
Pory, John, 47
Postlewayt, M., 54
power: cultural, 143; discourse as, 30;
   and gender/class, 24, 26, 68, 73;
   and sexual inversion, 71
Pratt, Mary Louise, 162n18
prejudice, 46, 53, 54–55, 142
Ptolemy: *Tetrabiblos,* 43
puns, 32, 33, 34, 36, 74, 90, 92, 167n18,
   173–74n28
Pygmalion (character), 4, 5–6

Quarry, Thomas, 23–24
Querini, Tomaso, 55

Raby, Peter, 187n37
race: early modern discourses, 43–47,
   54, 57–58; and femininity, 42–43
Racine, Jean, 142
racism: Derrida on, 45; and Rhymer,
   38, 41; and Ridley, 40–41
Rebhorn, Wayne, 2
recognition, 80
Regius commentary on Ovid, 4–5
Reich, William, 1
repetition, 80–83
Richard II (character): and clothing,
   123, 129, 130, 134
Richard II (Shakespeare), 127, 130–31,
   134–35. See also *specific characters*
Ridley, M. R., 39–40, 55
Rinaldo (character), 2
Roderigo (character), 41–42, 50, 52
Rosaline (character), 132
Rosyer, Nicholas, 23, 27
Rowe, Nicholas, 116
Royal African Company, 54
Rubin, Gayle: on sex/gender system, 61;
   on traffic in women, 59, 91
Rymer, Thomas, 38, 40, 50–51, 54–55

sartorial economies. *See* clothing
scapegoating, 9, 24, 121
Schleiermacher, Friedrich, 147
scolds, 28–29, 37
scopic economy, 51
Sedgwick, Eve Kosovsky, 62, 92, 93
Senden, Casper van, 46
Serres, Michel: and *le tiers exclu,* 93–94
Sewell, Arthur, 122
sex/gender system, 27, 29, 49, 61–62,
   66, 67, 69, 93–94
sexuality: ambiguity of, 11; bisexuality,
   34, 36, 37; black, 45, 46–47,
   49–50; and clothing, 132; and
   colonialism, 57–58; and comedy,
   173n17; and difference, 9, 10, 50,
   57, 87, 92, 93–94; and exchange,
   90–91, 93–94; homoeroticism, 108,
   109; homosexuality, 62, 92–93,

mother, 6–7, 9; and Myrrha, 4–5;
on sexuality, 9
Venus and Adonis (Shakespeare), 1–12;
antithesis in, 11, 12; incest theme,
3–5, 7–8, 9; Ovidian source, 1, 7, 10;
reading of, 7–10, 11. *See also specific
characters*
Venus and Adonis (Titian painting), 1
Vere, Elizabeth, 1
Vickers, Nancy, 90
Vigny, Alfred de: *Othello* translation of
Le more de Venise, 138, 145–47
violence, reciprocal, 9
Voltaire, 142

"wash the Ethiop white" (proverb),
38–39
Webster, John: *The White Devil,* 38–39
Weimann, Robert, 88
whiteness, 39, 50
Whitney, Geoffrey: *A Choice of
Emblemes,* 38–39
Williams, Deanne, 138
Williams, Raymond, 113
Wilson, F. P., 137
Wing, John, 65

witchcraft, 29, 30, 48, 56
women: ambitious fantasies of, 33;
desire of, 51, 58; and difference,
86; exchange of, 59–64, 75, 76,
90–92; and independence, 28;
and language, 28, 32, 72; myth and
desire, 10–12; objectification of,
62; as other, 60–61; overardent,
2, 8; passions of, 3; rebellious,
28–29; Renaissance ideal, 71–72;
representation of body, 90; role of,
28; as scolds, 28–29, 37; sexuality
of, 8, 48, 70–71; and silence, 30–36,
37; as spectacle, 31, 36–37; status
of, 27, 36, 61, 64, 93; subjection of,
67, 68; submission of, 34, 68; as
treasure, 31, 36; voice of, 27; and
witchcraft, 29, 30, 48, 56. *See also*
femininity
Woodstock, Thomas of, Duke of
Gloucester (character), 127–32,
133–34
Wrightson, Keith, 63

York, Duchess of (character), 131

Karen Newman is professor of English at New York University. She has written widely on Shakespeare and Renaissance letters and culture.